Land Information Management

An introduction with special reference to
cadastral problems in Third World countries

PETER F. DALE

Reader in Surveying
North East London Polytechnic, UK

and

JOHN D. McLAUGHLIN

Professor of Surveying Engineering
University of New Brunswick, Canada

CLARENDON PRESS · OXFORD

Oxford University Press, Walton Street, Oxford OX2 6DP

Oxford New York Toronto
Delhi Bombay Calcutta Madras Karachi
Petaling Jaya Singapore Hong Kong Tokyo
Nairobi Dar es Salaam Cape Town
Melbourne Auckland

and associated companies in
Berlin Ibadan

Oxford is a trade mark of Oxford University Press

Published in the United States
by Oxford University Press, New York

British Library Cataloguing in Publication Data
Dale, Peter F.
Land information management: an
introduction with special reference to
cadastral problems in Third World
countries.
1. Land use—Developing countries—
Data processing
I. Title II. McLaughlin, John D.
333.73'13'091724 HD1131
ISBN 0-19-858404-0
ISBN 0-19-858405-9 Pbk

Library of Congress Cataloging in Publication Data
Dale, Peter F.
Land information management.
Bibliography: p. Includes indexes
1. Land use—Developing countries—Data processing—
Management. 2. Land tenure—Developing countries—Data
processing—Management. 3. Cadasters—Developing
countries—Data processing—Management.
I. McLaughlin, John D. II. Title
HD1131.D35 1988 333.73'13'0285 87-28216
ISBN 0-19-858404-0
ISBN 0-19-858405-9 Pbk

Printed in Great Britain by
J. W. Arrowsmith Ltd, Bristol

Foreword

Shridath S. Ramphal
Commonwealth Secretary General

Land is the habitat of man and its wide use is crucial for the economic, social, and environmental advancement of all countries—indeed for human survival. Although it is part of man's natural heritage, access to land is controlled by ownership patterns; it is partitioned for administrative and economic purposes, and it is used and transformed in a myriad ways.

Population growth, technological and social hazards, and environmental degradation have all to be taken into greater account today by policymakers, resource planners, and administrators who make decisions about the land. They need more detailed land information than has been traditionally available. Although the printed map is still useful, computerized systems offer improved ways of acquiring, storing, processing, and retrieving such information.

Several countries of the British Commonwealth have pioneered systems for using new technology in land information. Their experiences need to be widely shared, so that countries do not have to experiment with expensive technologies or make costly mistakes.

This book, written by two experienced members of the surveying profession, serves that objective. It endeavours to guide those concerned with land management on some technical issues but, more importantly, on the implications and problems behind the use of modern techniques. It seeks to help those with poor infrastructure in assessing their requirements for land information, examining the technological choices available, and comparing their costs and benefits in relation to their technical and administrative implications.

By providing information that enables realistic decisions to be made on the technology that best meets their needs, this book should help governments in the prudent management of their land resources. I commend the initiative of the Commonwealth Association of Surveying and Land Economy (CASLE) in sponsoring its publication; it is a welcome example of professional co-operation in the service of the Commonwealth.

Preface

The modern age has a false sense of superiority because of the great mass of data at its disposal, but the valid criterion of distinction is rather the extent to which Man knows how to form and master the material at his command.

Goethe, 1802

The origins of this book may be traced to the fifth general assembly of the Commonwealth Association of Surveying and Land Economy (CASLE) held in Kuala Lumpur in 1985. At that meeting it was agreed that a text should be prepared on land information management that would be of particular interest to those charged with assessing the need for land-related information and with introducing land information systems into developing countries. It was anticipated that the text would serve as a source document for a series of workshops on land information management being organized by CASLE, and that it might also prove a useful reference for information policy makers and land administration specialists.

The authors have undertaken this assignment with more than a little trepidation. Land information management (LIM) is a rapidly evolving field, especially as it relates to the introduction and evaluation of new information technologies. At the same time, many aspects of the field, such as the economic assessment of land information systems, are still rather poorly defined and documented. We have been particularly concerned about the lack of documented LIM case studies and comparative analyses from developing countries. However, we would like to acknowledge the efforts of Mr Harold Dunkerley and his colleagues at the World Bank who have begun to address this concern through a series of studies and information management workshops.

We have also had to cope with a rather broad range of topics and concerns, ranging from the formulation of information policy through the design criteria for land information systems and networks to the specific data requirements of land valuers, registrars, and surveyors. Our approach has been to attempt to construct a broad conceptual framework for the study of LIM, and then to focus on the concerns of a specific land information community—the land administrators. This has been done in part because of the special requirements of the developing countries for improved land registration, land valuation, and land administration facilities. We were also concerned about the lack of published material in these areas as compared, for example, with the environmental information field, in which a series of important monographs and technical reports have recently been published.[1]

Thus this work must be viewed as an initial and tentative contribution to what promises to be an important and exciting field of study. We are very grateful to CASLE and especially to Robert Steel and Jane Woolley, who have provided continuous support to this venture. We would also like to acknowledge the very useful contributions and criticisms provided by the students and faculty in the Resource Information Management Group at the University of New Brunswick. Finally, we would especially like to thank our wives, Beryl Dale and Maggie McLaughlin, for their support and understanding.

London	P.F.D.
Fredericton	J. D. McL.
1987	

Reference

1. See, for example, (1) Burrough, P. A. (1986). *Principles of geographical information systems for land resources assessment*, Clarendon Press, Oxford; (2) *Resource inventory and baseline study methods for developing countries* (1983). American Association for the Advancement of Science, Washington; (3) *Information systems for urban and regional planning: Asian and Pacific perspectives* (1986). United Nations Centre for Regional Development, Nagoya, Japan.

Contents

1. Land information

In this chapter we examine the nature of land and the need for land information. We define the nature and objectives of information systems and distinguish between several types that relate specifically to spatial information. We then introduce the concept of land information management.

1.1 Introduction

Land is the foundation of all forms of human activity; from it we obtain the food we eat, the shelter we need, the space to work, and the room to relax. In a seminal report on land administration prepared for the Food and Agriculture Organization (FAO), Sir Bernard Binns observed:

The land is man's most valuable resource. It is indeed much more than this: it is the means of life without which he could never have existed and on which his continued existence and progress depend.

He then went on to warn that:

The resources of the land are neither inexhaustible nor indestructible, as many men and countries have already found to their cost. Resources that had taken many million years to accumulate have been squandered or allowed to waste away in a few decades, and this squandering and wastage is likely to continue on an increasing scale wherever definite measures to stop it are not undertaken.[1]

In the years since Binns wrote his report, the wastage and destruction have continued. More recently, however, the need for thoughtful and careful stewardship of the land, together with the more intensive use and management of its resources, has emerged as a matter of major global concern. This has led to a re-evaluation both of the need for information about land and of the strategies and programmes that may provide it. Increasingly it has been recognized that policy makers, planners, land administrators, and individual citizens all have a need for information about the land and make significant use of spatial data on a day by day basis. As Binns himself remarked:

Accurate knowledge of natural resources and accurate description and record of such knowledge are the first essentials to their rational use and conservation.[2]

In both the private and public sectors, land information is a prime requisite for making decisions related to land investment, development, and management. Information reduces uncertainty by helping to identify and

1

analyse problems. Strategies to overcome them may then be prepared and implemented. The value of the information and the effectiveness of the decision-making process are directly related to the quality of the information and the manner in which it is made available.

The responsibility for providing this information is being taken on by a complex, diverse group of individuals and institutions, who make up what may be described as the 'land information management community'. It is a community which includes geographers, surveyors, cartographers, foresters, valuers, and others who have traditionally played a leading role in the land information field, as well as systems engineers, computer scientists, records managers, land use planners, lawyers, and resource specialists. It is a community which is increasingly interested not only in the technology for gathering and processing information, and in the design and development of land information systems, but also in the policies and strategies for their effective use.

The chapters which follow are not primarily directed at the land information specialist. Rather, they are aimed at managers who are responsible for reviewing the requirements for land-related information, for assessing the adequacy of existing arrangements, and for commissioning new land information systems. They are directed at those who wish to understand the principles which underlie such systems, the components which go to form them, and the implications behind their use.

At the same time, in this text we will emphasize a particular subset of land information systems and arrangements—those related to individual parcels of land. Many less developed countries have a crucial need to modernize their basic administrative records, especially those relating to land tenure and land value. The UN Ad Hoc Group of Experts on Cadastral Surveying and Mapping has noted that the land forms

a base for most human activity. Obviously, therefore, systematic records of land and rights in land have great importance for public administration, land planning and land development, and private transactions in land. This situation is particularly true in those developing countries where the rapid growth of population has caused increasing pressure on rural land, while simultaneously a massive migration of people to cities and towns has led to the uncontrolled growth of urban centres. Nevertheless, the need for accurate land records is often ignored by policy-makers; and the cadastral systems of many countries are, in consequence, highly defective.[3]

It has been estimated that the United States will spend 90 billion dollars during the years 1986–2000 on the collection and management of spatially related information. For Third World countries, the potential for spending and wasting enormous sums of money on the development of their own systems is limited only by their lack of available funds. In Canada it has been calculated that 50 dollars per head of population are spent each year on surveying and mapping. Yet even 50 cents per person could barely be afforded in many countries of the Third World where the average per capita income of the poor is often less than a dollar a day. Such countries can least afford to waste resources and are most in need of the benefits of orderly land development. It is to help those who wish to understand the issues and implications of land information systems development that this book is written.

1.2 Land management

Land

Land management is the process whereby the resources of land are put to good effect. 'Land' is a term with many meanings. To the physical geographer it is a landscape, the product of geological and geomorphological processes. To the economist it is a resource which, along with capital and labour, is to be exploited or conserved in order to achieve economic production and development. To the lawyer land is a volume of space stretching notionally from the centre of the earth to the infinite in the sky, and associated with it are a variety of rights which determine what may be done with it. To many it is simply the space for human activity as reflected in the many different forms of land use. In the present context, land will encompass all those things directly associated with the surface of the earth, including those areas covered by water. It includes a myriad of physical and abstract attributes, from the rights to light or to build upon the land, to ground water and minerals, and the rights to use and exploit them (see Fig. 1.1,

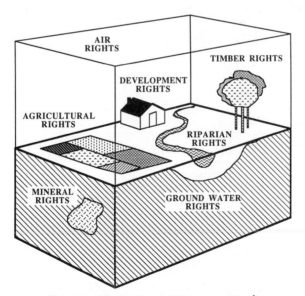

Fig. 1.1   *The land parcel (based on Platt[4])*

taken from Platt[4] and illustrating one land parcel). It includes all the material, biological, and chemical factors which surround humankind and which constitute the complex ecological system called the biosphere. It is thus:

'the air we breathe; the water we drink and use for recreation; the land we cultivate, mine and build on; the cities we flock to in growing numbers; and the wilderness we seek to enjoy today and to preserve for future generations.'[5]

The management of land

The resources and attributes of land need to be carefully managed if they are to be properly used and if waste is to be avoided. Land management entails decision making and the implementation of decisions about land (see Fig. 1.2). Decisions may be taken singly by individuals or collectively by groups. It is concerned with the stewardship of land, both for the present and for future generations. It includes the processes whereby land resources are:

allocated over space and time according to the needs, aspirations and desires of man within the framework of his technological inventiveness, his political and social institutions, and his legal and administrative arrangements.'[6]

At one end of the spectrum, land management may involve making fundamental policy decisions about the nature and extent of investments in the land. At the other end, it includes the routine operational decisions

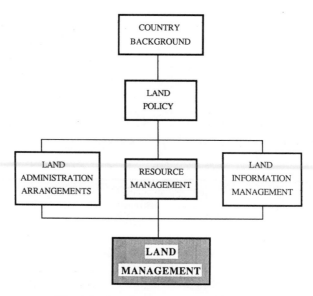

Fig. 1.2   *Land management arrangements*

made each day by land administrators such as surveyors, valuers, and land registrars. It embraces such matters as:

(1) property conveyancing, including decisions on mortgages and investment;
(2) property assessment and valuation;
(3) the development and management of utilities and services;
(4) the management of land resources such as forestry, soils, or agriculture;
(5) the formation and implementation of land use policies;
(6) environmental impact assessments;
(7) the monitoring of all land based activities in so far as they affect the best use of the land.

Stages in land management

As with all forms of management, land management necessitates the identification and ranking of goals, the cataloguing of alternative methods for achieving them, and an investigation of the consequences of each alternative. In theory, the steps involved in the management of land should include:

(1) a monitoring phase, in which information is gathered about the environment to identify where decisions and action are needed, (for example, detection of derelict land through the use of remote sensing techniques);
(2) a planning phase, when models are developed that permit the analysis of alternative courses of action;
(3) a policy-making phase, during which a particular course of action is selected;
(4) an operations phase, in which the chosen course of action is implemented (for example, building a new highway or carrying through some programme of land reform);
(5) a further monitoring stage, in which the results of the operations are reviewed. This latter activity is, however, all too often omitted.

1.3 Environmental and institutional perspectives

The management of land can be viewed both from an environmental and from an institutional perspective. The environment may be thought of as including all the physical, biological, and chemical factors that compose people's surroundings and that may be distinguished in terms of continuing, renewable, and non-renewable resources. While the focus of this text is not on the environmental perspective, it is important to acknowledge the role of land information in the environmental management process. Dr E. F. Roots, Scientific Advisor to Environment Canada, has noted:

Without accurate information about the lands and waters, and without an up-to-date inventory of the country's resources and what is happening to them and to the environment, the government and the people are handicapped in controlling their own destiny. It is not possible to make best use of the land and natural wealth, or to prevent its mis-use, without good factual knowledge of the country and its features.[7]

The institutional perspective, with which we shall be primarily concerned in this text, focuses on the various aspects of group, collective, or social action that influence and control people's use of the land. A primary, although not exclusive, institution in this regard is the system of land tenure. Professor Peter Dorner has described systems of land tenure as embodying:

those legal, contractual or customary arrangements whereby individuals or organisations gain access to economic or social opportunities through land. The precise form of tenure is constituted by the rules and procedures which govern the rights and responsibilities of both individuals and groups in the use and control over the basic resource of land.[8]

From this institutional perspective, land management includes the formulation of land policy, the preparation of land development and land use plans, and the administration of a variety of land-related programmes. It entails both government and private initiatives. Land policy consists of a whole complex of socio-economic and legal prescriptions that dictate how the land and the benefits from the land are to be allocated. Land administration includes the functions involved in regulating the development and use of the land, gathering revenue from the land (through sale, leasing, taxation, and so forth), and resolving conflicts concerning the ownership and use of the land (see Fig. 1.3). Increasingly, these activities are supported by a formal planning process.

Planning

Planning relates to all human activities and may be directed at personal survival, at optimizing the performance and profitability of an organization or company, or at securing benefits for the nation as a whole. In the case of land use, the responsibility for foreseeing and guiding change falls to the physical or land use planner. In the context of the urban environment:

planning is a reconciliation of social and economic aims, of private and public objectives. It is the allocation of resources, particularly land, in such a manner as to obtain maximum efficiency, whilst paying heed to the nature of the built environment and the welfare of the community. In this way planning is therefore the art of anticipating change, and arbitrating between the economic, social, political, and physical forces that determine the location, form, and effect of urban development.[9]

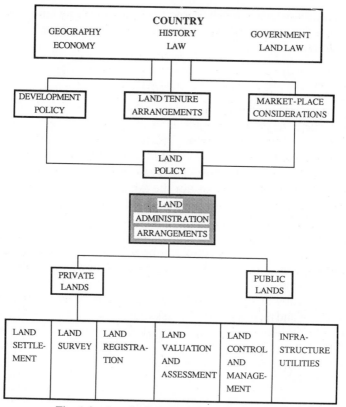

Fig. 1.3 *Land administration arrangements*[10]

In the rural environment the aims of the planner are similar, though the strategies for their realization will be different.

Planning is an interference in the free market in such a way as to persuade people to provide more universal benefits. When related to the physical environment, the process may be termed physical planning or sometimes town and country planning. Two separate activities are involved, namely the preparation of plans for the future and the implementation of what has been decided. The latter process is sometimes referred to as development control. Both activities must operate within a legislative framework that lays down procedures for planning and standards for implementing the design.

The first stage in the preparation of any plan is to review and hence to understand the present environment. The problems which must be addressed should then become more clear. In many areas of planning, the most difficult and important task is to turn a problem of which people are partially aware into a more precise definition of its underlying nature. Since the way a problem makes itself manifest is often mistaken for its cause, the initial task must be to isolate causes from effects. Planning must be based upon knowledge, knowledge depends upon information, and information depends upon the method of survey and the manner in which its results are communicated.

Information

The basic resource in all decision making is information. It is the function of a land information system to support land management at each of the phases indicated above. In practice, many decisions are made on the basis of inadequate information, in a disjointed and incremental way, and for reasons that are often subjective. The availability of good information can prevent neither mismanagement nor the taking of wrong decisions. It can, however, reduce the level of ignorance of the consequences of action or inaction. In India [11] where, in 1985, there were an estimated 300 million people who were undernourished, there were also grain surpluses amounting to 30 million tonnes that could not be sold because the poor were too poor to pay the price that was being demanded. Knowledge of the statistics does not prevent such situations. On the other hand, one key to the long-term solution of Third World problems is to increase awareness of the characteristics and magnitude of the tasks that have to be faced. This should, in turn, induce a better understanding of their true nature. Having information available is an important part, but only a small part, of the process of overcoming social and economic problems.

1.4   Land information systems

An information system may be formally defined as a combination of human and technical resources, together with a set of organizing procedures, that produces information in support of some managerial requirement. Data are raw collections of facts. Data relating to land may be acquired and held in alphanumeric form (for example, written in notebooks and surveyors' field books), or graphically (for example, as maps or aerial photographs), or digitally (for example, using electronic methods). To become information, the raw data must be processed so that they can be understood by a decision maker. A land information system gives support to land management by providing information about the land, the resources upon it and the improvements made to it.

The operation of a land information system includes the acquisition and assembly of data; their processing, storage, and maintenance; and their retrieval, analysis, and dissemination (Fig. 1.4). The usefulness of such a system will depend upon its updatedness, accuracy, completeness, and accessibility, and also upon the extent to which the system is designed for the benefit of the user rather than for the producer of the information.

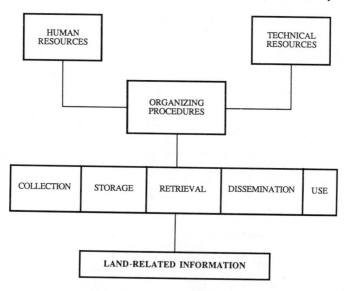

Fig. 1.4 *Land information systems*

S veral different categories of information systems can be distinguished, as shown in Fig. 1.5 and 1.6. These include systems designed to provide:

(1)   environmental information, whose primary focus is on delimiting environmental zones associated with some unique physical, chemical, or biotic phenomenon, such as areas liable to flooding;
(2)   infrastructure information, which focuses primarily on engineering and utility structures, such as underground services and pipelines;
(3)   cadastral information, which relates to zones where specific land rights, responsibilities, or restraints are recognized, such as areas subject to particular planning restrictions;
(4)   socio-economic information, which includes, for example, statistical and census-type data.

Land information systems may provide these data in the form of a product (such as a map or title certificate) or in the form of a service (such as professional advice). It can supply attribute data that may be presented in verbal or numerical form, spatial data that may be shown on maps, and temporal data that indicates their currency. The attribute or textual data may describe phenomena within a place, such as the characteristics of the soil and the activities which take place upon the land, or between places, as in networks and activity flows. The locational components of the data may be portrayed on maps in terms of points, lines, or polygons; they may incorporate three types of spatial relationships:

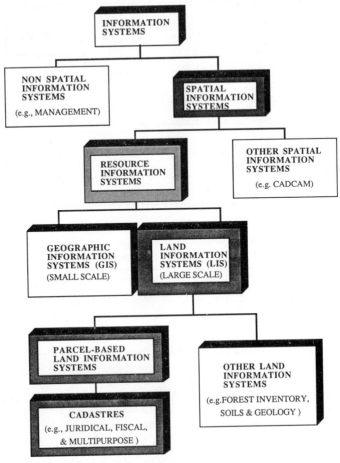

Fig. 1.5   *Information systems taxonomy*

(1) geometrical—where the data are referenced to a precise spatial framework, such as coordinates or grid cells;
(2) cartographical—where the data are generalized and symbolized;
(3) topological—where the relative location and the non-metric, spatial relationships of various data elements are defined.

Land information systems may be designed to serve one primary function, or they may be multifunctional. Some have been developed to support strategic planning. In these the focus is on determining organizational objectives and on the resources employed to achieve them. Some provide for management control and are concerned with the effective use of resources so as to accomplish an organization's objectives. Others have been designed for operational control so that specific tasks can be carried out effectively and efficiently (see Fig. 1.7). Each requirement dictates a special

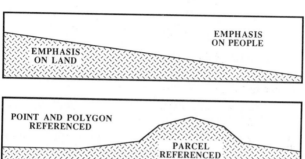

LAND-RELATED OR GEOGRAPHIC INFORMATION

LAND INFORMATION

ENVIRONMENTAL INFORMATION	INFRASTRUCTURE INFORMATION	CADASTRAL INFORMATION	SOCIO-ECONOMIC INFORMATION
Soils Geology Watercourses Vegetation Wildlife	Utilities Buildings Transportation & communications systems	Tenure Assessment Land use control	Health Welfare & Public Order Population distribution

EMPHASIS ON LAND / EMPHASIS ON PEOPLE

POINT AND POLYGON REFERENCED / PARCEL REFERENCED

Fig. 1.6   *Land-related information (based on Palmer[12])*

set of information criteria and hence a special type of information system. Some of the most important of these systems relate to land parcels. Many of the more broad-based systems are being developed around the land parcel as the basic spatial unit. Inadequacies in many of the present cadastral systems are, however, causing delays in their implementation.

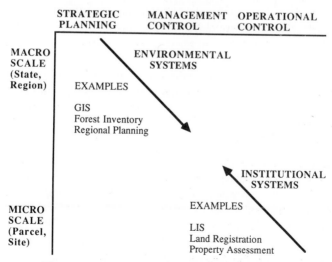

STRATEGIC PLANNING   MANAGEMENT CONTROL   OPERATIONAL CONTROL

MACRO SCALE (State, Region)

ENVIRONMENTAL SYSTEMS

EXAMPLES

GIS
Forest Inventory
Regional Planning

INSTITUTIONAL SYSTEMS

EXAMPLES

MICRO SCALE (Parcel, Site)

LIS
Land Registration
Property Assessment

Fig. 1.7   *Institutional and environmental systems*

1.5   The cadastre

Parcel-based information is required in a wide variety of activities. Frequent users range from existing or prospective landowners to lawyers, surveyors, valuers, real-estate managers, and agencies at all levels of government. During the last few decades, the demand for this information has expanded. This has extended the applications of existing parcel-based systems and created the need for new ones. Some of these changes have arisen because of:

(1)   a need for more efficient handling of land title documents to provide greater security of tenure for those in occupation of the land, and to keep pace with the greater demand for conveyancing;

(2)   a rise in property values, and a need for better support for mortgaging and investment;

(3)   a steady increase in the number of private and public users (from property developers to government lands officers and financial institutions such as banks) who make routine inquiries about land ownership;

(4)   the growing concern about the quality of the environment, and a transition in a number of countries from the perception of land as being a free commodity in plentiful supply to being a heritage for future generations and a resource requiring management for the public good;

(5)   the greater attention which has been paid to physical planning and to land development programmes, which in turn has resulted in a growth in the number of users and the variety of uses of cadastral information;

(6)   specific land-planning and management problems which have arisen in certain areas, such as the need to protect agricultural land around the edges of cities. In many Third World countries the greatest pressure on the land is in the urban fringe. Squatters move there from the rural areas in search of work and greater security, since the levels of starvation are often significantly less in urban than in rural communities. At the same time, the urban population is expanding because of the high birth rate. The solution to such problems requires new types of analysis based upon better information than has in the past been available.

In a parcel-based land information system, or cadastre, the data are organized around the cadastral parcel. This is generally the proprietary land unit, but it can be any tract of land that is part of an estate and has a separable identity. The principal function of a cadastre is the provision of data concerning such matters as land ownership, value, and use. It may, for example, provide the information component of land registration. This is the process whereby various rights in defined units of land are officially recorded. The information in a cadastre is collected, stored, referenced, and retrieved primarily at the land parcel level. Other referencing systems, such as coordinates, may then be added to facilitate data manipulation and the exchange of information with other systems.

The cadastral records consist of maps and text; these are linked by a unique property identifier such as the postal address, the coordinates of the parcel's centroid, or a sequential number assigned on a district by district basis. A graphical index, referred to as the property map or cadastral overlay, depicts all parcels in a given region and associates each parcel with its unique property identifier. The overlay should be based on a coordinate system so that other spatial information such as roads or administrative boundaries can be related to it. This graphical record may have a recognized legal status for property description, or it may merely serve as an index to other legal records. This is dependent on the purpose of the cadastre, the standards for its creation and maintenance, and the institutional and juridical environment in which it operates.

Parcel-based land information systems may be classified according to the information they contain or the primary purpose for which they have been developed. Three categories of cadastre are commonly recognized: the juridical cadastre, which serves as a legally recognized record of land tenure; the fiscal cadastre, which was developed primarily for property valuation; and the so-called multipurpose cadastre, which encompasses both the fiscal and the juridical with the addition of other parcel-related information. A more detailed analysis of each of these forms of the cadastre is given in later chapters. The multipurpose cadastre is the closest to the universal concept of a land information system. It is dependent neither on a particular level of technology nor on a specific type of land tenure system. Where private property rights are not recognized, as is the case in parts or all of many Third World countries, other parcels, such as units of occupation, can be employed. The multipurpose cadastre is also independent of the administrative structure: it may be centralized, decentralized, or both, and it may be implemented by one or more agencies at the local, regional, provincial, or even at the national level.

1.6 Land information management

As with other resources, land information needs to be carefully managed to maximize its potential benefits. Over the last two decades, new capabilities for data collection and processing, together with the expanding requirements of users, have directed attention to the need for improved land information management strategies. Such strategies are concerned with the effective organization of resources in order to achieve a set of objectives. These objectives may include improvements to the coverage, content, compatibility, and reliability of information, of access to it, and the possibility of integrating it with other data. The ultimate goal is to meet the needs of users more efficiently, effectively, and equitably.

Origins of land information management

The management of land information is not a new activity. Information systems have been in existence since people first took to sedentary agriculture. When the Babylonians occupied the lands between the Tigris and the Euphrates and the Egyptians cultivated the fertile regions of the Nile, the need for orderly land management was recognized. This in turn led to the development of rudimentary land information systems. More recent examples include topographical and geological mapping programmes, valuation and forest inventory surveys, and land title survey and registration systems. These systems provide both the information infrastructure necessary for land allocation and settlement and the additional technical and resource information needed for resource development.

What is new today is the quantity of data which can be handled, the speed with which these data can be processed, and the ways in which the data can be manipulated and analysed. The changes are ones of degree rather than of principle. The state has had a growing role in the processes of land administration through, for example, the granting of land titles, land taxation, and environmental regulation programmes. This, together with the gradual introduction of formal, systematic planning techniques, has focused attention on the need for new strategies and procedures for gathering, administering, analysing, and disseminating land-related information. This growth has in turn led to an emphasis on information as an important and expensive resource in its own right, and one that must be efficiently managed.

Management objectives

Land information management is directed at the effective use of information to achieve an objective or set of objectives. It entails:

(1) determining the requirements for land-related information;
(2) examining how the information is actually used in the decision-making process, how information flows from one producer or user to another, and what constraints there are upon that flow;
(3) developing policies for determining priorities, allocating the necessary resources, assigning responsibilities for action, and setting standards of performance and methods for monitoring them;
(4) improving existing land information systems or introducing new ones;
(5) assessing and designing new tools and techniques.

Manual and computer based systems

Land information systems may be computer based or manual. The traditional systems have been manually operated and in many cases will remain so for many years to come. In many traditional land information systems, the technical resources may be limited to a telephone, typewriter, and perhaps a photocopier. In a more sophisticated system, however, there will be elements of high technology applied to data storage, processing, and communications. The advantages of automation include:

(1) the physical compaction of data, so that less storage space is required and access to it is quicker;
(2) easier handling and manipulation, allowing for much more efficient and effective analysis;
(3) the possibility of merging graphic and attribute data in one set of operations; and
(4) the integration of data bases so that different data sets can be merged and processed together.

Technology, however, is only one component of a land information system. The disadvantage of using computers, particularly in Third World countries, is their relative complexity and their greater dependence on capital rather than labour. Where foreign exchange is in short supply and where labour is plentiful and cheap, the social and economic need may be to maximize local employment. Even where the investment can be justified, as Burch and others have remarked,

Merely computerizing an information system or an old process will not by itself improve effectiveness. To the contrary, the installation of a computer in a poorly designed information system will normally result in a perpetuation of the same types of errors and flaws as before.[13]

1.7   Land information and the Third World

Effective land information management is of particular importance to developing countries. As Repetto has noted:

especially in the Third World, where other concerns have had priority and capabilities are thinly spread, there are enormous gains to be realized by strengthening management capabilities for environmental protection and resource use. This involves putting in place the technical personnel, the management information systems, and the legal and administrative mechanisms to plan and guide resource use.[14]

Third World countries are arguably the most in need of land information systems to prevent wastage of their scarce resources. The cost of introducing

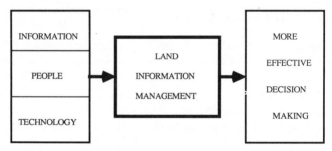

Fig. 1.8 *The land information management challenge*

or improving on existing systems is high and the availability of skilled manpower in such countries is almost non-existent. Even in more developed countries there is a shortage of trained and experienced personnel. The problems which have to be faced are partly institutional and partly technical and managerial. In the following chapters, the particular problems of parcel-based systems will first be examined. Technical issues will then be reviewed, leading to a discussion on institutional and managerial matters. Finally, some choices open to land information managers will be considered, and suggestions will be made for tackling problems associated with the development of a system. The challenge will be to produce better land information in support of better land policies (see Fig. 1.8).

1.8 Malaysia—a case history

Malaysia presents an interesting example of a developing country that is in the process of introducing new and innovative land information arrangements. This has resulted in part from a widespread concern about the *ad hoc* introduction of computers into various government departments. In 1984 a National Data Processing Committee, chaired by the Prime Minister's department, was set up to look into all aspects of computerization in the government. This committee was concerned with the hardware/software compatibility of the various computers being installed, the problems of data obsolescence and duplication, and the issue of data ownership.[15]

The Prime Minister's department has also been instrumental in creating a data bank and urban information system in the Kelang Valley, a system established 'to facilitate regional development planning, monitoring, and coordination'.[16] Growing interest in land information systems has also resulted from a specific concern for improved land administration.[17] In 1983 the Minister responsible for lands reported that the Cabinet had 'approved the setting up of a computerised land data bank to expedite and smoothen the administration and usage of land in the country'.[18]

Ung Cheng Pee, a prominent Malaysian surveyor, has written that the implementation of the land information program may follow the following scenario:[19]

(1) first, a computer-assisted land surveying system (CALS) would be developed in one of the states of Peninsular Malaysia as a pilot project;
(2) if successful, the CALS concept would then be gradually extended to the remaining states;
(3) at the same time efforts to develop a computerized legal cadastre would commence, perhaps by using microcomputers in each of the 99 land offices in Peninsular Malaysia (where the register documents of title are kept);
(4) attention would then focus on the development of a computer-assisted mapping system (CAMS) to increase the production and usefulness of topographic maps;
(5) this system would then be linked with the cadastral records.

It is hoped that such a system will be available to contribute to the Fifth Malaysia Plan 1986–1990.

Significant progress has been made towards achieving these goals. In January 1982 one of the first steps towards eventual computerization of land records was the introduction in Peninsular Malaysia of numerical codes whereby each parcel of land could be uniquely identified by its lot number and the area codes. Each of the 11 states of Peninsular Malaysia has been subdivided for administrative purposes into a number of districts, mukins or sections, and lots. In October 1983 a tender was called for the 'supply, delivery, installation, testing and maintenance of a computer system with supporting software and applications packages on a turnkey basis to meet the data processing needs of a Computer Assisted Land Surveying System in the Johor State Survey Department, Malaysia'.[20]

More recently, the Malaysian government has convened a national seminar on land information systems in Kuala Lumpur. Here it was resolved that the government should establish an integrated National Land Information System and institute a Central Policy Coordinating Committee to be situated in the Prime Minister's department 'to formulate and co-ordinate information system development among the Federal and State agencies as well as academic institutions'.[21]

References

1. Binns, Sir Bernard O. (1953). *Cadastral surveys and records of rights in land*, p. 1. F A O Land Tenure Study, Rome.
2. Binns, Sir Bernard O. *Op. cit.*, p. 1.
3. *Report of the meeting of the Ad Hoc Group of Experts on Cadastral Surveying and Mapping* (1974). U N publication E/CONF. 77/L.I., New York. pp. 25–6.

4. Platt, R. (1975). *Land use control: interface of law and geography*, Association of American Geographers, Resource Paper Washington. No. 75.1.
5. MacNeill, J. W. (1971). *Environment management*, p. 5. Privy Council Office, Govt. of Canada, Ottawa.
6. O'Riordan, T. (1971). *Perspectives on resource management*, Pion Ltd., London.
7. Roots, E. F. (1985). Surveys and mapping to aid environmental control and management of resources. *Proceedings of the United Nations Inter-Regional Seminar on the Role of Surveying, Mapping and Charting in Country Development Programming*, Aylmer, Canada.
8. Dorner, P. (1972). *Land reform and economic development*, Penguin, London.
9. Ratcliffe, J. (1974). *An introduction to town and country planning*, p. 4. Hutchinson, London.
10. Holstein, L., McLaughlin, J. and Nichol, S. (1985). Check-list for evaluating cadastral systems. Occasional paper, University of New Brunswick.
11. Brauer, D. (1986). Editorial in *Development and co-operation (D+C)*, Vol. 3/1986. Deutsche Stiftung für Internationale Entroicklung, Berlin.
12. Palmer, D. (1984). *A land information network for New Brunswick*, Technical Report No. 111, Department of Surveying Engineering, University of New Brunswick.
13. Burch, J. G., Strater, F. and Grudnitski, G. (1979). *Information systems: theory and practice*, John Wiley and Sons Inc., New York.
14. Repetto, R. (1986). *World enough and time*, pp. 38–9. Yale University Press, New Haven.
15. Ung Cheng Pee (1985). Towards a land information system in Malaysia. In Hamilton and McLaughlin (eds) *The decision maker and land information systems*, pp. 137–47. Canadian Institute of Surveying, Ottawa.
16. Johari, bin Mat (1986). Information system for regional planning in Malaysia: the case of Kevis in Kelang Valley. *Information systems for urban and regional planning: Asian and Pacific perspectives*, p. 305. UN Centre for Regional Development, Nagoya.
17. Kamarudin, R. (1973). Land administration in Peninsular Malaysia—a study on some critical areas. *Seminar on Land Administration*, Kuala Lumpur.
18. Ung. *Op. cit.*, pp. 137–8.
19. *Ibid.*
20. Seah Kok Seang (1984). Proposed computer assisted mapping system and cost benefit analysis. *The Surveyor*, Vol. 19, No. 1. pp. 33–8.
21. *Proceedings of the National Seminar on Land Information Systems* (1984). Ministry of Land and Regional Development, Kuala Lumpur.

2. Land registration

In this chapter we examine the particular problems associated with recording land ownership and managing the so-called legal or juridical cadastre. The chapter is concerned with the registration of proprietory interests in land.

2.1 Land ownership

In the dawn of history, when land for settlement and cultivation was plentiful in proportion to the size of the population, there was little need for land management or administration. With the growth of sedentary agriculture and of competition for the available space, land rights and controls over land use began to emerge. These rights initially applied to groups of people. However, with the passage of time in many societies they became vested in individuals. The juridical cadastre is concerned with documenting such rights and relating them to the land with which they are associated. It is concerned with all forms of property rights. The protection of customary rights may be as important as the protection of those of the individual, though the latter are the predominant concern in this chapter.

Land rights

Although the term 'land ownership' is in common use, it is not possible in a strict sense to own land itself. It is the rights to *use* the land that can be owned. Such rights may be held through custom or through the more formal processes of the law. The manner in which rights are held is known as the land tenure. In order to prove who owns the rights to any particular area of land, it is necessary to investigate the 'title' or entitlement. Title is the evidence of a person's rights to property. Land rights have been described as a bundle of sticks, each stick representing something which may be done with the land.[1] Each individual stick defines a way in which the land may be used, the profit which may be derived from it, or the manner in which some or all of the rights may be disposed of by transfer to other people or to organizations. For each right there will be an owner. Thus one person may own the overall rights but may have allowed another to lease the land and to use it for a defined period. Another may be allowed to take fish from the stream which passes through it, others to walk over the land by a right of way, and others to pipe sewage or gas from one side of it to another.

19

The land parcel

The cadastre is often the principal source of information about ownership of rights in land. Even when compiled for fiscal purposes, the record of payment of tax may constitute evidence of ownership of land. The basic unit of the cadastral record is the land parcel. Sometimes known as a lot, or plot, the parcel is an area, or more strictly a volume, of space recognized for recording purposes. It may cover many square kilometres, in the case of a farm or ranch, or may be as small as a square metre, for instance the land occupied by an electricity substation or telephone box.

In the context of the juridical cadastre, a land parcel is defined by a set of property rights. It extends notionally from the centre of earth to the infinite in the sky and as such should be regarded as a volume of space. In some Provinces of Canada, for example, special legislation relates to the use of air space and the height to which a landowner has a right to build. It is, however, more common to describe a parcel as the area where a particular volume intersects the surface of the earth. Exceptionally, the space may be divided horizontally into strata titles as in high-rise buildings, or into more complex forms as with mining rights. The recording and control of rights over such volumes of space cause particular problems, especially with regard to access and support.

In the present chapter, land will be taken to include all things attached to the soil whether above or below the ground. Thus crops growing in the ground and buildings erected upon it are considered to be part of the land. The parcel will be considered as a set of adjoining areas linked by a uniform set of ownership rights. Although a number of problems arise with such a definition of the parcel (see Table 2.1), it is the generally accepted basis for land registration.

Table 2.1 Parcel definitions

Parcels are:
Continuous areas (volumes) of land within which unique, homogeneous interests are recognized
Problems in defining parcels arise with:
• Non-contiguous areas
• Administrative boundaries
• Changes in natural features
• Differences in tenure and use
• Delimiting limited interests
• Delimiting public lands

Land is finite in extent and permanent by nature. This quality of permanence makes the land parcel an ideal basis for recording information since the rights, owners, and usage may change but the land remains for ever. Although parcels may be subdivided into smaller units or amalgamated with adjoining parcels into larger ones, the land which they cover remains unchanged. The need to record details of land parcels within a cadastre stems from a need for better administration of land. Land, after all, is the ultimate resource from which all wealth comes. Improvements in the management of land are essential for the betterment of both rural and urban poor. In most developing countries, the inadequacy of land information poses serious constraints on what can be done. Without knowledge of who owns the land, development cannot peacefully take place. In consequence, emphasis in many development programmes is now being placed on ensuring that rights in land are identified, recognized by the state, and recorded in some suitable form. The whole of this process is often referred to as land registration, the information component of which is the cadastre.

Urban expansion

At present more than half of the people in the world are directly involved with agriculture, most of them living in developing countries. Many of these people have rudimentary squatters' rights and little if any long-term security. In the urban sector, there is perhaps an even greater lack of security of tenure. It is estimated that in the last quarter of the twentieth century, the urban population of developing countries will increase by a further 1 billion people. In the city of Bangkok, Thailand, 40 000 new parcels are needed each year to keep pace with the estimated growth in the population. Much of the urban expansion is taking place at the edges of cities in what is sometimes referred to as the rural–urban or 'rurban' fringe. Squatter settlements and shanty towns grow up and cause social, political, and environmental problems. Good land records are on their own no solution to such problems, but they do provide a framework through which solutions can be devised and implemented.

2.2 Land transfer

Land is permanent but the nature, ownership, and extent of the rights associated with it change. When discussing the transfer of legal rights in land, it is customary to refer to three methods for processing the relevant records. These are: *'private conveyancing'*, in which the records and transfers of land are handled by private arrangement; *'registration of deeds'*, in which copies of such records are maintained by officials or by the state; and *'registration of title to land'*, where a state organization maintains the records of land ownership. With private conveyancing, the full cost of transferring the title to the land is borne by the land owner. Agents such as notaries or solicitors may be paid to oversee any dealings in land, and private surveyors may be employed to mark out and record the spatial limits of any property.

Security of title comes from the integrity of the professionals involved. It may be supplemented by the use of title insurance, in which an insurance company agrees to underwrite any loss if the title is proved to be defective.

Private conveyancing systems lead to duplication of effort, are generally expensive, frequently slow and inefficient, and provide little or no access to the information by the state. They are also open to fraud; a vendor may sell his land to several different purchasers without their knowing until too late that the vendor no longer has a right to sell.

2.3   Registration of deeds

The chances of fraud can be reduced under a system of registration of deeds, in which a copy of each deed of transfer is deposited in a public place. These registered documents then provide a priority claim to ownership. In many systems, records of mining claims are not registered in the Deeds Registry but elsewhere. In many systems, registration is not compulsory. In most, however, a search of the deeds register should ensure that no material factor has been overlooked in tracing the chain of title, thus saving both in time and cost whilst providing a substantial measure of security and protection to the would-be purchaser of the land. In addition, should the state need to acquire any land compulsorily for its own or communal purposes, it can ascertain the most recent purchaser directly from the registry.

Defects in deeds registration

The system does have a number of disadvantages. Deeds registration is a system for registering legal documents, not for registering title to land. A deed does not prove who owns the land: it only records an isolated transaction. The information in the deed may be inconsistent with previous transactions. Apparent consistency may be the result of copying from a previous deed that itself was in error. The information may then not agree with the facts on the ground. In England, Sir Charles Fortescue Brickdale, as Chief Land Registrar, once reported that when attempts were made to identify unregistered deeds of sale on the national Ordnance Survey large-scale plans:

about one in every four descriptions necessitates a visit to the ground to clear up some question of doubt, and this is not on account of slight imperfections in regard to the delicate points which do not really matter, but substantial doubt, for instance, as to which of two properties is intended to be conveyed, or as to whether some distinct portion of the land as it actually exists is or is not intended to be included. Properties are described by names long disused, by occupiers long since departed; wrong dimensions are inserted, wrong positions, wrong boundaries, no boundaries; half a house is conveyed as if it were the whole, six houses as if they were five, north appears for south, long for short, straight for crooked, a house on one side of the street conveyed by mistake for one on the other.[2]

Even today, nearly one out of every eight plans accompanying title deeds presented for first registration in England contains some fault which must be corrected by the Land Registry. Conditions in many other countries of the world are little different. It is rare for a conveyancer to visit the ground and to see exactly what land is subject to the conveyance. None the less, deeds registration systems can operate efficiently if there is full and careful documentation, as is, for example, practised in parts of southern Africa. Although the deed is the essential item that is registered in this system, there is strong supporting evidence from detailed surveys of the parcels that clearly define the land concerned.

Improving deeds registration system

Many deeds registration systems can be improved through the use of better techniques. In particular, as summarized in Table 2.2, improvements can come through:

(1)   better basic records management, including better administrative and accounting arrangements;
(2)   standardization of forms and procedures to expedite the routine processing of documents;
(3)   physical improvements to record keeping and document storage so that there is easier access;
(4)   the use of microfilm for both archiving and retrieval of data;
(5)   more realistic and more flexible standards for surveying and mapping, so that cheaper survey methods become possible;
(6)   partial examination of cadastral surveys and greater flexibility in the methods used;
(7)   partial examination of title documents, sampling rather than fully

Table 2.2   Improving a deeds registration system

1. Improve basic records management
2. Standardize forms and procedures
3. Improve physical storage facilities
4. Make microfilm copies
5. Adopt more flexible survey standards
6. Adopt more flexible survey procedures
7. Partially examine title
8. Make registration compulsory
9. Computerize access to indexes
10. Computerize abstracts of title

scrutinizing their contents, and hence taking a reasonable degree of
risk;
(8)　compulsory registration so that there is a complete record of all
transactions in land;
(9)　automation of indexes to provide quicker document retrieval;
(10)　computerization of the Abstracts of Title to provide quicker access to
the important pieces of information.

2.4　Registration of title to land

The improvements listed above can lead to a process of registration of title.
Many of the defects in deeds-based systems currently in operation can be
cured by changing to registration of title, under which the basic unit for
registration is the land parcel not the deed. Each parcel is identified on a map
or plan that is cross-referenced to the registers that list the name of the
owner, the nature of the tenure, and other ancillary information. The
registers must be kept up to date at all times and be a reflection of the legal
position on the ground. It is then only necessary to consult the current entry
on the proprietorship register to find the name of the owner. Under most
systems of registration of title, the information on the registers is guaranteed
so that, in the unlikely event of fraud or error, anyone inadvertently
suffering from the incorrectness of the information will be compensated.

Each system of registration of title has its own characteristics, derived
from its historical and cultural background. The two best-known systems are
the one that developed in Australia and has been named after its instigator
Sir Robert Torrens and the one that evolved in England. Though often held
to be in contrast because of the different approaches they appear to adopt
with regard to the recording of boundaries, they are in many respects
similar. Both share the overall objectives of operating a system that provides
security while being simple, cheap to operate, accurate, expedient, and
suitable to the particular environmental circumstances.[3] Both are primarily
concerned with the protection of the rights of the individual—though an
adaptation of the English system has been used in Kenya to protect
communal rights in tribal areas.[4]

Arguments in favour of a system of registration of title have been
advanced elsewhere.[5] In practice, there is a continuum as improvements to a
system of registration of deeds can make it almost as effective as registration
of title. Henceforth, the term 'land registration' will be used to cover both
systems.

Land titling programmes

Theoretically at least, unless part of a deliberate land reform programme,
land registration should not change any rights in land but rather give them

stability and provide a framework for land administration. Where changes are planned, the associated programme may be described as land reform. In the United States however the verb 'to title' has been widely adopted and is used to embrace not only the processes of registration of title but also the processes of land reform.[6] So called 'land titling' programmes have been used to bring about major social changes by using the instrument of land registration to shape a new social or economic order. In this treatise, the advantages and disadvantages of using the tool in such a way will not be discussed. The point at issue is that land registration is a powerful tool which can influence not only the physical and legal but also the social and economic environments. In addition, the land information system which supports land registration may also support many other land-related activities.

2.5   Juridical cadastres

The information system which underpins land registration is known as the juridical cadastre. Land registration cannot operate effectively without some form of cadastre. Although cadastral systems already exist in many countries, few operate efficiently. Many are out of date, expensive to maintain, inefficient or largely ineffective in practice, and irrelevant to modern conditions and requirements. In some countries, alternative unofficial systems have developed to meet local needs. In Turkey, for example, many people who are technically squatters (and known as the '*gececondu*') have established patterns of land use and land rights that operate outside of the national cadastral system; many have sufficient confidence in their customary rights to construct substantial but unauthorized high-rise buildings within the main urban centres. Few Third World countries have documented the various forms of existing land rights, few can afford more than the most rudimentary cadastral system, and none can afford the wastage that arises from the misuse of the land.

Benefits of cadastral systems

The juridical cadastre has as a rule two parts. The first is a written record or register containing information about each parcel, such as the name of the owner and the rights which appertain to the land; the second is cross-referenced to the first and contains a detailed description of the parcel, in the form of either maps or survey measurements. The introduction or upgrading of such a cadastral system has been reviewed by Williamson.[7] When combined with registration of title, it should bring a number of benefits, as summarized in Table 2.3, including:

(1)   *Certainty of ownership*. The compilation of land records will necessitate the formal identification and recognition of the ownership of the land, a process known as adjudication. This should provide certainty

Table 2.3   Benefits of a land registration system

1. Certainty of ownership
2. Security of tenure
3. Reduction in land disputes
4. Improved conveyancing
5. Stimulation of the land market
6. Security for credit
7. Monitoring of the land market
8. Facilitating land reform
9. Management of state lands
10. Greater efficiency in land taxation
11. Improvements in physical planning
12. Support for land resource management

not only as to the landowner but also about what other rights exist in the land. This in turn should lead to greater social cohesion.

(2) *Security of tenure*. Through the adjudication process, existing defects in any titles to land can be cured by the judicious use of appropriate powers. In many countries the official record is supported by a state guarantee of the title to the land. Greater security should in turn lead to greater productivity, especially in rural areas where farmers have an incentive to take greater care of the land and to invest their capital and resources in it.

(3) *Reduction in land disputes*. Disputes concerning land and boundaries can give rise to expensive litigation. The settlement of such disputes should be part of the process of adjudication and will not only lead to greater productivity from the land but also reduce court costs and money wasted on litigation.

(4) *Improved conveyancing*. The costs and delays in transferring property rights can be substantially reduced through the operation of a land registration system. Duplication of effort, for instance in the repeated investigation of old titles, can be avoided, thus saving on costs.

(5) *Stimulation of the land market*. The introduction of a cheap, secure, and effective system for recording and transferring interests in land should improve the operation and efficiency of the land market. It should not only lower transaction costs but also permit the market to respond effectively to all the needs of users.

(6) *Security for credit*. The land title can be used as security against any loan. Evidence suggests that the combination of a sound title with the ability to raise long-term credit can give rise to a substantial increase in productivity from the land.

(7) *Monitoring of the land market*. The cadastral system may be used to monitor and if necessary to control land transactions and ownership.

(8) *Facilitating of land reform*. Land redistribution, land consolidation, and land assembly for development and redevelopment can be

expedited through the ready availability of information on who currently owns what.

(9) *Management of state lands*. The state is often the major landowner in a country. The development of a cadastral system, and in particular the creation of cadastral maps in a systematic manner, will benefit the state in the administration of its own land, which will often give rise to improved revenue collection from the land that it leases. Also, the public acquisition of land through compulsory purchase prior to redevelopment can be expedited.

(10) *Support for land taxation*. The potential benefits that accrue from establishing an efficient and equitable land tax system are discussed in Chapter 3. Many countries have some form of land assessment and derive revenue from charges made on the land. Often the cost of improvements in the cadastral system are offset by greater efficiency in tax collection and the consequential greater rate of recovery of tax.

(11) *Improvements in physical planning*. The cadastral system may be used to support physical planning in both the urban and rural sectors. Better land administration should lead to greater efficiency in local government. Many development programmes have failed or been unnecessarily expensive because of a lack of knowledge of existing land rights. The cadastre also provides a basis for restricting certain uses of the land, for instance those that might give rise to pollution.

(12) *Recording of land resource information*. The development of the multipurpose cadastre is described in Chapter 4. The availability of up to date large-scale cadastral plans can lead to the creation of an efficient land information system that services a variety of land resource management activities.

Some of the problems of quantifying these benefits are examined in Chapter 9. In many Third World countries the benefits are obtainable only at a price that they are unable to afford. As Moreno has remarked, many systems are:

too costly, too complicated and too time consuming . . . the cost of precise boundary surveys, coupled with the operation of the prescribed title registration systems inherited by the countries, is out of proportion to the benefits to be derived therefrom, while the cost and time required for extending such a system to cover an entire country, is beyond the resources of almost every developing country . . . Many newly-independent countries inherited colonial land administration systems, which long ago lost touch with modern methods of land management and even with realities in the countries themselves. On the one hand, countries are advised to undertake cadastral surveys and land registration as indispensable for their land administration, but on the other hand, the techniques and operations required are too costly and time consuming for any of them to do so. We might, therefore, have to adjust and adapt our technologies, or alternatively, have to change our recommendations to accord with realities.[8]

Cadastral components

The issues which must be tackled if the benefits of land registration are to be realized are in part legal, in part technical, and in part institutional. Within the juridical cadastre there are four main operations, each of which provides land information (Table 2.4): adjudication, which is the official determination of rights in land; demarcation, which is the marking of the limits of each land parcel on the ground; survey, which entails measurement and mapping; and description, which entails entering relevant information into the official recording system such as in registers. Adjudication takes place during the initial compilation of the registers; the other processes are ongoing and take place initially and as and when there are changes in land ownership. Although each of these processes has a separate identity, they are interdependent. For instance, the determination of the position of a boundary is a matter of adjudication but will depend upon the nature of the boundary. The procedures adopted will differ between boundaries marked by an imaginary line between corner beacons and those marked by the physical presence of a hedge. Such differences will in turn affect the manner and accuracy of the survey used to record its position.

Table 2.4   Components of a juridical cadastre

Adjudication
Demarcation
Survey
Registration
Information management

Unlike other forms of survey (except those practised underground where for health and safety reasons there have to be stringent controls) cadastral surveying has been carried out within a tight framework of legislation. In topographic mapping, any method of survey is normally permissible within the general terms of a contract, provided that it can be shown to give the requisite standard of accuracy. In the cadastre, all stages of the operation may come within statutory regulations. In West Malaysia, for example,[9] it is necessary for all properties to be described by straight lines between turning points, thus making it necessary for all properties to be marked by pegs at all boundary corners. As a consequence, the limits of each parcel must be precisely determined and the survey able to locate the small pegs buried in the ground. This effectively excludes the use of all photogrammetric methods.

2.6 Boundaries

The four processes of adjudication, demarcation, survey, and parcel description are closely influenced by the nature and definition of boundaries.

In a legal sense, a boundary is (except in the case of strata titles) a vertical surface that defines where one land owner's territory ends and the next begins. It may be likened to a bead curtain suspended from the sky such that anyone passing through it from one side to the other passes from one set of property rights into another. The boundary surface intersects the ground along the legal boundary line; stepping over this line is equivalent to passing through the bead curtain. The legal boundary is an infinitessimally thin surface extending from the centre of the earth to the infinite in the sky and is essentially an abstract concept. In practice most people mark the limits of their property on the surface of the earth either with linear features such as fences or hedges or with point features such as wooden pegs, iron bars, or concrete marks. These physical objects may also be referred to as the boundary, though they may not follow the same line in space as the legal limit. Therein lies the seed of confusion.

This confusion is reflected in the terms 'fixed' and 'general' boundary. The distinction between the two has often been a matter of acrimonious debate amongst land surveyors, especially between those with a Southern African or Australian background and those more familiar with the English system. In simple terms, there are at least three concepts of a fixed boundary and three of a general boundary.[10]

Fixed boundaries

To some a fixed boundary (sometimes referred to as a specific boundary) is one which has been accurately surveyed so that a surveyor can, from the survey measurements, accurately replace any corner monuments that might get lost. Although such boundaries are sometimes said to be guaranteed, no legislation gives such a guarantee within any precisely defined limits.

The term fixed boundary is also used to describe a boundary corner point that becomes fixed in space when agreement is reached at the time of alienation of the land; the location of the legal boundary cannot then change without some document of transfer. This is the principle that is adopted under the so-called Torrens system. The surveyor's measurements may provide useful evidence of the boundary's location but the boundary is fixed whether or not there has been a survey.

Under both the systems just described, the evidence on the ground takes precedence over what is actually written down. Under the English system, however, a boundary is fixed when agreement is reached between adjoining owners and the line of division between them is recorded as fixed in the register. From then on the evidence on the register normally overrides whatever is on the ground. The exact line of a boundary under dispute is then determined by reference to the documentary evidence in preference to either long-term occupation and possession of the land or the position of well-established physical features such as hedges, which may be inconsistent with any registered plan.

General boundaries

Under the English general boundary system, the precise line of a boundary between adjoining parcels is left undetermined—it could be one side of a hedge or fence, or the other side, or down the middle. There is, in effect, a strip of unspecified width and uncertain ownership left between each parcel. To others a general boundary is a 'euphemism for an indefinite boundary'[11] such as one which is uncertain and variable like the line of high tide in coastal regions or the edge of a forest. To yet others, as is the case for example in Kenya, it is an approximate line that is deliberately kept vague to prevent argument and the proverbial splitting of hairs. It is as if the line of a boundary as marked on a map is placed out of focus—the open spaces either side of it are clear but the centre of the blurred line is indeterminate. Provided that there is good monumentation, for instance fences or iron stakes driven into the ground, then the parcels define themselves on the ground and all that is needed by the Registrar of Titles is a pointer to ensure that the correct parcel has been referred to. Inspection on the ground can reveal the precise alignment of the boundaries, should it be needed.

The advantages of general boundaries lie primarily in the less demanding standards of survey (see Fig. 2.1), and the manner in which the Registrar of Titles can ignore small changes in the position of a boundary agreed between two parties, whilst still guaranteeing the title of each. The cadastral records may therefore be compiled more cheaply and maintained within defined limits more accurately. If, for example, a fence between two properties falls down and is re-erected along a slightly different line there would be no need to alter any cadastral map or filed plan. In the case of strata titles, the

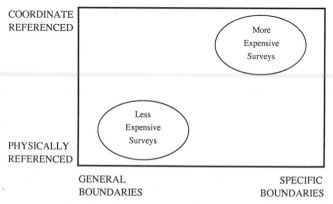

Fig. 2.1   *Cadastral survey systems: boundaries and surveys*

ownership of parts of buildings can be defined and guaranteed without the precise determination of where, within the walls and floors, one set of property rights changes into another. General boundaries are also particularly useful when the ownership of properties is being determined in isolation, as in sporadic adjudication, for the ownership of land can be ascertained without it being necessary to consult the owners of the adjoining properties. The advantage of more specifically defined boundaries, on the other hand, is the confidence which parties can have as to the precise spatial extent of their properties.

2.7 Adjudication

Adjudication is the process whereby existing rights in a particular parcel of land are finally and authoritatively ascertained.[12] It is a prerequisite to registration of title and to land consolidation and redistribution. There is a cardinal principle in land adjudication that the process does not alter existing rights or create new ones. It merely establishes what rights exist, by whom they are exercised and to what limitations if any they are subject.[13] As such, it should introduce certainty and finality into the land records. Unfortunately in areas of customary tenure where the manner of holding of rights in land may be undocumented and uncertain, distortions in the land ownership pattern have sometimes been introduced. A classic example of this distortion occurred at the turn of the century in Buganda, the central region of Uganda, where the British administration mistook the trusteeship of the land by the chiefs for outright freehold. The chiefs became the registered owners of many square miles of land, giving rise to the Mailo system,[14] thus dispossessing the peasant population of their prior customary rights.

Sporadic and systematic adjudication

The determination of land rights presupposes that the land parcels associated therewith have been defined either prior to or concurrent with the ascertainment of those rights. The process may proceed sporadically or systematically. By sporadic is meant 'here and there', 'now and then', namely whenever or wherever there is a demand or other reason for determining the precise ownership of an individual parcel. The sequence in which parcels are brought on to the register is piecemeal, haphazard, and unpredictable. The systematic approach, on the other hand, implies a methodical and orderly sequence in which all parcels are brought on to the register area by area. In the longer term systematic adjudication is less expensive because of economies of scale, more safe because it gives maximum publicity to the determination of who owns what within an area, and more certain because investigations take place on the ground with direct evidence from owners of adjoining properties. Sporadic adjudication can be used selectively to encourage specific categories of land ownership and is cheaper in the short term because adjudication of the rights to many parcels can be deferred. It also permits the cost of the whole operation to be passed directly on to the beneficiaries.

Sporadic adjudication can be applied voluntarily whereas, with the systematic approach, it will be necessary to summon all persons within a designated area to give evidence. Hence systematic adjudication must be compulsory. As such, in order to obtain local co-operation, the process must be subsidized by the state. Experience has shown that, without some degree of compulsory adjudication, registration of title will almost certainly fail and complete registration of all land is never likely to be achieved. Furthermore, disputes over land are more difficult and expensive to resolve if the sporadic approach is adopted.

The adjudication process

The standard procedure for systematic adjudication begins with the promulgation of a law defining the powers of those who will take part; this provides a framework within which they will work. Normally there will be an adjudication officer who is responsible for making the necessary decisions. He or she may be guided by local committees of non-officials. In addition, there will be a demarcation officer who is responsible for marking out the parcels, a survey officer who will survey the boundaries, and a recording officer who will take note of all the decisions reached. One officer may undertake more than one of these functions.

Once the necessary legislation has been passed, the adjudication process can commence. If it is intended that the cadastre should become an inventory of land resources then it must be extended to more if not most of a country. As Dowson and Sheppard wrote: 'one of the supreme advantages of a complete land register and one utilized for all purposes is that it must inevitably take so much that is disputable out of the region of controversial opinion'.[15]

The whole process of adjudication will, depending on the size of the country and the complexity of the land ownership pattern, take many months or years to complete. Some principles must be established for the selection of those places that must be tackled first.[16] Priority should be given to areas where land reform programmes are being planned, where government is intending to dispose of its own land, where litigation over land is frequent or disputes and uncertainty as to the ownership are holding back development, where there is need to guarantee credit, where land values are high or there is cultivation of valuable and permanent cash crops, where there is an increasing number and complexity of land rights, or where it is intended to introduce or improve the basis of tax collection. Political expediency may also need to be considered.

Not all areas will be worth incorporating into the system. There will be areas of low land value or low development potential where there is little or no justification for introducing registration of title. Although the total completion of the cadastral mapping of a country appears on the surface to be an ideal, it may in practice be long delayed and in some areas may never be completed, for to do so would be an unjustifiable use of resources.

Once an area is selected the adjudication programme must be publicized by announcements over the local radio or in the local press and public meetings to explain what is happening. It is essential that the landowners have an understanding and confidence in what is going on, for without their co-operation the adjudication will fail. They must know at what time and on what day their land will be visited by the adjudication team so that they can prepare and present the necessary evidence. At the appointed time they will explain their claim and the adjudication officer's decision on it will be recorded by the recording officer. If the boundaries are determined concurrently, then they will need to be demarcated and, at the earliest possible subsequent date, surveyed. If there is too much delay the survey officer may be unable to relocate the boundary beacons. The results of the adjudication should then be displayed in some public place and landowners permitted a limited period of time—usually between 30 and 60 days—to appeal against the decisions if they have grounds for doing so. Once any appeals are settled, the results can be entered into the land registers as the definitive statement of the official rights in the land.

Where deeds registries are already in existence, recourse to adjudication in the field may be avoided. If there is adequate mapping of the physical boundaries then careful examination of the deeds should be sufficient to identify the parcels and their associated sets of property rights. If, however, the physical evidence is at variance with the documentary then investigation on the ground may still be necessary. In England, for example, there is good basic large-scale mapping. Although there is no longer any Registry of Deeds within the general boundaries rule the old deeds and documents used in private conveyancing can be used in First Registration, which is when land is first brought on to the register. Where necessary, field visits are made to clear up uncertainties but a substantial number of conversions to registration of title can take place solely on the basis of the documentary evidence.

2.8 Boundary monumentation

The monumentation of parcel boundaries is generally achieved in one of two ways: the emplacement of corner beacons and pegs in the ground, or the construction of linear features such as walls and fences or the growing of hedges.

Pegs

The advantages of pegs are that they are cheap, have a low maintenance cost, are easy to emplace, and indicate the precise location of the corner points of property boundaries. As part of the survey process of setting out, their positions can be precalculated, which is a matter of increasing convenience with the extension of computer technology and the use of computer-assisted design for the layout of new housing estates. Their major disadvantage is that they are easily moved or lost either deliberately, carelessly over time, or inadvertently during site construction (for example when bulldozers are used to build roads or dig drainage ditches). Boundary marks should be visible at all times. Pegs buried flush with the ground soon become hidden by vegetation or soil and can be expensive to find.

Hedges and fences

In rural areas the growing of hedges often provides a simple and practical means whereby boundary lines can be made visible, especially from the air, thus allowing the use of cheaper photogrammetric methods of survey. Such methods of monumentation do not, however, provide a universally accept-able solution to the problems of land demarcation. Hedges may conflict with local agricultural practice, they may take nutrients and moisture from the soil which could be more productively used, they may be socially unaccept-able (in some societies the concept of a fence or hedge as a barrier against intrusion is contrary to customary law and practice), or they may form barriers which are resented by pastoralists who have established rights to move freely through the land. Hedges may fundamentally change the nature of the landscape, they may alter their positions over time by reseeding themselves downwind causing a dynamic change in the location of bound-aries, they require labour both to introduce and then to maintain, and of course they may wither and die. Similar objections can be levied against the use of fences, which may be more expensive to construct and to keep in good order. On the other hand, if such methods naturally occur within the community, then advantage should be taken of them. Even though fences are primarily items of defence and guards against intrusion and are often erected for social rather than for legalistic reasons, the general boundaries rule will permit their use for registration purposes. In urban areas the most permanent monument is often the building itself and the actual boundaries can be referred to it. In rural areas, in spite of the objections above, fences and hedges are more advantageous.

Hedging was the key to success in Kenya where millions of hectares of rural land were brought on to the register in a relatively short period of time. In a major land reallocation scheme, each prospective new landowner was required to grow hedges along his boundaries so that these could be photographed from the air and subsequently mapped. A hedging inspectorate was set up within the Survey of Kenya and charged with ensuring that the hedges were in fact planted and properly maintained. Inevitably there were problems. During the growing season, priority had to be given to growing cash crops and to subsistence agriculture, to the detriment of the hedge plants. In general, however, the landowners were sufficiently convinced of the importance of hedging their land that they co-operated with the authorities. As a result, the granting of title proceeded on the basis of effective and extremely cheap surveys.

2.9 Boundary surveys

There is some evidence that, in the short term, adjudication of the ownership of parcels and the location of their boundaries, followed by suitable monumentation, provides the necessary and sufficient conditions for secure tenure. Such appeared to be the case in south-west Uganda.[17] Here, after adjudication, demarcation, and survey, the landowners declined to collect their title deeds, for which they had to pay a small fee, on the grounds that paper documents would add nothing to what everybody had by then come to know. The publicity that normally accompanies the adjudication process, and the firm monumentation of points on the ground so that adjoining neighbours can see the agreed limits of their land, resolves many disputes. Prevention of future disputes, however, requires the cadastral survey (Table 2.5) of the boundary beacons or lines.

Surveying represents a long-term investment; its advantages, though real, are not immediate. A geometrical framework provides a basis for producing maps which can assist in the administration of the land—for planning and controlling its development, for redefining disputed or uncertain boundaries, and for structuring geographical or land information systems. In many Third World countries, however, the techniques of mapping have to be such as to meet the minimum necessary and sufficient conditions using the minimum of resources at minimum cost, producing results with maximum

Table 2.5 The functions of a cadastral survey

1. Definition, demarcation, determination, and retracement of boundaries
2. Subdivision, assembly, and reallotment
3. Spatial organization of resources (political, administrative, and land tenure boundaries)
4. Provision of land information

speed. Technical aspects of survey are examined in more detail in Chapters 5 and 6.

Accuracy standards

A major determining factor in the cost of a survey and the speed with which it may be completed is the accuracy standard that it is deemed necessary to sustain. Historically this has often been determined by what is technically possible rather than by what is necessary and sufficient for the operation of the cadastre. The regulations that govern the conduct of surveys have more often reflected the state of the art in surveying at the time they were introduced than, for instance, the quality of the monumentation that is used. Thus at a time when traversing was considered the most appropriate method of cadastral surveying, the necessary standards were determined by what it was technically reasonable to achieve—for instance in Nigeria a proportional error of 1 part in 3000 in rural areas and 1 part in 4000 in urban. A more reasonable approach would be to have flexible standards that could be adapted to the local land use, land value, or the type of boundary beacons most appropriate for the area.

Survey regulations

In order to improve efficiency and productivity, amendments may be needed both to the land law and to any regulations currently in force relating to the manner in which surveys must be carried out. In recent history, the introduction of such techniques as electronic distance measurement was in some countries long delayed because the regulations governing the conduct of cadastral surveys laid down that all distances were to be measured directly using chains or tapes. Although such restrictive regulations have in most cases been repealed, it is still possible to find that photogrammetric methods fall outside the list of permitted survey techniques.

Additional constraints on what can be done to simplify surveys stem from planning legislation, especially that relating to the size of plot frontages or the width of roads. The initial compilation of registers is primarily concerned with recording what already exists. The maintenance phase predominantly consists of setting out new boundaries in conformity with subdivision rules or planning regulations. These regulations may imply levels of precision where none is needed. Thus a road reserve width of 20 metres can become 20.00 metres or a width of 50 imperial feet can become 15.24 metres, and surveyors attempt to maintain a standard of precision of 1 centimetre. Although this is not required by the legal cadastre for the purposes of registration of title, it can have a significant influence on costs.

Additional pressures come from high technology. With the increasing use of computers for design purposes, the precision of the computing process tends to be forced on to those responsible for laying the design out on the ground. This inevitably increases costs to a level which can only be justified on very high density development sites.

2.10 Parcel records

A register of titles normally contains two elements: a record of the attributes associated with each parcel and a description of the land to which they refer. In the compilation of the registers, the cost of survey and the preparation of the parcel descriptions may account for around 40 per cent of the total costs of the land title registration scheme. As such, a 10 per cent saving in the costs of survey may produce an overall saving of only 4 per cent. None the less this may be a significant figure.

Parcel attributes

The attributes that may be recorded in the registers include the name of the owners, the nature of the tenure (such as freehold or leasehold), the price paid for the land on transfer, any restrictions on the use of the parcel (such as restrictive covenants or charges where the land is subject to mortgage), any exclusion of rights to minerals below the soil, and any caveats or cautions which may require a third party to be informed if any dealings in the land are proposed. Depending on the legal system, certain categories of overriding interests may be assumed to apply but not be included within the entries on the registers. These include the rights of others to light or the restrictions imposed on all properties by town and country planning legislation. Additional information of a multipurpose nature, such as the land use or the soil type, may also be included. In many cases, for example where a right of way over certain parts of the land is in existence, the entries on the register which are written in verbal form may be supplemented by evidence on an attached plan. This plan then becomes a formal part of the description.

Parcel descriptions

The function of a cadastral plan is first and foremost to identify the parcel of land which has been referred to in the written parts of the registers. This may of course be achieved by a simple parcel reference number relating to the house, street, and town in which the property is located. '23 Acacia Avenue, Newtown' would identify a parcel whose limits may be determined by inspection on the ground. Frequently, however, this is insufficient and the parcel description should provide additional information such as the shape and size of the property and at least the approximate location of its boundaries. It should also show the relative location of the property by providing some details about adjoining parcels. The description should enable the boundaries to be relocated in cases of dispute or uncertainty, enable subdivision to take place within or up to the limit of the existing plot, and permit areas to be calculated for the purposes of planning or assessment. In addition it should form a basis for land information management and the multipurpose cadastre, as will be discussed in Chapter 4.

Verbal descriptions   Parcel descriptions may be verbal—for example 'all that land between the river Exe and the main road between Newtown and Wyemouth'; numerical (including the coordinates of or the bearings and distances between corner monuments); or they may be graphical, with the information plotted on a plan. Verbal descriptions on their own are inadequate for most purposes. An exception is where they refer to the bounds or abuttals, that is, the details of what adjoins the property—for example, 'up to the edge of the land owned by Mr. Jones'. Such descriptions reflect the importance of occupation and use of the land and may help in determining boundaries on the ground. In general, however, they are significantly inferior to the other methods and produce little information of value for other applications.

Graphical plans   Graphical methods are the most effective and easy to comprehend; they communicate quickly and cheaply most of the relevant information. A cadastral plan should be at a scale that is large enough for every separate parcel to appear as a recognizable unit. However, the larger it is, the more expensive in general it becomes. Suggested scales are indicated in Fig. 2.2. The plan should show not only the boundary monuments such as pegs but also relevant topographical features such as buildings and fences. These will help in the identification of the boundaries. In urban areas, a scale of 1:1000 is almost always sufficient. There are of course exceptions but even in central London, where land values are amongst the highest in the world, a scale of 1:1250 is often sufficient. In rural areas a scale of 1:5000, 1:10 000, or even 1:20 000 may be adequate (depending on the size of the parcels and the manner of their demarcation).

SUGGESTED SCALES

TYPE OF AREA	CUSTOMARY PLOT FRONTAGE	IMPERIAL MAP SCALES	METRIC MAP SCALES
Urban	5m to 15m	1:600 (1"=50')	1:500
Urban	15m to 30m	1:1200 (1"=100')	1:1000
Suburban	30m to 60m	1:2400 (1"=200')	1:2000;1:2500
Rural	60m & greater	1:4800 (1"=400')	1:2000;1:5000
Resources		1:12 000;1:24 000	1:10 000;1:25 000

Fig. 2.2   *Property maps*

Numerical descriptions Property descriptions may also be based on numerical information. Modern field survey techniques normally produce numerical data, whilst with the increasing use of computers even graphical information tends to be converted into digital form. From such data it is relatively easy to produce the description of property boundaries either in terms of coordinates or by reference to the metes, that is, the bearings and distances between adjoining points. In some jurisdictions the metes are combined with the bounds, but in such cases it is normal for the bounds to take precedence if there is any conflict of evidence. The numerical data may be held within a computer or on printed lists.

The relative weight given to different types of evidence varies between jurisdictions. In most countries the marks found in the ground take precedence over the numerical values. If a peg is found at a measurement that differs from that shown on the record then, unless there is other evidence to show that the peg has been moved, its present position will be accepted. Historically, this has been in part because the quality of some survey measurements was not good, but more particularly because pegs generally represented the limits of possession and occupation of the land. Measurements were more open to dispute. Today, however, many land surveyors argue that the quality of survey measurement is now such that greater certainty can come from trusting the record, as in the English fixed-boundary approach, rather than the pegs on the ground, which are at all times subject to movement. This argument is reinforced by the confidence which many people have in the quality of data held in numerical form. Though a plausible argument, the traditional view that 'marks come before measurements, pegs are paramount to plans' is based on common and customary law and in most cases on everyday experience.

2.11 Parcel reference systems

The various methods for describing the limits of each parcel must include an element that refers uniquely to the parcel as a whole. Even with a graphical system it is necessary to have a parcel indicator (sometimes referred to as the PID) or a unique parcel reference number (UPRN) that identifies the parcel and allows for cross-referencing within the registers and any other filing systems. Given the parcel reference number, it should be possible to access all the details of the parcel, including its attributes and its spatial description. A number of alternative referencing systems have been adopted, and these include:

(1) *Grantor/grantee index.* This gives the name of the vendor and of the purchaser, such as Smith A. B. and Jones C. D. If either of these is known then the details of the title can be found under the relevant

heading. Such an approach was used in the Maritime Provinces of Canada prior to the introduction of the Land Registration and Information System (LRIS).[18] It does not uniquely define a parcel, nor does it provide locational information.

(2)   *Title number.* This is usually allocated in sequential order so that the next title after number 123456 would be 123457. If the plot whose title number were WX11122 were subdivided in two, it could then become plot WX88563 and WX88564, the WX being an area code. The English system uses such an approach cross-referenced to a postal address system.

(3)   *Volume and folio.* This is used in the Torrens system and in the Federal Republic of Germany and comprises the volume of the register and the page in which the parcel details are given. Thus Vol. 989 Fol. 60 would be the 60th page in the 989th volume of the registers.

(4)   *Subdivision name and plot number.* The subdivision may be an administrative area such as a parish or farm, individual parcels within that area being given a consecutive number. Unlike the simple title numbering system, this introduces some spatial identity.

(5)   *Block and plot number.* This is similar to the above but with the blocks chosen for the convenience of registration and not necessarily coinciding with other administrative boundaries.

(6)   *Post office address.* Where there is a plot number and street address system this can be used to identify the parcel within the registers. Although not easy to computerize, it can be supplemented by a post code as used for the automatic sorting of letters.

(7)   *Street index and parcel address.* Here every street is given a reference number and the parcel is located within it. This can be in alphanumerical form such as 555554444A333 where 55555 is the street code, 4444 is the plot number, A indicates abnormalities such as properties more particularly known by a name (for example The White House), and 333 is a further subdivision for strata titles.

(8)   *Grid coordinate or geocode.* This may be based on latitude and longitude or more conveniently on the national grid mapping system (see Fig. 2.3). The use of a grid system requires the adoption of a particular map projection, which will in turn transform measured quantities on the ground to mathematically derived equivalents on the projection. Although the difference between the two sets of values gives rise to some confusion, the disadvantages of using a projection system are far outweighed by the advantages.

In selecting a method for parcel referencing (see Table 2.6) it is desirable that the system should be:

(1)   easy to understand, making confusion and mistakes less likely;

(2)   easy to remember so that landowners can recall their references;

A PARCEL IDENTIFIER WHICH GIVES THE GEOGRAPHIC
LOCATION OF A CONVENIENT POINT WITHIN THE PARCEL
(SUCH AS THE VISUAL CENTRE). IT IS EXPRESSED AS
X, Y COORDINATES

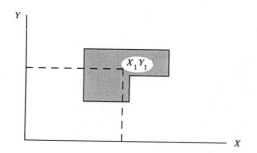

EXAMPLE   X = 1 732 000
           Y = 0 218 532
XY PAIR   10, 72, 31, 28, 05, 03, 02
GEOCODE = 10 . 7231 . 28 . 0503   (Last digits can be dropped if redundant)

Fig. 2.3   *Geocodes*

(3) easy to use both by the general public and administrators;
(4) easy to process in computers;
(5) permanent so that, for instance, the parcel reference does not change
     with the sale of the property;
(6) capable of being updated when there is a subdivision or amalgamation
     of two adjoining properties;
(7) unique so that no two parcels have the same reference and there is a
     one to one correspondence between the property on the ground and
     the property referred to in the registers;
(8) accurate and unlikely to be transcribed in error;
(9) flexible so that it can be used for a variety of purposes from regis-
     tration of title through to all forms of land administration;
(10) economic to introduce and to maintain.

There is no perfect answer to what system to choose; much will depend
upon what is already available. If there is no street-numbering system, it will
be impossible to incorporate a street address without significant administrative effort; if there is one, then the address will need to be recorded if it is to
be processed by computer. In most cases it will be necessary to have a unique
parcel reference number that can be linked manually or through a computer
to separate lists containing the name of the owner, the postal address, the
geographical or grid coordinates, and any other references that are linked to

Table 2.6   Choosing a land parcel identifier

Design criteria:
- Uniqueness
- Simplicity
- Flexibility
- Permanence
- Economy
- Accessibility

Used for:
- Referencing records to individual parcels
- Indicating spatial location of each parcel
- Linkages to other parcels

the parcel. The system may then be entered in a variety of ways so that, given one piece of information, the unique parcel reference number can be used to locate all other associated data.

2.12   Improving systems

The various components outlined above form separate stages in the compilation of a legal cadastre, but they are not independent. The optimum methods of survey will depend upon the type of monumentation. Boundaries that are not visible from the air cannot, for example, be surveyed by photogrammetric methods unless all the corner points are marked on the ground with signals of sufficient size to appear on the aerial photographs. If the legislation requires that boundaries be defined and described by straight lines between corner pegs then ground survey by traversing along the property boundaries will be the most likely solution, and the adjudication process will need to identify all turning points along the boundary perimeter. If, however, the custom is to grow hedges along the boundaries or if a sporadic approach is to be adopted then a general boundaries system may be used, leaving the ownership of the bounding features undetermined. The corollary of this is that changes in one part of the cadastral system may require or may bring about changes in other parts.

In many countries the cadastral system is basically sound. Its failure to work properly stems more from issues of practice than from issues of principle. Small changes in the specifications of surveys and minor amendments to the legislation may bring about significant improvements. It is better if a system can be subject to evolutionary rather than to revolutionary change. The key to this incremental improvement lies in the hands of management, who must assess the minimum that is both necessary and sufficient for the system to meet most practical needs.

In some countries, however, a more radical overhaul of the system is necessary, with new procedures and new technologies being introduced. Whilst the compilation of new registers is being undertaken, it will be necessary to update the completed records so that changes resulting from transfers or subdivisions can be incorporated. Failure to keep the records up to date often occurs from the very beginning. Maintenance and up-dating of systems must be operational from the very start if the investment in the cadastre is not to be wasted. Governments must be made aware not only of the size of the capital investment necessary to produce and maintain the system, but also of the length of the time over which funding will be needed before the systems can be financially self sufficient.

Although the location of boundaries is important to the legal cadastre, there is, in general, little need for precise measurement. The primary objective is a system for recording of rights in land to standards which ensure the good management of the land and the people who occupy it. The system should be capable of solving most of the problems most of the time at the minimum of cost. No system has ever been able to solve all of the problems all of the time. Provided that there is the support of an insurance fund to compensate anyone who suffers as a result of any defects in the system, then, contrary to much that has been attempted in the past, the system can operate by taking calculated risks. It can then provide the necessary security of tenure and a sound basis for land management and development whilst operating at a lower level of costs both in the short and in the long term.

2.13   Thailand—a case history

Thailand is a country that presents an interesting 'land-titling' case study. Currently there is a major project under way to upgrade its cadastral and land registration systems. Details have been provided by Angus-Leppan and Williamson.[19] At the outset of the project, 15 per cent of the country was held by title deed, 52 per cent was under certificate permitting certain usage of the land, and the remaining third was undocumented. Pressure on rural land has been steadily increasing; over the last two decades the demand for land for cultivation has grown at an annual rate of 4 per cent.

The cadastral development project has been supported by the World Bank and the Australian Development Assistance Bureau. The aims have been to:

(1)   establish a spatial reference system by upgrading the present survey network through the extension of geodetic control;
(2)   produce cadastral mapping in rural areas, based upon rectified photo-maps; these are generally at a scale of 1:4000, though larger scales are necessary in villages and where land parcels are small;

(3)   produce urban mapping at scales of 1:1000 and 1:500 as appropriate, again based where possible on rectified aerial photographs;
(4)   adjudicate and survey developed areas (priority being given to privately held land and to state land used for administrative purposes);
(5)   upgrade the data held for land and property valuation and taxation.

The need for improvement has stemmed in part from the inadequacies of existing cadastral maps, many of which are between 30 and 50 years out of date. The project has been designed to make use of existing skills and procedures by concentrating on those activities that have so far been most cost effective. It has been possible to avoid major changes in legislation and technology by adapting existing methods. It is accepted that the physical boundaries of the parcels in general define the legal limits, thus allowing the use of aerial photographic methods in most areas. Where vegetation cover prevents their effective use, simple ground survey methods are adopted. Changes have been incremental and evolutionary. Computerization has been introduced only into proved and operational systems.

Priority has been given to:

(1)   areas where the confirmation of land titles should help the provision of credit for agricultural improvements;
(2)   areas where there is a large amount of undocumented land;
(3)   areas where there is to be a rural poverty eradication programme;
(4)   areas where the number of boundary disputes is high.

The whole programme is being carefully monitored to evaluate its overall costs and benefits. The evidence to date is that the increased productivity from the land, combined with greater social stability, more than justifies the reforms which have been undertaken.

References and notes

1. Simpson, S. R. (1976). *Land law and registration*, p. 7 Cambridge University Press.
2. Fortescue-Brickdale, Sir C. (1914). *Methods of land transfer*, London.
3. Fortescue-Brickdale, Sir C. *Op. cit.*
4. Simpson, S. R. *Op. cit.*, p. 257.
5. Simpson, S. R. *Op. cit.*
6. Stanfield, D. (1984). Rural land titling programs in Latin America. *Proceedings of the International Workshop on Land Tenure Administration*. Salvador, Brazil. p. 207–27.
7. Williamson, I. (1986). Cadastral and land information systems in developing countries. *The Australian Surveyor*, Vol. 33/1, pp. 27–43.
8. Moreno, R. (1984). Cadastres and land registration. *Proceedings of the International Workshop on Land Tenure Administration*. Salvador, Brazil. pp. 409–16.

9. For instance, section 396(1) of the Malaysian *National Land Code* states that for any property:

   (a) its boundaries have been determined by right lines;
   (b) its boundaries as so determined have been demarcated on the surface of the land by boundary marks or, if by reason of the configuration thereof or for any other cause the placing of boundary marks on the actual line of the boundaries is to any extent impossible or impracticable, boundary marks have been so emplaced as to enable that line to be ascertained;
   (c) the area enclosed by its boundaries as so determined has been calculated;
   (d) a lot number has been assigned thereto by the Chief Surveyor; and
   (e) a certified plan, showing the situation of the land, the position of its boundaries as so determined and of the boundary marks placed thereon and the area and lot number thereof, has been approved by the Chief Surveyor.

10. Further details of this and other cadastral systems are given in Dale, P. F. (1976). *Cadastral surveys within the Commonwealth*, Her Majesty's Stationery Office; Overseas Research Publication No. 23, London.

11. Dowson, Sir E. and Sheppard, V. L. O. (1952). *Land registration*, Her Majesty's Stationery Office, Colonial Research Publications No. 13, London.

12. Lawrence, J. C. D. (1985). Land adjudication. Paper presented at World Bank Seminar on Land Information Systems, Washington D C.

13. Simpson, S. R. *Op. cit.*, see Chapter 15.

14. West, H. W. (1969). *The Mailo system in Buganda*, Cambridge University Press.

15. Dowson, Sir E. and Shepperd, V. L. O. *Op. cit.*, p. 72.

16. West, H. W. (1969). 'The role of land registration in developing countries'. *Chartered Surveyor*, Vol. 102, pp. 211–21.

17. Dale, P. F. *Op. cit.*

18. Simpson, R. L. (1985). LRIS—the basis for land information systems. In Hamilton A. and McLaughlin, J. (eds) *The decision maker and land information systems*. Papers and Proceedings from FIG International Symposium, Edmonton, 1984. The Canadian Institute of Surveying, pp. 88–93.

19. Angus-Leppan, P. V. and Williamson, I. P. (1985). A project for upgrading the cadastral system in Thailand. *Survey Review* Vol. 28/215, pp. 2–14; Vol. 28/216, pp. 63–73.

3. The fiscal cadastre

In this chapter we review some of the basic approaches to property valuation and the kind of land information that is required to support them. We also examine aspects of the organization and management of the fiscal cadastre.

3.1 The origins of the fiscal cadastre

The fiscal cadastre may be defined as an inventory of land parcels that provides the information necessary to determine the value of each parcel and the tax due on it. The applications of the fiscal cadastre are, however, more widespread and relate to a variety of land management functions (Table 3.1). There are three major steps in operating the fiscal cadastre. Firstly, it is necessary to discover and identify all parcels that are to be valued. Secondly, each land parcel must be classified and its value determined. Thirdly, the taxes must be collected from those who are responsible for the property. The actual person or persons who must pay the tax may not necessarily own the property. The fiscal register may, however, be a primary source of evidence as to the true owner. There should therefore be a connection between the management of the fiscal registers and the so-called juridical cadastre.

The earliest cadastres were developed for taxation purposes. Rudimentary cadastral arrangements have been traced to the early agricultural settlements along the Tigris, Euphrates, and Nile Rivers, where revenues for the Pharaohs and the priesthood were met principally by an assessment of land income as revealed by the cadastral survey. The tax was based on the principle that all land belonged to the king and all those who cultivated his land had to pay taxes in the form of rent. In later times, the Greeks and Romans developed elaborate land records and survey systems in support of land taxation.

Table 3.1 Functions served by the fiscal cadastre

- Information base for property taxation
- Support in financial allocation programmes
- Monitoring and support for land market
- Aid to land use development control
- Provision of land information

Modern fiscal cadastral systems can be traced to the tax mapping of the Italian provinces of Milan and Mantua between 1720 and 1723. Following this the Austrians carried out a cadastral survey between 1785 and 1789 of the entire territory included within the Austro-Hungarian Empire. In 1807, Napoleon appointed the mathematician Delambre to chair a commission whose task was

To survey . . . more than 100 million parcels, to classify these parcels by the fertility of the soil, and to evaluate the productive capacity of each one; to bring together under the name of each owner a list of the separate parcels which he owns to determine, on the basis of their total productive capacity, their total revenue and to make of this assessment a record which should thereafter serve as the basis of future assessment.[1]

Much of the impetus for the development of fiscal cadastres in Europe in the eighteenth and nineteenth centuries has been attributed to the French Physiocrats. They argued that, since landed property is capable of producing an income over time and is the basis of all wealth, the revenues necessary for administering the state should be derived from taxing that wealth at source, namely by taxing the land. This approach became widely accepted in Europe, where most state revenues came to be obtained by levying a ground tax. This tax was ultimately based on the estimated taxable revenue of each parcel, the amount depending on the particular use of the land. The physiocrats' methods later provided much of the stimulus for large-scale tax mapping in North America and elsewhere, since maps are a means by which all properties can be identified and recorded.

3.2 Land and property taxation

Two different methods are used for raising revenue from land: property-rating systems and land value taxation. With a property-rating system governments raise revenue by assessing and taxing improvements, such as buildings and the uses to which they are put. Thus a property used as a shop will be taxed differently from one used solely for residential purposes. With land-value taxation, on the other hand, the tax is based on the value of the land itself as determined from either its improved or its unimproved state. Both systems become instruments of land policy, inevitably influencing the manner in which the land is used.

Taxation objectives

Some authorities have expressed concern about the efficiency and effectiveness of land value and property taxes and have advocated the greater use of value-added taxes, poll taxes, or local sales and local income taxes. The concerns have revolved around the basic principles of taxation, as well as the

Table 3.2   Objectives of a taxation system

- Meet social objectives
- Produce significant revenue
- Be under full governmental control
- Be simple, easy to understand, and efficient to collect
- Make tax evasion difficult
- Be equitable, sharing the tax burden fairly
- Give incentive to employment
- Make best use of resources

mechanics and cost of administering the tax. The objectives of any taxation system are partly political and partly administrative. As matters of general principle (Table 3.2), the tax should:

(1) be seen either to serve clearly identifiable social objectives or else to produce significant sums of revenue;

(2) be exclusively controlled by the political authority imposing the tax (unlike India, for example, in the early days of the British administration when the local tax collectors, called Zamindars, often collected excessive amounts of tax and retained the surplus for their personal use);

(3) be administered in a way that is understood both by the taxpayers and by their political representatives;

(4) be relatively simple and cheap to collect;

(5) be designed so that it is difficult to avoid payment;

(6) distribute the tax burden in a way that is seen to be equitable (for example by relating the tax to what the individual can afford);

(7) encourage high and stable levels of employment;

(8) ensure the best allocation and use of resources.

Property tax

Some critics consider that property taxes are not necessarily related to the ability of the taxpayer to pay, since the occupation of a property does not necessarily affect the income that is derived from it. Some consider that the tax has a depressing effect on incentives and productivity and that it can be relatively expensive to collect. (In parts of the Indian subcontinent the cost of administering the fiscal cadastre can exceed the revenue collected.) On the other hand, property tax can be a productive tax, capable of generating a significant amount of revenue. In many countries it is already well established as a system and the taxpayers have become accustomed to it. It broadens the tax base so that the majority of people have to pay at least some tax. When it is properly administered, there is little opportunity for tax evasion, since property and land, unlike income, are difficult to hide.

Property taxes can also play an important role in controlling the use and development of the land, since they provide a stimulus to landowners to use their land optimally. If the land is taxed on the basis of a more profitable use, then the taxpayer has an incentive to use the land that way. The property tax can also be related to the benefits received. These benefits may be in the form of services or of an increase in the land value resulting from action taken by the community rather than by the landowner. The tax can thus be used to recapture for the community some of the windfall profits that can accrue from land use planning decisions. This is sometimes referred to as 'betterment'. For example, land valued at $1000 per hectare as agricultural land may suddenly become worth $50 000 per hectare to the owner if he or she is granted permission to build houses upon it. The increased value is created by the community, but unless it is subject to specific taxes the benefit will all go to the landowner.

Property and land value taxes are of course only two ways to collect revenue. As McGlade comments:

a more enlightened approach to funding of local revenue involves the whole basket of taxes available and certainly involves the continuance of the property tax system in co-ordination with wider use of other taxes such as sales, income and poll taxes. If valuation administration were strengthened together with the enlightened use of a minimum number of differential rates, a greater equity in tax treatment amongst taxpaying groups would result.[2]

In Singapore the property tax is the second largest source of tax revenue. In 1979, it contributed 15.5 per cent of the tax and 11.3 per cent of the total government revenue.[3] In general, however, the importance of property taxation has declined in comparison with taxes on income (both of individuals and corporations), on capital transfer, on capital gains, and on sales and expenditure. In the United States, property taxes yield a sum equal to 3.6 per cent of the Gross Domestic Product (GDP); in Britain local rates account for 3.3 per cent; in New Zealand the figure is 2.27 per cent. In Australia, local rates and state land tax yield 1.46 per cent of the GDP. In Germany, the property tax levied by municipalities accounts for 12.6 per cent of their revenue but represents only 0.37 per cent of GDP.[4]

Land tax

Whereas property taxes are essentially concerned with improvements to the land, land taxes are generally based upon a valuation of the productive capacity of the land itself. For agricultural land, for example, this would require a direct survey of a farm at harvest time, or an indirect assessment based upon the area and estimated yield. The latter has been the case on the Indian subcontinent, where only income above a certain threshold is now subject to tax. Estimates of yield can be obtained from past experience or, increasingly, from aerial photography or remotely sensed imagery.

Land taxes based upon estimates of productive capacity have at one time or another been imposed in Australia, New Zealand, Denmark, South Africa and East Africa, Jamaica, Barbados, Hawaii, and western Canada. In New Zealand, the taxation of land was introduced in 1878, with the aim of breaking up the large individual holdings of agricultural landowners. Many countries still retain some variant of a land tax, though most now tax both the land and the improvements to it. Less developed countries tend to tax agricultural land, while developed countries often concentrate on the taxation of urban land.

3.3   Property valuation

Property taxes can be imposed on the land, on improvements to the land, or on both. They may be based on the capital value or on the rental value of the property. Finally, they may be a charge on the owner, on the occupier, or on both. The level of the taxation in part depends upon what is construed as the value of property. According to the United Nations: 'property has value because it provides amenities and satisfactions of living, as in the case of residences; services in the production of goods, such as a manufacturing plant; and income in the form of rents or leases.'[5]

The value of any tract of real estate depends upon a variety of factors, which include the use and enjoyment of the land, the income arising from it, and the rights to alienate or transfer it. The value depends in part upon conditions inherent in the property and in part upon factors which are extraneous to it. Intrinsic factors include the topography of the land, the nature of the soil, and the design and condition of the buildings. Extrinsic factors include the environment in which a property is located, the proximity to other land resources, the availability of transport, and the adequacy of public services. More particularly, however, the value of land depends upon the economic climate and government fiscal policies. The value is often only minimally influenced by the actions of the landowner and may be largely dependent on the administrative and legislative framework.

The process of valuation may be described as the carefully considered estimate of the worth of landed property based on experience and judgement. The purpose of valuation is to determine 'value', a term generally prefaced by some description such as market value or benefit value. A major distinction can be made between capital and rental value. The capital value is what would be paid to build or buy the property; the rental value is the income that can be expected from it. The advantage of basing taxes on the rental value is that the value assessed is the value in use, and includes no element of potential value such as what the land might be worth if it were used in some other way. The method is convenient for properties such as flats or apartments, especially where charges made on occupiers can be more easily recovered than those sent to landlords. The disadvantage is that there is often a lack of reliable information on the rents that are being paid; the assessment may therefore be arbitrary.

Market value

For taxation purposes, the concept of market value is generally used. Market value may be defined as:

the most probable price in terms of money which a property should bring in a competitive and open market under all conditions requisite to a fair sale, the buyer and seller each acting prudently and knowledgeably, and assuming the price is not affected by undue stimulus.[6]

In simple terms, the market value is what it is reasonable to expect the land would fetch if it were sold in the market-place. This, however, may be assessed in a number of different ways.

Valuation Methods

The valuation is usually derived from the market price, expressed as either a capital sum or a potential income. Where there has been no sale and the property itself has not changed hands then one or more of the following methods may be used (Table 3.3):

(1) The *comparative method*. This assumes that the market value is equal to the price recently paid for a similar property or interest in land. The valuer's problem is to determine what the market considers to be recent and similar. Adjustments may need to be made for differences between the properties used in the comparison and changes that have subsequently taken place in the market or are of a structural nature. If an almost identical house were recently sold next door for a known price but which lacked a particular facility such as a garage or central heating, then a slightly different assessment would be expected. The approach is often the most simple and efficient means of determining market value, especially for single-family residential properties in an active market.

(2) The *income method*. This is also a comparative method and holds that the market value of an interest in land is equal to the present value of the net income that should in future come from the land. The net income is the gross

Table 3.3 Site and property valuation methods

- Comparison with other properties
- Determining income generated from the property
- Estimating costs for rebuilding
- Determining value of site if fully developed

income less the cost of overheads, such as depreciation of the building stock and its maintenance and upkeep. It is equivalent to a notional rent and must be discounted at an appropriate rate. The valuer's problem is to determine the net benefits that should come from the land by comparison with similar properties; and then to determine the market discount rate by analysing recent sales of similar assets.

(3) The *cost method*. This is also known as the *contractor's method* or the *quantity survey approach*. It assumes that the costs of replacement, less appropriate depreciation, are equal to the value. The problem is to assemble suitable cost data, including the cost of the site, and to estimate depreciation rates. The method is particularly useful for insurance purposes, where the cost of site clearance may be added to cover the possibility of a building being destroyed by fire, and for valuing new constructions.

(4) The *residual method*. This represents a combination of the three methods listed above. The value of the site is assessed as if it had been developed. The method may be applied either to the land itself or to the improvements upon it. It involves no new problems for the appraiser, save that of estimating the date of development completion. Its importance lies in that it should encourage land to be brought up to its full potential. Land that is derelict can then be taxed as if it were fully productive, thus providing an incentive for the owner either to develop the land or to sell it to someone else who will use it more beneficially.

Rating

While an increasing number of jurisdictions base their taxation on the capital or market value of the property, several still use some variation of a rental value approach. For example, the system of local taxation of property in the United Kingdom, which is called rating, is based upon an assessment of the occupiers of the land and buildings according to an estimated rental value. Except for industrial properties, the basis for the annual value for rating purposes, is the estimated rent that the property might reasonably be expected to yield from year to year, assuming that the landlord undertakes to pay the cost of repairs, insurance, and other expenses necessary to maintain it in a satisfactory state and that the tenant undertakes to pay the rates and taxes. This produces a 'gross value' from which a standardized deduction is made for the cost of repairs and other outgoings, to arrive at the net figure of 'rateable value' on which the rates are charged as a percentage of the assessed value. Industrial properties are assessed on the assumption that the tenant bears all outgoings so that a net assessment of rateable value is arrived at directly.

In order to carry out each of the above forms of appraisal, there is a need for records of recent sales of similar interests in land and the type and costs of any constructional improvements such as buildings. The data on construction costs are generally easy to ascertain, given the size of the property and the nature of the materials used. The determination of recent and similar sales and valuations is often more difficult and may require the use of statistical techniques to determine market trends.

3.4 The creation of fiscal cadastres

The fiscal cadastre is an instrument for administering land tax policy. Although primarily a support for land value and property taxes, the data that it records can be used in the determination of other forms of tax, such as those imposed on personal wealth or income derived from real estate. The data also provide fiscal information for the expropriation of land for government purposes and for revenue transfers between different levels and departments of government.

The creation of a fiscal cadastre entails a number of operations (Table 3.4), all of which must be carried out within the framework of the law. These include:

(1) The identification and mapping of all properties that are to be subject to tax. A primary requirement for an efficient and effective fiscal cadastre is a set of current property maps that provide an index for compiling and maintaining valuation information. The maps are necessary to ensure that all parcels are identified and that no parcel is taxed more than once. The approximate size, shape, and location of the parcel, as depicted on the map, may be used in the actual valuation process.

(2) The classification of each property in accordance with an agreed set of characteristics relating to such matters as its use, size, type of construction, and improvements.

(3) The collection and analysis of relevant market data. This may include data on sales prices, rental charges, or building maintenance costs, together with details of the dates when these applied.

(4) The determination of the value of each parcel in accordance with one or more of the principles outlined under 'Valuation Methods'.

Table 3.4 Creating a fiscal cadastre

1. Identify and map all properties
2. Classify each property
3. Analyse market data
4. Value each property
5. Identify owners and tax payers
6. Prepare valuation roles
7. Send out bills and collect taxes
8. Establish appeals procedures

(5)   The identification of the person or persons who will be responsible for paying the tax. It is also important to identify the legal owner in case the property is forfeited through non-payment of tax though, as Dillinger has noted:

> tax legislation can be written so as to make the property itself liable for taxation, sparing the tax office the problem of tracking down an owner or occupant. Such legislation, termed *in rem*, specifies that a property failing to pay its tax will be seized and sold. The expectation is that the threat of losing the property will bring forward an owner, tenant, or anyone else in beneficial occupation of the property, to pay the tax . . . Tax offices have generally found that the *in rem* definition is not sufficient. The seizure of property is too drastic a remedy for most governments to take on a regular basis. Once a tax office neglects to seize delinquent properties, the threat loses its force, and delinquencies become common. Tax offices instead need the name of an individual, to whom bills can be addressed, and less drastic penalties applied.[7]

(6)   Preparation of the valuation roll.
(7)   Billing and collecting, which are the tasks of notifying the individual property taxpayer what he has to pay and collecting the appropriate taxes.
(8)   Appeals procedures.

Many of the components of the fiscal cadastre are closely allied to those of the proprietary records discussed in Chapter 2. Indeed in Canada, for example, the fiscal record is often treated as supporting evidence of ownership. As Dowson and Sheppard have remarked,

> it is impossible to give a definition of a Cadastre which is both terse and comprehensive, but its distinctive character is readily recognized and may be expressed as the marriage of (a) technical record of the parcellation of the land through any given territory, usually represented on plans of suitable scale, with (b) authoritative documentary record, whether of a fiscal or proprietary nature or of the two combined, usually embodied in appropriate associated registers.[8]

Many countries where there is some rudimentary form of land register lack a fiscal cadastre. Yet the often high capital investment needed to establish an effective land information system may be more than offset by the increase in revenue resulting through improved tax collection, as a number of examples from North America have shown.[9] However, such an approach raises major institutional and political issues, especially where the data held for fiscal purposes are confidential. Difficulties can also arise where the proprietary parcel differs from that used for tax purposes, a matter that is causing some concern in the development of land information systems in Australia. None the less, if such problems can be resolved, the potential for saving in administrative costs and for generating marketable information is considerable.

3.5   Site data

The information required to develop and maintain a fiscal cadastre may be collected directly through surveys and indirectly from other sources, such as the land registration office for details of ownership and sales price and the planning office for building permits. In many jurisdictions, for example, affidavits attached to property-conveyancing documents provide the primary source of sales data.

Table 3.5   Site information (see *N R C Report on Procedures and Standards for a Multipurpose Cadastre*[10])

Site/location:	**Construction quality:**
Topography	Quality of materials
Soil characteristics	Workmanship
Usable land area	Architecture
Building setback requirements	
Landscaping	
Cul-de-sac location	**Construction materials:**
Corner location	Foundation
View	Framing
Street and alley access	Floors
Railroad and waterway access	Walls (exterior and interior)
Available utilities	Ceilings
Distance to shopping etc.	Roofs
Nearby nuisances	
Zoning	
	Other building features:
Building size:	Number of rooms by type
Ground floor area	Heating, ventilation, air
Total floor area	conditioning
Leasable area	Plumbing facilities
Volume	Fireplaces and similar
Building height	amenities
Ceiling height	Additions and remodelling
Clear span	Porches and patios
Number of stories	Swimming pools
Number of apartments	Shelters for automobiles
	Elevators
	Power equipment
Design:	
Intended use	
Architectural style	**Age/extent of depreciation:**
Shape of building	Chronological age
Roof type	'Effective' age
Story height	Remaining economic life
	'Percent good'
Shape:	Condition
Floor area/perimeter ratio	Extent of remodelling
Number of corners	

The valuation process depends upon the availability of such site data as the frontage, depth, and width of the parcel, its topography, shape and area, the drainage and soil conditions, and details of any off-site improvements. Typical information relating to both site and improvement characteristics is listed in Table 3.5.[10]

In a site survey, all properties in a jurisdiction may be visited in a systematic and cyclical fashion, or individual parcels may be visited on a sporadic basis. The approach and rationale are similar to that for systematic adjudication of title to land, as discussed in Section 2.7. When valuing buildings, the valuer may carry out a short visual inspection of the exterior of the property or may undertake a detailed room by room survey. Valuers often do not have the time or resources to carry out quantity surveys or to develop separate cost estimates for each individual building. Instead, they generally employ standardized building cost tables. These include unit cost tables, which give the rate per square metre or cubic metre for different classes of building according to their type and grade of construction, and individual tables, which show the cost of construction for various parts of a building.

The points system

The simplest form of urban valuation, often employed in developing countries, is known as a points system. It is based upon the assessment of a small number of building characteristics that may or may not have any relation to market value. A typical example of such a system is that employed in Ibadan, Nigeria,[11] where residential valuations are based on only two characteristics of the building, both of which are visible from the street. One is the classification of the materials used for the exterior construction and the other is the number of floors. Mud buildings without cement plastering are valued at ¾ of a point for the ground floor, and ½ point for each additional floor. Mud buildings with cement plastering are valued at two points, with one point for each additional floor. The tax is then calculated by applying the rate to the number of points. While such systems may be easy to administer, they can lead to serious inequities and abuse.

Rural properties

The valuation of rural properties poses different problems from that in urban areas. Agricultural property assessment is usually based in large measure on the productivity of the soil. Factors considered in the rating of productivity may include the climate and details of the soil profile such as its thickness, colour, chemical composition, texture, moisture content, and structure. These in turn may be modified according to the salinity, topography, stone and rock cover, tree cover, natural and man-made hazards, and the distance to markets. In southern India, for example, the potential yield is calculated from the simple classification of the soil, the water supply, and the average market price over the past 20 non-famine years. The tax is derived from this figure and is then applied to all similar lands, with an adjustment based on the distance that grain will have to be carried to the market.[12]

In the Canadian province of Saskatchewan, detailed mapping of soils is carried out by teams of agronomists on the staff of the Saskatchewan Assessment Authority, who keep current soils and valuation information on nearly 70 million acres of agricultural land. For valuation purposes, maps are prepared on overlays to aerial photographs at a scale of 1:20 000. Aerial photographs provide much valuable information in support of agricultural assessments. They may be used to:

(1) assist in determining land forms, soil types and textures, vegetation, erosion, drainage, and use patterns;
(2) aid in accurately transcribing land use patterns and acreages to the assessment field sheets;
(3) help in accurately locating and mapping physical features such as ravines, gullies, sloughs, creeks, and lakes on the field sheets;
(4) help in locating and mapping man-made features and hazards such as road diversions, highways, irrigation ditches, farm buildings, and other types of encroachments on agricultural land;
(5) aid in determining the density and species of wooded areas;
(6) help in delineating and mapping peat and muskeg areas;
(7) help in determining and mapping areas where survey markings are at a minimum or absent and roads and trails do not follow survey lines;
(8) assist, on both an actual and comparative basis, in resolving disputes over assessments that have resulted in appeals;
(9) enable much preliminary work to be done in planning field work.[13]

Further details of the use of aerial photography are given in Chapters 5 and 6.

3.6 Administrative matters

In many countries there is a central valuation authority responsible for administering government valuations and, where such exists, the fiscal cadastre. Such an authority may, as in England and Wales, provide a comprehensive land valuation service both to departments of central government and to local authorities. The valuation department has to advise government on matters affecting the value of land, and to carry out valuations where appropriate. Valuations may be required, for instance, for taxation, for calculating the compensation to be paid where land is acquired for public purposes (either by compulsory purchase or by agreement), for determining compensation for any adverse consequences of planning decisions, and for such purposes as fixing the rent on government-owned property.

Central valuation authorities

Many developing countries, however, do not yet have a central valuation authority. In Malaysia, for example, the National Valuation Division carries out valuations for such matters as stamp duty and estate duty and provides advice to government, but about 300 local authorities are responsible for valuations for ratings. They have, in the past, carried out their respective functions without any common form of standards, control, or co-ordination. In the view of Dass,[14] who was formerly the Director-General of Valuations for Malaysia, a central valuing authority provides:

(1)   a uniform application of laws and standards;
(2)   greater economy, by reducing the duplication of records, staff, and effort and by greatly improving the capacity to employ specialist valuation expertise;
(3)   an opportunity to introduce advanced office or mapping techniques, including computers for analysis, recording, and valuation;
(4)   better research facilities;
(5)   greater independence for authority;
(6)   a more adequately staffed service;
(7)   better property management—a central valuation organization can achieve considerable savings in national expenditure by providing proper property management services to the government;
(8)   greater potential for specialization in such areas as plant and machinery, agricultural, mining, and goodwill valuations, where small organizations cannot afford to train and employ specialists;
(9)   overall co-ordination of land sales data.

As Dass has observed:

In many developed and developing countries, Valuation Courts and other appellate bodies appear to strongly support the comparable sales approach method of valuation. In order to be able to defend such valuations in Court, organizations should be able to collect, analyse and store effectively all available sales data . . . Such projects can only be undertaken by large centralized organizations. Land sales data collection and storage into a National Land Sales Data Bank can be established to function effectively, provided there are proper legislations and qualified staff to handle such projects. Such a bank, in addition to its obvious functions, can also help in the monitoring of land speculation trends and changes in patterns of ownership. This form of information could prove extremely useful to national policy makers in formulating sound land taxation and land ownership policies.[15]

Use of computers

One of the chief problems faced by a developing country trying to create a better valuation service is the lack of qualified manpower. One potential solution is to use computers. Many of the data tend to be uniform in character, the processing is highly repetitive, and quite complex analyses are often required. Computers may be used to create and maintain valuation data bases, to analyse price and cost data, to determine general market trends, to carry out investment and statistical analysis, and to maintain departmental accounts and personnel records.[16] Their use should lead to improvements in the accuracy and speed with which valuations can be undertaken. They should reduce clerical costs and eventually reduce the unit cost of an appraisal or assessment. More efficient scheduling of the workload of each assessor should become possible and more and better information should be available for decision making and administrative control.

In Kenya, where the form of rating is based on the unimproved site value, most local authorities obtain their main source of revenue from land taxes. Although there are more than thirty rating authorities in Kenya, only two, Nairobi City Council and Mombasa Municipal Council, have their own valuation staffs. For the others, ratings are carried out by the Government Valuation Office. The law requires revaluation once every five years. Kigunda, then a Deputy Chief Valuer, explained that while the concept of unimproved site value is simple,

the exercise entails colossal amount of rather repetitive work by valuers . . . That is why it is suggested that rating is one area where computer assistance in both establishing a complete data base and in actual valuations should be seriously considered. Once the valuer has been relieved of the routine aspects of the valuation he can focus his attention on the more analytical aspects of the exercise. . . . This analysis would provide a complete valuation base which would be easy to update wherever a revaluation becomes due. . . . It must be emphasized that even if the valuer were to adopt computer assisted methods of valuation, the final judgement and responsibility for the professional standard of the product lies with him, as they in turn depend on the quality and quantity of research carried out to provide the basic data.[17]

3.7   The German cadastre—a case history

The German cadastre, as applied in the non-urban areas, provides a good example of the way in which a system for the classification and valuation of rural land can operate. The present system was introduced in 1934 and began with the passage of legislation on soil classification (*Bodenschatzungsgesetz*) which was used to classify all non-urban land so as to distinguish different soil types. This was used to assist in land use planning, land taxation, probate assessment, and in determining rents and sale prices. The objectives were to provide a fairer distribution of taxes, an improved basis for the distribution of grants and loans to agriculture, a basis for planning and managing food production, the amalgamation and drainage of farms, and the provision of a basis for land use planning. It has since been suggested that, during a time of high unemployment, it was partly introduced because of its potential to increase the level of employment.

Soil categorization

The categorization of soil required the precise identification and description of the nature and character of the soil (*Bestandandsaufnahme*). The results were presented as maps together with an estimate of the potential yield, based upon the nature and condition of the soil, the topography and climatic conditions. First, the long-term use of every hectare of land (*Kulturart*) was recorded and charted on maps (*Katasterkarten*). Since, however, a large portion of German agricultural land had already been charted in the nineteenth century, only the changes had to be considered. Then the nature and condition of the soil was identified and described. This information was combined with data on climate and water condition to develop a soil–climate index. The categories of land considered in 1934 and still used are:

(1) *Acker* (arable use), 'A';
(2) *Garten* (garden and horticultural land), 'G';
(3) *Grunland* (grassland, permanent pasture for grazing), 'Gr';
(4) *Wiese* (grassland, permanent meadows), 'Gr W';
(5) *Streuwiese* (small meadows, mainly in forests), 'Gr Str';
(6) *Hutung* (rough grazing), 'Gr Hu';
(7) *Acker-Grunland* (temporary grass break on arable land), 'A Gr';
(8) *Grunland-Acker* (temporary arable, arable crops sometimes grown between grass breaks), 'Gr A'.

The real-estate registers

As soon as the results of the soil classification were complete, they were made public on a parish area basis. After allowing for a period for objections, the results were passed to the surveying authorities and recorded in a real-estate register (*Liegenschaftskataster*). This register is an inventory and description of real estates, including fields and buildings. It is supplemented by the land charge register (*Grundbuch*), which provides information about the legal conditions of ownership, loans on real property, real servitudes, and easements. Before 1934 there were more than forty systems of real-estate and land registry in Germany, which were mainly established for taxation purposes. In 1934, with the soil classification legislation and new legislation for surveying, a new real-estate register (the *Kataster*) was introduced and made common to the whole of Germany. This register had four main elements:

(1) location maps of all field plots (*Flukarkartenwerke*);
(2) a register of location of all field plots (*flurbuch*);
(3) the cadastral register (*Liegenschaftsbuch*); and
(4) a catalogue of ownership and a directory of the names of owners (*Eigentumerverzeichnis und Namenskartei*).

The location maps

The location maps consist of two combined maps: the field map (*Flurkarte*) shows only the field boundaries and corner marking points; the field classification map (*Flurschatzungskarte*) provides information about the soil valuation. Both are at the scale of 1:5000. The location register includes all fields of a parish district, divided into sections and smaller units. Each field is given a number, a description of its location, its principal use, its size, the soil classification, and any special circumstances.

Land and cadastral registers

Every page in the land register (*Grundbuch*) has an equivalent page in the cadastral register, which is kept by the district authorities (*Kreise*) and is organized in separate card-index systems on a parish basis. The land register provides, through its filing system, a list of the names of all owners and parcels of land in two sets of card indexes. All changes in ownership have to be reported and all buying or selling transactions must be authenticated through the land register. The descriptive parts of the cadastral register that relate to the fields and soil are much more comprehensive than in the location register. The names and addresses of the owners are included, together with the parcel number in the land register. The complete system thus provides at least three institutions with the same basic information about the land, namely the tax office of the district where the field is located, the tax office where the owner lives, and the land registry. The updating of each of these registers calls for a degree of co-operation and organization. Computers have a particularly valuable and important role to play here.[18]

References

1. Quoted by Simpson, S. R. (1976). *Land law and registration*, p. 405. Cambridge University Press.
2. McGlade, A. J. (1984). Alternatives to the land taxation system. *Report on the*

3rd Conference of Heads of Commonwealth Valuation Departments, p. 12. Hong Kong.

3. Geok, N. T. (1980). Property tax assessment in Singapore. In *Report on Second Conference of Heads of Commonwealth Valuation Departments*, pp. 79–80. Ottawa.

4. McGlade, A. J. *Op. cit.*, pp. 10–11.

5. UN (1968). *Manual of land tax administration*, p. 17. Dept. of Economic and Social Affairs, United Nations, New York.

6. Boyce, B. N. and Kinnard, W. (1984). *Appraising real property*, p. 6. D C Heath and Company, Lexington, Mass.

7. Dillinger, W. (1986). Property taxation and the fiscal cadastre. Paper presented at World Bank Seminar on Land Information Systems, Annapolis, p. 9.

8. Dowson, Sir E. and Sheppard, V. L. O. (1952). *Land registration*, p. 47. Her Majesty's Stationery Office, Colonial Research Paper No. 13, London.

9. Several examples are given in Hamilton, A. and McLaughlin, J. (eds) (1984). *The decision maker and land information systems*, papers and proceedings from the FIG International Symposium, Edmonton, Alberta, Canada.

10. Taken from National Research Council (1983). *Procedures and standards for a multipurpose cadastre*, p. 73. National Academy Press, Washington D C.

11. Dillinger, W. *Op. cit.*, p. 5.

12. Dale, P. F. (1976). *Cadastral surveys within the Commonwealth*, pp. 228–9. Her Majesty's Stationery Office, Overseas Research Publication No. 23, London.

13. *Saskatchewan rural land assessment manual*, 1st Edition, (1979). p. 81. Saskatchewan Assessment Authority, Regina.

14. Dass, R. (1977). The organisation and establishment of central valuation departments and its problems. *Report on First Conference of Heads of Commonwealth Valuation Departments*, p. 46. Kuala Lumpur.

15. Dass, R. *Op. cit.*, p. 51.

16. Hamilton, S. (1980). Real estate valuation and computers. *Report on Second Conference of Heads of Commonwealth Valuation Departments*, Ottawa.

17. Kigunda, R. (1980). A case for computer application in valuation. *Report on Second Conference of Heads of Commonwealth Valuation Departments*, pp. 201–2. Ottawa.

18. Weiers, C. J. and Reid, I. G. (1974). Soil classification, land valuation and taxation. 'The German Experience'. Centre for European Agricultural Studies, Wye College, Ashford.

4. The multipurpose cadastre

In this chapter we define the multipurpose cadastre and describe its components. We then identify the data that may be included within or related to the cadastre.

4.1 The concept

The forms of the cadastre discussed in the preceding chapters are all subsets of a land information system. Their particular function is to support either the recording of rights in land or the values associated with it. Each contains a set of land records, which can be expanded into the multipurpose cadastre. In such a system, information pertaining to land ownership, land economics, planning, statistics, and management may all be combined, either in one unified system or through a network of smaller systems linked together. The multipurpose cadastre may support:

(1) land transfer by holding the records relevant to land ownership;
(2) land taxation by recording details of owners, occupiers, properties, and values;
(3) general land administration by providing land-related information in an integrated form, making possible both complex forms of analysis and a broader understanding of land issues.

The multi-purpose cadastre may be defined as a large-scale, community-oriented land information system designed to serve both public and private organizations and individual citizens. Its distinguishing characteristics[1] are that it:

(1) employs a proprietary land unit (the cadastral parcel) as the fundamental unit of spatial organization;
(2) relates a series of land records (such as land tenure, land value, and land use) to this parcel;
(3) is wherever possible complete in terms of spatial cover;
(4) provides a ready and efficient means of access to the data.
Its chief components are a spatial reference framework, a base mapping programme on top of which cadastral information can be overlain, and a series of files relating various types of information to each parcel (Fig. 4.1).[2]

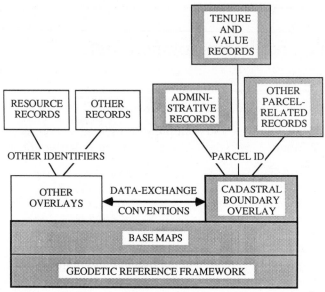

Fig. 4.1   *Multipurpose cadastre components (based on NRC^2)*

It differs from other forms of the cadastre in its breadth. It differs from other forms of land information system in that it is parcel based.

Hub systems

Even though the items of land information are parcel specific, it may be desirable or necessary to compile the records separately and to link them together on demand. So-called 'hub systems' contain separate files for groups of topics, linked together through the use of a unique parcel identifier. The total information for one parcel can then be obtained by a series of enquiries to the different files rather than by retaining all the information on one record. The advantages of operating the system in such a way are partly technical—a system which is too big and complex tends to generate its own special problems—and partly administrative in that specialists in one area, such as in valuation or in public-housing administration, can be responsible for the collection and collation of data within their own field of expertise. This can be done without interfering with other parts of the system, leaving the land information manager to act as overall co-ordinator.

4.2   Components of the multipurpose cadastre

The development of multipurpose cadastres has in general been evolutionary and has been based on the refinement or improvement of existing land records and of the surveying and mapping base. Initially there must be a spatial framework, which should normally be in the form of a geodetic network (Chapter 5). A geodetic network makes it possible to establish spatial linkages between all relevant land information so that any one item can be related in space to any other. The spatial framework should be supplemented by a series of large-scale maps or plans that are up to date and accurate, portraying important topographic features, including the physical positions of boundary fences and beacons. As Binns, writing in the light of experience with the Food and Agricultural Organization, commented:

1. It is important—and to a progressive economy, absolutely necessary—to have a full and accurate knowledge of the natural resources of the land.
2. Maps are the best means of obtaining, recording and analysing such knowledge.
3. Maps are absolutely necessary to the success of schemes for planned development of natural resources.
4. The complexity of human relationships with the land is such that it is essential to record in detail these relationships as represented by public, communal and individual rights in land.
5. Large scale maps are the only sound basis for such a record.[3]

The development of computers and digital mapping, as discussed in Chapter 7, has opened up further opportunities for analysing and displaying spatial data. The advantage of holding maps in digital form is that not only can they be transmitted for display on graphic screens or as hard-copy prints but also, more importantly, they can be kept up to date more easily.

Within the multipurpose cadastre there should be maps showing the location of physical features and a set of map overlays or layers portraying such matters as land ownership and administrative boundaries. Details of the boundaries may be related to the parcel record either by plotting them on a map overlay or else holding them as a string of coordinate values in a separate computer file. The attributes of each parcel may be stored on paper files, in microfilm records, or in a computer data base, the relevant records being cross-referenced through the unique parcel identifier. This should be designed so that, within the registers and records, the details appertaining to each parcel can be readily and quickly extracted. The layers of information held within the system may be independently collected and collated. These layers refer to attributes or objects which represent all the same feature, as illustrated in Fig. 4.2.

The relationships between the different types of data in a multi-purpose cadastre can be portrayed on maps or processed through a computer to give answers to specific questions, or handled in both ways. Consider Fig. 4.2 and Table 4.1. The data in such a system may either provide information on all details relating to a given parcel (parcel 3 is leasehold, there is no mortgage on the land, the buildings are of wattle and daub, it is used for agriculture, its value is L$60 000, and 8 people live on it with a total income of L$28 000); or it may provide details on individual themes (parcels 5, 6, and 8 have incomes

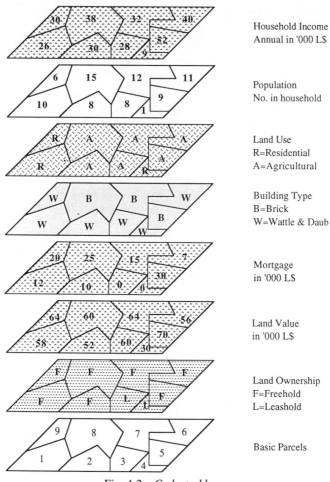

Household Income
Annual in '000 L$

Population
No. in household

Land Use
R=Residential
A=Agricultural

Building Type
B=Brick
W=Wattle & Daub

Mortgage
in '000 L$

Land Value
in '000 L$

Land Ownership
F=Freehold
L=Leashold

Basic Parcels

Fig. 4.2   *Cadastral layers*

in excess of L$35 000); or it may combine data (the only residential properties built of wattle and daub and with annual income of over L$25 000 are plots 1 and 9).

The multi-purpose cadastre is in part concerned with the physical attributes associated with each land parcel, including man-made objects such as buildings, pipelines, and structures, and natural features such as the vegetation, water, or geology. It is also concerned with abstractions such as property and administrative boundaries, land value, and land use. It may also contain data about surveying and mapping, including measurements and cartographic information. Not all of these items will be included initially within the cadastre; some may never be incorporated and others may be added only in the distant future. The multipurpose cadastre is essentially a

Table 4.1 Cadastral information in relational record

				Cadastral layers				
Parcel	Income	Pop.	Use	Bdg.	Mort.	Value	Tenure	Abuts
1	26	10	R	W	12	58	F	2,8,9
2	30	8	A	W	10	52	F	1,3,8
3	28	8	A	W	0	60	F	2,4,7,8
4	9	1	R	W	0	30	L	3,5,7
5	52	9	A	B	30	70	F	4,6,7
6	40	11	A	W	7	56	F	5,7
7	32	12	A	B	15	64	F	3,4,5,6,8
8	38	15	A	B	25	60	F	1,2,3,7,9
9	30	6	R	W	20	64	F	1,8

tool that can grow and be adapted in the light of economic pressures and local needs. As such, it is a basis for planning and managing the development of land.

4.3   Information in a multipurpose cadastre

A multipurpose cadastre must produce information that satisfies users' needs. It must distinguish between what it is necessary to know, for the purposes of planning and land administration, and what is merely interesting.—This is sometimes referred to as 'the need to know versus the nice to know'! The list of possible features and attributes that may be recorded within any land information system is effectively endless. If, for any item, the question can be asked 'where is it?', then it becomes a candidate for inclusion within the system. If the location is ephemeral then it can be ignored; if it is semi-permanent then the next question is 'how often is the locational attribute required and how often does it change?' Archives of data collected for posterity rather than for the present may serve the needs of the historian and may be justified on that basis alone. However, both these and items of pure scientific interest are difficult to evaluate in cost/benefit terms.

One critical test for determining whether to include any category of information is whether the user is prepared to pay the price for gathering, storing, and updating it. The market for information does not, however, operate in a simple way, especially where government-held information is concerned. The distinction between the 'need to know' and the 'nice to know' is not always clear. The primary beneficiaries are often the state and related bodies, who may be both producers and users of the system and be sheltered from market forces. Undoubtedly the greater the use to which the information is put, the greater will be the benefits even though it may be impossible to quantify these. Some information may be rarely used but none the less worth holding within the system so that it is available at short notice when required.

4.4   Items for possible inclusion in the multipurpose cadastre

The multipurpose cadastre will contain a core set of data related to land tenure and land value, and such additional data as can usefully be referenced to the parcel.

Land rights and restrictions

The special relationship between people and the land is manifest in rights to the land and restrictions that may be placed on its development and use. Land tenure records will thus be of primary importance. Rights to surface materials and to subsurface materials such as minerals and hydrocarbons will need to be included. These may lie either with private individuals and organizations or with the state. In either case, their limits will need to be defined and recorded. Rights to the land where boreholes are sunk for exploration or extraction will need to be protected. In each case the information should be cross-referenced to the record of land parcels.

Land values and tax assessments

The maintenance of adequate land records for tax assessment can bring significant revenues to government. Land value and tax records may be the most important economic factors in justifying the multipurpose cadastre. Details of land assessment are discussed in Chapter 3. A list of site date that might be stored within the cadastral record system is given in Table 3.5.

Rural and urban land use

Land use is a combination of human activities that are carried out on the land and are specifically related to that land, together with the natural physical characteristics of the earth's surface. An indigenous forest is not a human activity, yet it represents a form of land use. The distinction between a retail and a wholesale shop is a matter of activity, not physical structure. The administration of the land is primarily concerned with controlling its use. The ultimate objective is to maximize the benefits that can be gained from it. Some record of land use is therefore desirable. In practice, specific land use records throughout the world are usually poor or non-existent. Much land use information has had to be deduced from topographic maps that were not designed with this in mind.

    In many societies the pattern of land use has evolved on a free market basis with little or no governmental control. With the increasing pressure on land because of high population densities, this is no longer necessarily the best way to proceed. Information is needed when changes in land use are planned or proposed, for such changes may require the approval of some authority, for instance to build a house or to dispose of waste products.

The land parcel The basic spatial unit upon which records of land use can be compiled is the land parcel. In urban areas this may be subdivided into parts of buildings—a shop on the ground floor may be separated from the residential accommodation above it. In rural areas, however, the full parcel is more appropriate. Thus the records of title or assessment need only have an additional entry for the land use classification for a powerful tool to become available to the administrator. Once the initial land use data have been acquired, the entry can be updated whenever a change of use is approved. Not all changes of land use are, however, subject to approval; many go unreported, especially in rural areas. Some monitoring may be possible using land tax assessment information but there is an inherent danger that land use mapping will not be kept up to date.

Land use data may be obtained from satellite images, though the interpretation is not very reliable, or from aerial photographs, though again there are limitations to what can be deduced even by a skilled interpreter, or by inspection on the ground, though even then two land use surveyors may classify the same information in a different way.

Classifications of land use Central to any land use mapping is the need for a clear and precise system of classification. The World Land Use Survey, which was a Commission of the International Geographical Union, adopted a classification in 1949 that was oriented towards agricultural interests (see Table 4.2). The nine first-order categories covered settlements and associated non-agricultural land, horticulture, trees and other perennial crops, cropland, improved permanent pasture, unimproved grazing land, woodlands, swamps and marshes, and unproductive land. These could then be

Table 4.2 World land use survey classification system

First-order categories:
1. Settlements and associated non-agricultural land
2. Horticulture
3. Tree and other perennial crops
4. Cropland
5. Improved permanent pasture
6. Unimproved grazing land
7. Woodlands
8. Swamps and marshes
9. Unproductive land

broken down into a finer classification system on a hierarchical basis. Individual countries could thus adapt the system to their own use.

The United States Standard Land Use Code, on the other hand, is highly oriented towards human activities. It, too, uses nine categories, namely residential, major manufacturing, minor manufacturing, transportation and communications and utilities, trade, services, cultural and entertainment and recreation, resource production and extraction, and undeveloped land and water areas. An alternative classification for the United States was produced by the US Geological Survey in 1976 (see Table 4.3). This illustrates the difficulty of getting a universal system of classification that will stand the test of time. In the United Kingdom, the National Land Use Survey Classification was produced in 1975 to meet the specific problems of administering the town and country planning legislation. As its use was not mandatory, its impact was limited. Further details of land use mapping can be found elsewhere.[4]

Issues relating to standards, codes, and the transfer of data between systems are referred to in Chapter 10. Within the multipurpose cadastre, it is desirable to record the current land use and to indicate the land use zone within which every parcel lies. This information has an inevitable impact on the value and potential of any property and is of historical value in land use planning. Where planning applications are submitted or approved, the information should be registered in the cadastre. Where licenses are granted for business or industrial premises, these too may be linked to the cadastral record.

Housing and buildings

Planning regulations are concerned as much with the quality as with the type of land use. Records are often maintained not only of the number of dwelling units but also of the number of stories or the height of the buildings, the floor area, the type of construction, and the general physical conditions of the

Table 4.3   United States Geological Survey land use classification system

First-order categories:
1. Urban or built-up land
2. Agricultural land
3. Range land
4. Forest land
5. Water areas
6. Wet land
7. Barren land
8. Tundra
9. Perennial snow or ice

buildings. Building permits can also be recorded and any progress in new building monitored by development control officers and by tax assessors.

Population and census data

Many countries carry out a census every decade. The arguments for registration of title to be based on the land rather than less permanent features can also be applied to census collection. Virtually all human activities take place within a land parcel, which can thus form the basic spatial unit for recording census data.

Administration

Administrative boundaries defining political subdivisions, town boundaries, planning zones, census enumeration districts, and other units affect each land parcel. These have traditionally been shown on maps by a series of lines. In a computerized system, they need to be stored in such a form that, when enquiries are made about an individual parcel, the administrative region that it lies within can be readily determined.

Antiquities

Cultural features of particular historical interest may require special protection. Some record of their nature may be implicit in the land use classification, but special legislation is usually in force to protect them. The features may be within a general conservation area, or may be individual objects subject to special treatment.

4.5 Items that can be linked to the multipurpose cadastre

There are many other types of land data that can be linked to the multipurpose cadastre through mapping overlays, by reference to coordinates, or in some other fashion (see Fig. 4.3). The more important of these are listed below.

Topography

The traditional cadastral plan treats the earth as flat and shows limited topographical detail. The plan may show the location and dimensions of the property boundaries without indicating the existence of development on the site or the nature of the terrain. Topographic maps are produced separately, often by separate sections of the national mapping agency. The cadastral plan rarely provides details of land forms, slopes, or the elevation of the

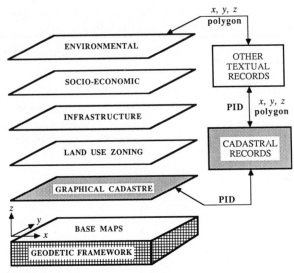

Fig. 4.3   *Linkage mechanisms*

land. Although such plans may be produced in overlay form (overprinting the cadastral detail on top of the topographic map), defects in the printing process, or a failure to co-ordinate both forms of survey on the same system, can lead to the appearance in the records of gaps and overlaps that do not in fact exist.

Developments in digital mapping and the extension of unified geodetic survey control systems are reducing the disparity between topographic and cadastral maps. Through an integrated system, it is possible to link the physical details of a site with its boundaries as defined by law. This linkage is perhaps the most fundamental and important step in the construction of a multipurpose cadastre.

Geological and geophysical data

The mapping of the underlying geological structures of the earth is normally based upon topographic maps. Although the pattern of such structures rarely coincides with the boundaries of proprietary units, the overlapping polygons that can be used to represent rock type or land parcel can be graphically displayed and analysed by computer. Site-specific information is, however, needed where there are mines or quarries, or where there is sand or gravel extraction. Each area may be subject to special environmental controls or to restrictions on the access to the site. Where a site is to be filled after completion of mining or other extractive processes, records should be maintained so that, after land reclamation, there is knowledge of what has happened in case of future construction on the site. Subsidence of buildings is a particular problem that can occur if the records of past land use are not consulted. Similarly, records of the earth's gravity or the strength of its magnetic field may need to be integrated so that, for example, suitable sites for oil exploration can be linked to the land parcels concerned.

Soils

In countries such as Norway and Denmark, the categorization of soil types appears on the cadastral record and has been used in the assessment of the value of the land. In India, as noted in Chapter 3, a rudimentary classification of the land into wet paddy and dry paddy fields is made and used in the calculation of tax, the assessment being based upon the estimated productivity of the land.

Maps of soil types and of land capability based on soil types may be produced. In many countries, both rich and poor, urban expansion has taken place upon land of good agricultural potential, although less fertile land may remain undeveloped because it would be more expensive to build on. This can result in immediate savings for the construction industry but continuing long-term financial loss to the nation. Although a knowledge of land potential will not prevent the use of agriculturally productive land for residential or industrial development, it will reduce its abuse. The cadastral record, as with other forms of land information system, can provide a framework for monitoring the causes and effects of soil erosion by relating the past and present land use to the past and present state of the soil.

Vegetation

Forests Many countries have incomplete and inadequate soil maps; many more have little if any mapping of vegetation other than, perhaps, forests. Some information about vegetation can be gleaned from topographic maps, which may, for example, distinguish between deciduous and evergreen forests, orchards and horticultural areas, cropland and pasture. Much of this information may be interpreted from the aerial photographs used in the compilation of the topographic maps. Relevant information tends to be produced as a by-product, there being an assumption that the foresters will overlay their own more detailed information on the topographic base as do the geologists with rock-types. As computerization is introduced into the forestry records and the underlying topographic maps are digitized, so the opportunity grows to assess the impact of forest management on the general environment and conversely the impact of certain activities in the environment upon the forests. Sources of air pollution and other causes of environmental damage need to be identified and their effects monitored. Once again the cadastre provides a framework within which this may be organized.

Some countries describe their inventory of forest resources specifically as a forest cadastre.

Other vegetation   Ideally there should be records of existing vegetation types so that, in combination with soil and other data, the potential for improvements in agricultural practices can be evaluated. In the initial stages the records may be incomplete or, indeed, sparse. The data will, however, relate to land parcels. They may be the subject of annual returns by the landowner or tenant farmer and may be ideally suited to processing by computer. Such records may at first sight appear an expensive luxury. On the other hand, most countries collect statistics on agricultural production and have some information on the crops that are grown and the livestock reared. The multipurpose cadastre may then be an extension of something already in existence that requires greater efficiency and economy of operation.

Conservation   Certain land parcels may be of special scientific interest, containing rare or endangered species of flora or fauna. Special legislation may govern the conservation of such sites, restricting what may be done on them. Individual items may also be protected. In the United Kingdom, for example, tree preservation orders may forbid specified trees from being cut down. Items of this kind are related to land parcels and should be recorded on the registers, for their existence affects any site development.

Wildlife

Whereas vegetation is attached to the soil and therefore is, by definition, part of the land, animal forms of wildlife cannot be considered in the same light even though they too may need protection, especially in the case of endangered species. The land that they inhabit may, however, be protected as in wildlife parks and nature reserves. The conditions governing their protection are essentially restrictions on the rights of people to use the land and have a logical connection with a land-parcel record system.

Hydrology

Fresh water is one of the resources that are essential for survival. Water is used for drinking, for irrigation, for domestic and industrial purposes, for fishing and for recreation. Each use may be subject to a separate set of rights. The sources of water need to be identified, and the rights of access to and use of the water need to be controlled. The locations of springs, wells, and boreholes need to be mapped and records maintained of the depth of the water table. During a drought in England in 1976 it was realized that, had adequate records of old well sites been available, reserve sources of water could have been tapped.

Rain may fall equally across adjoining land parcels but the extent to which the riparian owners may draw that water from streams, rivers, and channels is generally subject to some form of control. Riparian rights may be subject to statutory or customary law, as may the rights to fish and to navigate upon the waters. Many countries have legislation to ensure that groundwater does not become polluted. Many industries have nevertheless discharged dangerous toxic wastes into major waterways. The multipurpose cadastre can be a tool in the administration of appropriate controls.

Protection is also needed in time of floods. Areas of land liable to flooding should be identified and recorded so that a landowner may know the risks. The appropriate authority can likewise plan preventive measures and emergency relief actions. Similarly, when land is reclaimed from the sea, the rights to that land and the physical problems associated with its use need to be documented.

In more affluent countries, pressure is growing on the inshore environment from the increasing use of beaches and near-shore waters for recreation. Erosion increases round the water's edge and health and safety standards can be put in danger. Further offshore, there is a need to control the rights to mineral and hydrocarbon exploration and exploitation. The extension of the cadastre to that environment thus needs to be considered.

Climate

Weather records do not usually belong to the multipurpose cadastre, although their evidence may be needed in considering the location of industries. If the records can be based on the national grid coordinate system, linkages can be established between the two information systems when required.

Pollution, health, and safety

Reference has already been made to water and air pollution. The boundaries of smoke control zones need to be recorded so that any landowner will know about restrictions on the use of particular types of fuel. Similarly, where special health and safety protection regulations are in operation, details of the areas affected must be readily available.

An area of growing international concern has been the impact of development projects on the environment. This has, for instance, given rise to a directive of the Council of the European Communities which requires member nations to prepare an: 'assessment of the environmental effects of those public and private projects which are likely to have significant effects on the environment'.[5]

Member states are required to ensure that, before planning consent is given to any project likely by its nature, size, or location to have significant effects on the environment, an environmental impact assessment be carried out which:

will identify, describe and assess in an appropriate manner, in the light of each individual case . . . the direct and indirect effects of a project on the following factors:
—human beings, fauna and flora,
—soil, water, air, climate and the landscape,
—the interaction between the factors mentioned in the first and second indents,
—material assets and the cultural heritage.[6]

The list of projects that must be assessed includes agriculture, extractive industries, energy industries, processing of metals, manufacture of glass, chemical industries, food industry, textile, leather, wood, and paper industries, rubber industry, infrastructure projects, and other (specified) projects. The preparation of assessment reports will need the support of a range of land information.

Industry and employment

Within the urban environment, many authorities keep records both of industrial activities and of present and predicted levels of employment. Economic data on production may be needed, especially if it supports the local land tax or rating system. Since the records relate to land parcels, it is logical that they should be cross-referenced to them. If the number of people living in each residential property is also on the record, the information can be used in studies of the distances to shops or journeys to work, or the estimated levels of demand for additional services such as schools, hospitals, and transport facilities.

Transport

A railway line, a road, and a parking space are all examples of land use. Although the latter is more clearly an individual parcel, concern for the network of roads and railways within both the urban and rural environments is an integral part of land administration and management. A line of transport communication represents a set of rights of way that are subject to laws and planning restrictions as much as any other feature. For some road sections, the adjoining owners own the land up to the centre line—or, in Latin, 'ad medium filum viae'. Other roads may have been adopted by the state and hence alienated from the adjoining owners, thus becoming a separate land parcel.

Water and sewerage

Certain categories of data can be described under the general terms 'utilities', 'facilities', and 'services'. These include water and waste disposal, which are items of major importance especially in the urban environment. Most urban land parcels have piped water and sewerage facilities. Most urban roads are served by storm drains for the prevention of flooding and the dispersal of rain water. The availability of existing water and sewerage facilities may have a major influence on the shape and scale of development. The cadastre can either provide the necessary information or can be linked to a data base that does.

Unlike many of the items referred to under hydrology, most of the features belonging to the public utilities are buried in pipes under the ground. They may be subject to easements that should be documented on certificates of title. Those responsible for water management will need to know where the pipes are buried, how far below the ground they are, how old and in what condition they are, what capacity they can carry, and where access to the network is possible. Although man-hole covers may mark the sites of such access and are relatively easy to map, the alignment of the buried features may remain uncertain and their survey can be difficult. Few countries can boast adequate records of their water and sewerage pipes and drains, and many have to resort to techniques of uncertain scientific principle such as dowsing to locate them. The costs of these inadequacies are rarely evaluated or admitted. For instance, a water board that fails to find the outlets of 30 per cent of the water that is known to enter its system may not wish the facts to be made public.

Gas, electricity, and telephones

Similar deficiencies in recording underground services exist in the gas, electricity, and telephone services. Here the consequences can be more dangerous, for explosions and electrocution have occurred when digging machines have struck such utilities. Electronic devices assist in the detection of some buried features but are not fully reliable. Many holes are dug in the ground to locate utilities, only to reveal nothing at the bottom. In the United Kingdom alone such activities cost many millions of pounds sterling each year. The availability of good records of underground services will not necessarily prevent such outright waste but should reduce it. The closer co-operation between different authorities responsible for the utilities becomes easier if facilities exist for sharing information. It is not uncommon to find that, soon after a road has been resurfaced, a succession of authorities come along and dig it up to renew or mend the infrastructure. The cadastre can operate as a focal point through which information may be passed from one utility to the next, especially when linked to a digital-mapping data base. It is difficult, using conventional graphical mapping systems, to display all the related underground facilities in a clear and concise way. Digital mapping allows data to be held as scale free, that is, in one to one relationship with the ground. The data may then be analysed and displayed without the restrictions of normal map scales.

Emergency services

A particular administrative problem arises with the emergency services where a rapid response will be needed in case of fire or some natural or man-made disaster. Although not an individual category of information, it deserves special attention. The computer, in particular, allows for the rapid assembly of essential information, all of which can either be built into the system or else linked to it as part of a network. In Australia, for example, fire is a particular danger at certain times of the year; in some states, the cadastral records of ownership have been linked through planning and development controls to vegetation and other characteristics that constitute a fire hazard.

4.6   Quality of information

The categories of data referred to above indicate a range of topics that may be included within the multipurpose cadastre or related to it. Not all items are specific to land parcels, although all have a direct effect upon their operation. The line between the parcel-based land information system, one example of which is the multipurpose cadastre, and the geographical information system is thin. In general, the cadastral version is more detailed, more complex, more complete, and open to public scrutiny.

Fig. 4.4   *Characteristics desirable in information*

Within any land information system, the data held must have a number of characteristics (Fig. 4.4) other than their relevance to the land. These include:

(1) *Currency*. The data must be accessible in an up to date form within a time frame that meets the needs of the user.
(2) *Precision*. The data must provide measurement information to the standard that is required. Thus underground facilities, for example, must be recorded to a precision which they can be dug up expeditiously.
(3) *Accuracy*. There must be little or no error in the information extracted from the data. Where possible error exists, the degree of probability of its correctness should be available. There should be guarantees, as in the registration of title, in which anyone who loses because of errors in the registration process can receive compensation.
(4) *Verifiability*. Different users should be able to get the same answer to the same question.
(5) *Clarity*. The information must be free from ambiguity.
(6) *Quantifiability*. Where appropriate, numerical information should be obtainable.
(7) *Accessibility*. It should be possible to extract information quickly and easily.
(8) *Freedom from bias*. There should be no alteration or modification to the raw data in order to influence those who receive them.
(9) *Comprehensiveness*. The data should be complete in spatial cover and content. Financial constraints may, however, prevent this and priority areas must therefore be completed first.
(10) *Appropriateness*. The information derivable from the data should relate to the potential users' requirements.

4.7 LRIS—a case history

One of the earliest and best-known efforts to develop the multipurpose cadastre concept has been under way for the last two decades in the Maritime Provinces of Canada. This initiative, under the auspices of the Land Registration and Information Service (LRIS), is a particularly interesting case study given:

(1) the rather primitive nature of the land administration arrangements previously existing in the provinces;
(2) the institutional as well as technical reforms that have been introduced;
(3) the extensive project documentation that has been made available for review.

The Canadian Maritimes consist of the three small Atlantic coastal provinces of New Brunswick, Nova Scotia, and Prince Edward Island, having a total area of 130 000 square kilometres (not including the offshore) and a population of approximately 1.7 million. The economies of these provinces are based on primary resource exploitation, principally forestry, fishing, and agriculture. The land tenure system is in the Anglo-American tradition and the administrative arrangements have included an unsystematic land survey fabric, metes and bounds descriptions, and rudimentary deed registration.

Surveys in the Maritimes

The first step in a very long process of land records modernization in the Maritime Provinces was the preparation of a report by the New Brunswick forest industry to a government Committee on Post-War Reconstruction in the 1940s for:

the organized and supervised survey of property boundaries with adequate monuments so that boundaries can be renewed without dispute . . . for up-to-date accurate property maps for municipal taxation purposes. Control surveys are necessary as a framework for making line maps, and the survey of municipal and property boundaries can be combined with control surveys and used for this purpose.

While a need for a densified control survey system was recognized by surveyors, forestors and others in the 1940s, the actual establishment of such a system was to prove prohibitively expensive until the mid 1950s, when the development of electronic distance measuring equipment made it economically feasible. In 1958, the New Brunswick Coordinate Survey Program was formally organized within the provincial Department of Land and Mines. In 1967, a provincial Surveys Act was passed, legally defining a control coordinate system and providing for its continued maintenance.

In 1968, the Canadian federal government committed $4 million to the Atlantic Provinces to underwrite a two-year effort for a control surveys, base mapping, and land registration programme, followed by another $5 million in 1970. The objectives of the day were:

(1) to enable more efficient use of the natural resources in the provinces;
(2) to enhance security of tenure and bring down the cost of property conveyancing by the conversion of the present system of land registration to a land titles system;
(3) to contribute to more effective planning for and implementation of economic development programs.

The Council of Maritime Premiers

At about the same time, the provincial governments of New Brunswick, Nova Scotia, and Prince Edward Island agreed to establish the Council of

Maritime Premiers, through which they could provide a formal framework for promoting unity of purpose, for improving intergovernmental communications, and for implementing joint programmes. An early area of interest for the new Council was the matter of land use and land ownership. In 1973, the staff previously employed in survey programmes by the provinces formed the nucleus of a new regional organization, the Land Registration and Information Service. The Council of Maritime Premiers initially succeeded in gaining strong support from the federal government, which provided funding for 75 per cent of the programme cost through to mid 1979. The programme then received a potentially devastating blow in 1979 when the federal government withdrew its funding. However, by then the provincial governments had acknowledged the importance of the LRIS programme and were prepared to assume full responsibility.

The LRIS programme

The Land Registration and Information Service programme has consisted of four component phases:[7]

phase I—the extension and densification of a second-order control survey system;

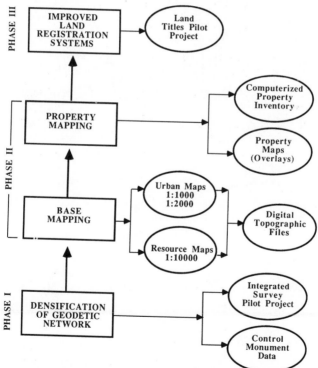

Fig. 4.5 *LRIS—Maritime provinces, Canada*

phase II—the development of a large-scale planimetric and topographic mapping programme throughout the Maritime Provinces, and the introduction of a large-scale cadastral mapping series;

phase III—the gradual replacement of the existing rudimentary deed registry system in each province with a computer-based land titles system;

phase IV—the creation of a series of integrated land records.

The first three phases are illustrated in Fig. 4.5.

The control survey and base-mapping programmes are now effectively in place. Approximately 50 000 control monuments have been established and 11 000 map sheets prepared. The control programme is now in a maintenance mode, while a 'second-round coverage' mapping of the entire land mass at 1:10 000 and urban areas at 1:1000 and 1:5000 using digital technology has been underway since 1984. Cadastral maps and computer files have been

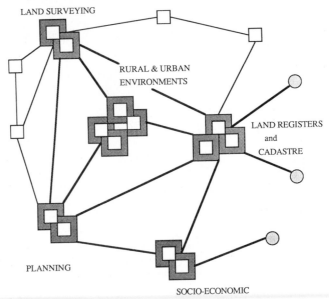

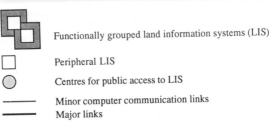

Fig. 4.6   *A design for a land information systems network*

created for more than 750 000 parcels. Prince Edward Island became the first province/state in North America to have complete cadastral mapping coverage, and since has created an innovative one-stop shopping approach (using microfiche records) for accessing land information.

Land titles legislation, after many setbacks and despite initial opposition, has been passed; a demonstration project commenced in New Brunswick during the summer of 1984. This project has proved a success and it appears that the province is going to support a comprehensive title conversion programme.[8]

The fourth phase of the LRIS programme has been substantially modified over the years. Initially it was envisaged that the service would create and maintain a large, centralized land data bank. This concept, for a variety of economic and institutional reasons, was not accepted. Many government agencies and private organizations have established their own computer-based data files over the years. The government of New Brunswick, for example, automated its valuation records in the 1960s and currently manages a province-wide, on-line property valuation data base. Similarly, the province has a comprehensive digital forestry-mapping data base. In recent years, efforts have shifted in all three Maritime Provinces to the development of distributed land information networks, in which each organization will maintain responsibility for its own data. But a co-ordinated approach is being developed for the exchange and use of the data (see Fig. 4.6).[9]

Evaluation of LRIS

Over the years a number of formal and informal socio-economic evaluations of the LRIS programme have been undertaken by external management consultants. Some of the findings of these studies have included:

(1) The major anticipated benefits from the control survey phase have been greater cadastral and engineering survey efficiency. The documention of these benefits has proved to be very difficult, however, and LRIS has continually had difficulty in obtaining funds for implementing and maintaining their control frameworks.

(2) For phase II mapping activities, significant savings have accrued to public agencies and private firms that would otherwise have contracted for mapping services. The cadastral mapping programme in particular has met with widespread public support and has quickly become a necessary product.

(3) For phase III, the benefit to cost ratio for converting to land titles with guaranteed titles has been deemed acceptable, although an initial proposal to guarantee boundaries also was considered unfeasible and was dropped from further consideration.

(4) The benefits to be gained by integrating land records, either in a

centralized data bank or in a distributed network, have been almost universally accepted—for example, in minimizing duplication and improving access to the data. However, it is still not clear to what extent the LRIS programme has contributed to more effective resource management and to promoting regional economic development.

With the surveys and mapping framework now in place, and the development of distributed land information networks well advanced, the Maritime Provinces have provided, and will continue to provide an especially important laboratory for testing the principles of land information management over the next decade.

References

1. Oliver, V. G. (1985). *Digital cadastral mapping: design and development considerations*, Master's Thesis, Department of Surveying Engineering, University of New Brunswick, Fredericton N B.
2. Based on National Research Council (1980). *Need for a multi-purpose cadastre*, p. 47. National Academy Press, Washington DC.
3. Binns, Sir Bernard O. (1953). *Cadastral surveys and records of rights in land*, p. 4. FAO Land Tenure Study, Rome.
4. See, for example, Rhind, D. W. and Hudson, R. (1980). *Land use*, p. 272. Methuen, London and New York.
5. From the European Economic Community Directive 85/337/EEC.
6. Article 3 of the Directive 85/337/EEC.
7. Simpson, R. L. (1984). LRIS—the basis for land information systems. In Hamilton, A. and McLaughlin, J. (eds) *The decision maker and land information systems*. Papers and Proceedings from the FIG International Symposium, Edmonton, October.
8. McLaughlin, J. and Williamson, I. P. (1985). Trends in land registration. *The Canadian Surveyor*, Vol. 39(2), pp. 95–108.
9. McLaughlin, J., Dickson, P. and Morrison, W. (1985). Building the New Brunswick land information network: the property assessment component. In *Computers in public agencies: sharing solutions*, Vol. I. Papers from the Annual Conference of the Urban and Regional Information Systems Association, Ottawa, Ontario, July, pp. 96–103.

5. Frameworks for spatial referencing

In this chapter we consider the nature of control frameworks and the manner in which they can be surveyed. A framework for spatial referencing is a necessary part of a land information system if different layers and levels of information are to be interrelated.

5.1 Geodetic networks

At its simplest level, the function of a spatial information system is to answer two questions: 'what is where?' and 'where is what?' Expressed in another way, given a particular object or set of objects, the system should be able to determine where those objects are in space; or given a particular location the system should be able to specify what occurs at any given point. Implicit in such a simple concept is the existence of a frame of reference that can define the 'where'. This may take the form of:

(1) Geographical coordinates—examples are latitude and longitude.
(2) Rectangular coordinates—these are based on a transformation or map projection of the basic geographical framework on to a plane surface.
(3) Rectangular sections—these are used in western Canada and parts of the United States where large areas are subdivided into quarter sections, quarter-quarter sections, and so forth (see Fig. 5.1). The rectangular section approach imposes a grid-iron pattern on the land-scape, which is often unsympathetic to the topography and natural land forms. Coordinates provide much greater flexibility; when tied to a geodetic framework, they have many different applications in surveying and mapping.

Geodesy is the scientific study of the size and shape of the Earth. It is also concerned with establishing the precise location of points on the surface of the Earth. This has traditionally been done by creating a framework of points known as a geodetic control network. The network consists of physical features such as triangulation pillars, which mark the planimetric position of points, and benchmarks, which mark their height. The description of the points, their coordinate values, and reliability may be stored in a geodetic data base.

Geodetic networks are designed to serve a wide range of users and uses, ranging from reconnaissance-level surveying, through small- and large-scale

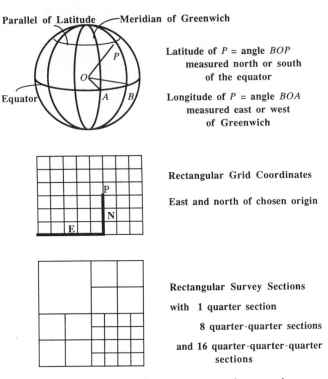

Fig. 5.1   *Spatial coordinate referencing frameworks*

mapping, engineering and land surveying, to scientific research, for example in geophysics and the study of plate tectonics. In the context of land information systems, the function of such a network is to define a unique reference framework through which all mapping, field surveys, and other data collection activities in any given area can be spatially integrated. A control network is needed so that the relative positions of different features can be established or compared. Dowson and Sheppard have commented:

it is the points in the reference framework fixed on land throughout the territory concerned that constitute the indispensable links between (a) the measurements made and recorded on paper, in field books, or plans etc., in the course of land survey and (b) the ground itself. It is only through the establishment and maintenance of those ground points, in enduring form and suitably distributed, that the land parcels defined during the process of cadastral survey can be located again reliably and authoritatively at need . . . boundary beacons on erection should be tied in by appropriate measurements to the adjoining points on the original reference framework and become incorporated in it. In this way the boundary beacons are made to serve a wider public purpose.[1]

Individual landowners need to know the size and shape of their parcels and their location relative to their neighbours' parcels. As such, a description by 'metes and bounds' may satisfy the necessary and sufficient conditions, the metes giving the size and shape and the bounds indicating details about the adjoining properties. For isolated surveys to protect the rights of individual landowners, little more may be needed. Within groups of co-adjacent parcels, as in a township, or where others need to use the information, for spatial analysis or inquiry, such an independent approach is inadequate (see Table 5.1). In the long term, isolated surveys are also more expensive when compared with the adoption of a more unified approach. In Canada in the 1970s it was shown that the restoration of boundaries using a co-ordinated control network was 25 per cent cheaper than when using the isolated-survey approach.[2] On this basis it was possible to reinforce the arguments in favour of establishing a geodetic network, the initial and maintenance costs for which are inevitably high.

Within a limited area, it is possible to establish a local survey network unconnected to any national system. In a country such as Nigeria this was for many years the only rational approach, as the size of the country and the difficulties in communication were so great as to preclude any alternative. A local network provides a number of fixed points to which all surveys, both topographic and cadastral, can be connected so that land parcel boundaries can, for example, be related to the physical objects appearing on the topographic maps. For most land information management purposes, where townships are well separated and where no national geodetic control exists, a local network is adequate. Existing map series can be used as the basic framework. If coordinate values have been established on the local system, they can, at some future date, be transformed to the national system as and when such becomes available. Ideally, however, a national network should be established first, so that all areas in a country can be cross-related. This avoids the inevitable confusion that will otherwise arise when, for every point, there are two sets of coordinates, the old and the new.

Table 5.1 Spatial references

Referencing systems should be able to:
1. Identify points, lines and areas (and hence parcels)
2. Indicate size and shape of features
3. Permit calculation of areas
4. Show relative and absolute positions
5. Help in the location and relocation of boundaries
6. Aid subdivision work and setting out new estates
7. Aid engineering and underground services work
8. Support land information system development

5.2   Principles of surveying

A concern for accuracy and the determination and analysis of errors in measurement are central to land surveying. It is known that errors in measurement accumulate in proportion to the square root of the number of compound observations taken. For example, if the expected error in measuring a distance of 30 metres is ±0.01 metre, then when using a tape of 30 metre to measure a line 3 kilometres long (that is 100 tape lengths) the expected error would be 10 times that of a single length, or ±0.1 metre. Some of the errors would cancel each other out and some would tend to accumulate. The converse of this is that the random nature of the error can be reduced by repeated observations. Measuring a single line 100 times, each time independently, would give an expected error of one over the square root of the number of observations times the expected error of one single measurement. Thus if the expected error of each single measurement were, as above, 0.01 metre then the mean or average of the 100 measures would have an expected error of 0.001 metre. This calculation does not, however, take account of non-random effects such as a tape whose nominal length is consistently different from its actual value.

The methodology behind most forms of land surveying is based on five principles, which are often referred to as those of control, consistency, economy, independent check, and maintenance. The principles apply to small isolated surveys as well as to major national ones and are as important to engineering and detail surveys and to hydrographic work as to cadastral surveys. They are designed to ensure that the quality of a survey is maintained so that the final product meets the requirements of the task for which it was undertaken.

5.3   The principle of control

The traditional approach to land surveying operates, as the saying goes, by 'working from the whole to the part'. A framework of points across the whole area to be surveyed is laid down, the points being well separated and carefully measured. For a national geodetic network, the points would be 50 to 100 kilometres apart. This initial framework is known as the primary net. The positions of these points are then calculated and held fixed. A secondary network is then established. For a national survey, the points would be about 20 kilometres apart. This secondary network is connected to and adjusted within the primary control. This net may then be further 'broken down', by subdividing it into tertiary and fourth-order points so that the accumulation of error within each level of the network cannot exceed that of the higher order. From these lower-order points, the position of points of detail such as property boundaries or hedge junctions may be fixed.

Triangulation

The points in a national geodetic framework are often referred to as triangulation or 'trig' points; before the 1960s the network was normally observed in the form of triangles whose shape could be determined accurately. Theodolites were used to measure the angles to high levels of precision. For instance, they might measure to 1 second of arc, which represents the angle subtended by 1 centimetre at a distance of 2 kilometres. Up until the late 1950s, long distances were very difficult to determine accurately and hence shorter lengths, known as baselines, were carefully and painstakingly measured and their lengths magnified by simple triangulation to determine the lengths of the sides of the triangles in the primary network. Since the late 1950s it has been possible to observe lines of up to 50 kilometres or longer by electronic means. The time taken for an electromagnetic wave to pass from one end of a line to the other and back to the start again is accurately determined. By accurately measuring the interval of time for the wave to travel over this double journey, and knowing the velocity of the wave from estimates or measures of the atmospheric conditions, the distance between the end-points can be calculated. Using this method, distances can be determined with a precision that is commonly of the order of 1 part in 200 000 of the length. This is equivalent to 20 centimetres over a distance of 40 kilometres, or better than half a centimetre over a range of 1 kilometre.

Traversing

One immediate result of introducing electronic distance measurement (often referred to as EDM for short) has been to replace triangulation by traversing. In this technique, points are fixed by measuring successive angles and distances. The disadvantage of triangulation is that the shapes of the triangles must be carefully selected and each triangulation station must be visible from several directions. As a result, the points are often located on the tops of hills that may be remote and inaccessible. With traversing, the minimum requirement is to have one line of sight into and one line out of a control station. This gives greater flexibility in the selection of points. It is then possible to traverse along roads or through townships, establishing points where they may be of greater use for subsequent detail surveys. The unit costs of traversing are much lower than for triangulation and the process is much quicker: a surveyor would need to spend several hours or even days, depending upon the weather conditions, trying to complete his observations on some remote hill top, whereas for traversing, fewer observations are needed and access to each control station is generally much easier.

In flat areas or those with dense vegetation, triangulation is usually uneconomic or impractical, even if tall towers are erected to provide all-round visibility. Long before the use of EDM for major control networks, it was common practice to carry out traversing with short lines, using graduated steel tapes to measure the distances. In countries such as Ghana, this was the only practical way of providing the control. It is still the most commonly used technique in cadastral surveying. The term 'taping' or 'chaining' describes this form of measurement. (In the early days, steel chains were used to determine the distances.) Many traverses were run with a compass and chain—the compass to give the bearing of the line and the chain to measure the distance. The compass is now rarely used; its inherent accuracy is poor and more sophisticated instruments for measuring angles, such as the theodolite, are now readily available.

5.4 Map projections

Old survey measurements and data may be on a different projection from the one that is currently in use. A map projection enables measures of angle and distance to be transformed from the values measured on the ground to those that would be calculated from the coordinates, and vice versa (Fig. 5.2). Over a small area, even the size of a small town, it is possible to treat the earth as flat and to use the two sets of values as if they were the same. This is true for the average land parcel, treated in isolation. When the size of the area being processed is large, problems arise because the earth is round and not flat. Differential adjustments to the distances must then be made. In one part of an area covered by a particular projection, a true ground distance of 1

Spheroidal-shaped Earth   Flat surface transformation

 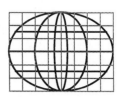

Map projections are transformations so that true distances on the Earth's surface are stretched and compressed in order to fit on to a plane, that is flat, surface.

The ratio between the Earth distances and the projection equivalent is called the SCALE FACTOR. The scale factor varies across the area of the map.

To convert true distances to map projection distances, multiply by the scale factor. The resulting value may subsequently be reduced further for plotting by, for example, reducing it to 1 part in 50 000 for a 1/50 000 scale map.

Fig. 5.2 *Map projection scale factors*

kilometre might be represented as 999.5 metres, whereas in another part it could be 1000.5 metres.

For a plot with a true frontage of 40 metres, this means that in one part of the country the landowner would appear to lose 2 centimetres from the front of his or her land, whereas someone in another place might gain the same amount. Put in such a way, the problem might not seem worthy of concern. In practice, not only do the land owners become confused but, from a technical point-of-view, the accumulation of such differences soon becomes significant when attempts are made to connect the surveys to a national control system and to link together information from different areas. These differences are sometimes referred to as projection errors. The term is, however, a misnomer, for they become errors only if they are ignored.

The basic problem arises when using a geodetic network. The magnitude of the differences between the observed and the computed values will depend on the projection system adopted and the area covered. 'Surveyors projections' are generally used, namely those classified as 'conformal' or 'orthomorphic'. Details are given in standard textbooks.[3] Such projections retain the shape of small areas, thus preserving the angles that are measured from any point. With a conformal projection, the numerical value of any angle as measured with a theodolite can be used directly in the system. The linear scale, however, changes from point to point and hence any distances measured must be adjusted using local 'scale factors' to compensate. This entails multiplying every observed distance by a factor which, in the example given above, would be 0.9995 or 1.0005. By applying such scale factors directly or inversely (according to whether the transformation is to or from the computed values), true distances and projection distances can be interchanged. Full advantage can then be taken of a rectangular coordinate system for calculating bearings, distances, and areas.

5.5 Coordinate systems

Rectangular coordinate systems are those based on a rectangular grid. Points are then described in terms of their distances east and north of a given point, called the origin. Rectangular coordinates have a number of advantages. They enable the surveyor to use simple survey methods and simple computations and yet to achieve the equivalent of geodetic accuracy. Traverses may be run between previously established points, providing additional control stations for future surveys. The quality of any work can be quickly and easily checked and any gross errors can be isolated and eliminated.

Because of the way that errors tend to accumulate, the relative accuracy between two points will be greater than the absolute. For most practical purposes it is their positions in relation to neighbouring points that is more important than their absolute positions in space. With a coordinate system, the relative accuracy is effectively maintained. The coordinate values of points of detail can be easily stored, retrieved, analysed, processed, and updated in a computer. They can be cross-referenced to data for other points, lines or areas, enabling spatial searches to be made within the data base. Thus it becomes possible, for example, to find all land parcels within a specified distance of some specific point such a school or a hospital.

5.6   Electronic position fixing

Up to the 1950s, the two techniques for tying surveys into control were triangulation and traversing. More recently, new techniques based upon electronic position fixing have emerged. These may be ground based or make use of artificial earth satellites. Ground-based systems, such as those used in hydrographic surveying, require a limited number of fixed points: three are essential and a fourth is desirable to give an independent check. Each base station transmits a signal. The difference in time between the receipt of the signals from a pair of stations is a measure of the difference in the distance to them. This can be used to calculate a locus of points which form a mathematical curve known as an hyperbola. From two pairs of control points, two hyperbolae can be calculated. These will intersect at the point whose position is to be fixed. Over long ranges the accuracy is not very great because of the frequencies that are used.

The Doppler Transit Satellite System

Although adequate for navigation, such systems are generally unsuitable for use on land. High precision can be obtained by replacing the fixed base stations by satellites in orbit and by using signals of higher frequency. Using a technique such as the Doppler Transit Satellite System, measurements can be taken to the US Navy Navigation Satellite System (NNSS) as the satellites pass overhead. In 1986 there were six operational satellites. Several days are needed to acquire enough data (between 30 and 50 passes are normally desirable) for a good positional 'fix'. A transmitter aboard the satellite sends out two signals, one of nominally 400 MHz and the other of 150 MHz. Both frequencies are highly stable. They are modulated to carry specific information about the orbit of the satellite, known as the *ephemeris*, and pulses to mark the time. Because the satellite is moving in relation to the ground station, the frequency of the signal that is received is slightly different from the frequency transmitted. The instant at which it is received also differs from the instant of transmission by an amount which changes as the satellite moves along its orbit.

The change in frequency is known as the *Doppler shift*. It is measured by comparing the incoming signal with a constant reference frequency, which is generated at the receiving station. From these measurements, and by knowing the relative times at which they are made, it is possible to calculate changes in the distance or range to the satellite that have taken place. From these range differences and from the estimated position of the satellites, three-dimensional coordinates of the receiver station can be derived (Fig. 5.3).

As the satellite moves in its orbit, measurements are made to it from known ground stations. These provide data from which the orbit of the satellite can be computed. The data are computed for 12 hours in advance and are sent to the satellite, which in turn transmits them every two minutes. These data are referred to as the 'broadcast ephemeris'. They contain enough information to enable the position of any point to be computed to within 3 to 5 metres. By taking measurements from a global network of tracking stations, a more precise estimate of the parameters of the satellite can be obtained. The relevant data are known as the 'precise ephemeris'. They can be used to improve the ground position accuracy of points to between 1 and 1.5 metres.

Greater relative accuracy is possible by observing simultaneously at two or more stations and by comparing their relative positions. This eliminates many systematic effects due to errors in the ephemeris or uncertainties in the atmospheric corrections that need to be applied. With more advanced processing, the relative accuracies can be improved to about 30 centimetres for baselines up to 200 kilometres in length and 60 centimetres for baselines up to 600 kilometres. In 1982, the costs were estimated to be about $75 000 to

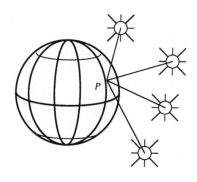

The range, that is distance, to three satellites provides
three pieces of information to fix point *P* in three
dimensions. A fourth satellite is, however, needed
to determine clock differences.

Fig. 5.3   *Satellite Global Positioning System*

fix 18 points (or $4000 per point).[4] The technique can therefore be considered as relevant only for establishing a few primary control points in a country, perhaps allowing for the connection of existing local networks into a national framework.

NAVSTAR Global Positioning System

More recently, the NAVSTAR Global Positioning System (GPS) has been developed. Although the 18 satellites that were planned to form the basis of the system had not all been launched by 1987, experience with those that are in orbit has been encouraging. When all 18 satellites are in orbit, it will be possible to have a minimum of four satellites in view anywhere in the world where there is a clear view of the sky. Each satellite will transmit both identification and positioning information. The carrier waves of the signals from the satellites are modulated to include coded messages and a precision code (P) and a coarse/acquisition code (C/A) from which, as with Transit Doppler observations, ranges to the satellites can be determined. The ranges are calculated from comparisons between the clocks in the satellite and in the receiver unit. This comparison introduces a bias: any two clocks may be slightly out of agreement. The actual distances as measured to the satellites are therefore referred to as 'pseudo-ranges'. At least four satellites must be observed to calculate the three-dimensional coordinates of the receiver station and its unknown clock bias.

When enough satellites have been launched, it will be possible to measure absolute position anywhere in the world. Given access to the P code, observations spread over an hour or so will give a precision of the order of 1 metre or better. Using the C/A code, effectively instantaneous coordinated positions will be possible to a precision of 10 to 20 metres. This is more than adequate for most navigational purposes. Because of the military implications, access to the P code may be restricted and the C/A code may be down-graded to reduce the accuracy to about 200 metres. On the other hand, in surveying and mapping there is no need to work instantaneously and, once a few absolute positions are established, many more can be added by observations of relative position.

It is here that GPS comes into its own: it marks a revolution more than an evolution in land surveying. By using differential measurement methods, similar to those for Transit Doppler, relative accuracies of the order of a few centimetres can be achieved with about 15 minutes of observation. Refined techniques have already demonstrated that accuracies of a few millimetres are possible. At least two receivers are needed, each at present costing about $50 000, though the price is falling. The relative-measuring technique can use the C/A code, or no code at all, so dependence on more precise information from the United States military does not arise. The only assumption is that the satellites continue to operate.

GPS therefore offers an opportunity to connect a large number of points into a minimum number of primary control stations. In many less developed countries, there are already some primary triangulation stations that were established for strategic or other purposes. In Africa, for example, there is a chain of triangles that runs north to south approximately along the line of the 30th meridian and another running east to west along the 12th parallel north. There is also a range of additional points that have been established by the Transit Doppler Satellite System. GPS observations can now be used to transfer these values by differential or translocation techniques to all areas of a country.

Discounting the initial capital outlay, the unit cost for fixing a point becomes relatively cheap. Points can be measured with relative ease. In practice, a receiver is placed on one of the primary stations and another on the point of interest. With 15 minutes observing time and some subsequent processing, which can be done on a computer, the distance to a new point can be 'fixed'. All that is needed is a clear view of the sky. Lines of sight between distant ground stations are no longer necessary in order to fix the points. Line of sight is, however, still needed between each station and at least one other known point so that a surveyor can subsequently set up a theodolite at the control station and find the orientation of the observations relative to the grid network. Theodolites cannot measure bearings directly: they can measure only the difference in angle between two pointings.

5.7   Inertial surveying

Although GPS is one of the most promising systems, a variety of other methods can be used to densify control networks. Of these, inertial surveying and photogrammetric aerial triangulation have the greatest potential. The concept of inertial technology is relatively simple, though the actual hardware is expensive and needs further development. The basis of the system is to combine the behaviour of gyroscopes with the ability to measure intervals of time very precisely. Because gyroscopes try to hold a fixed direction, it follows that when they are moved, a resistive force is set up which can be measured in the form of an acceleration. This can be mathematically integrated over time to give velocity; a second integration gives distance. Thus the instrument can be set up at a known point before being moved to a new station; its sensors will then determine how far it has gone. Because of hysteresis, which is the effect of the system lagging behind as strains are released, the instrument has to be allowed to stop every 3 to 5 minutes if accurate results are to be achieved. Such stops are known as zero-velocity updates. Given these, and some fairly substantial post-processing of the data by computer, accuracies of point fixes of the order of 20 to 30 centimetres are possible over a range of 40 kilometres or so. These accuracies do not quite meet the needs of the cadastral surveyor, and the cost at several hundreds of thousands of dollars per unit makes them unattractive at present. Another drawback is that the instruments are relatively heavy to carry, requiring two strong men to lift them into a helicopter or onto a motorized vehicle.

5.8   Photogrammetric control surveys

An alternative method for establishing the relative positions of control points is by photogrammetry. An aerial photograph is a record of the bundle of rays of light which pass from points on the ground through a camera lens to form an image on the so-called negative plane. If all the rays of light pass through one point in the lens of the camera, (because of its compound nature this is not strictly correct but is in effect what happens), then the angles subtended at this point, between objects on the ground and their corresponding images on the negative, will be the same. By taking measurements on the photographs, it is possible to deduce the relative directions of objects on the ground as viewed from the focal point of the camera; given two sets of directions by using overlapping stereophotographs, the relative positions of the ground points themselves can be ascertained.

Aerial triangulation

If the position of some of these points is measured on the ground, then the actual position of many others can be calculated from measurements on the photographs. This process of extending ground survey control is known as aerial triangulation. Given good equipment, a precision of better than 10 micrometres at the photographic scale is possible. With photography taken from a height of 1500 metres with a camera having a focal length of 150 millimetres, the photographic scale would be 1 in 10 000 (this is the ratio of the focal length of the camera to the flying height). Clearly identifiable points could then be fixed to an accuracy of better than 10 centimetres.

Aerial triangulation is a process whereby ground control can be extended by photogrammetric methods. It is generally a more economic method for coordinating points than ground survey on its own, given economies of scale and reasonable standards of accuracy. An overlapping pair of vertical air photographs, when viewed stereoscopically, forms an optical model of the ground. In order to determine the scale of the model, the ground distance between two points on it must be known. To determine differences of height and to ensure that the distances measured are horizontal distances, three 'height points' are needed since three points define a plane (see Fig. 5.4). In practice, to provide an independent check, three points are normally fixed to control the scale and orientation and four points are used to provide height

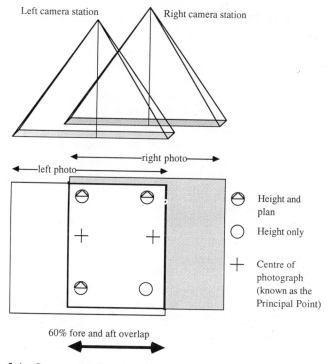

Left camera station   Right camera station

◄——left photo——————►   ◄————————right photo————►

⊖ Height and plan

○ Height only

+ Centre of photograph (known as the Principal Point)

60% fore and aft overlap
◄————————►

Fig. 5.4   *Stereo pair of aerial photographs (single air photo overlap)*

control for levelling the model. Given a single isolated model, these must be measured using ground survey techniques. If, however, there is a strip of photographs or a series of overlapping strips forming a block, then only a limited number of models need be controlled by ground survey, the remaining control being derived from measurements on the photographs themselves.

Photogrammetric techniques are essentially mass production methods and their cost effectiveness depends upon there being a sufficient number of points to be fixed. Greater precision than that indicated above is possible using larger scale photography, the best equipment available, and appropriate computer software. The penalty to be paid for greater precision is greater cost, which, in unit terms, can only be reduced by fixing more points. Each point must be clearly visible on the aerial photographs, which may require 'premarking' or 'presignalization'. This entails marking the points out clearly on the ground, for example by painting white stones or by laying out white crosses of an appropriate size centred on the ground mark. In practical terms this is expensive, time consuming and difficult, for any mark that is not visible at the instant when the photographs are taken cannot be used in the aerial triangulation. If the position of the ground mark is needed later on, then it can only be fixed by subsequent ground survey, which increases the overall costs.

Until the advent of computers, the reconciliation of the photogrammetric measurements with the ground control was carried out by analogue methods. Analogue representations of the models were physically adjusted until the right size, orientation, and level of the model were established. Subsequently, a process known as 'independent models' was developed, in which each model was set up in a stereo-plotting machine and the relative positions of each overlapping pair of photographs were established by analogue means. Measurements were then taken from each model and processed in a computer. No attempt was made to join the models together by mechanical means. Instead, the join was formed mathematically and corrections were calculated for each model to transform its coordinates through a shift in origin, a scale change, and a rotation of the three-dimensional axes to which it was referred. After this, measurements could be taken from each model in turn to provide more detailed mapping.

The modern method is to take measurements on each of the photographs and then to compute not only the absolute but also the relative position of points, the latter having traditionally been done by analogue methods. Two approaches are adopted in the adjustment process—the use of polynomial equations and the so-called 'bundle method'. In the former, polynomial equations are used to adjust the coordinates of the points measured on the photographs; in the latter, the bundles of rays that are formed by these points with the camera station are manipulated. Standard computer packages exist in both cases; the methods are described in detail in standard photogrammetric textbooks.[5] The effect in either case is to provide three-dimensional coordinates with a precision of a few centimetres.

5.9   Ground marks

Control networks have two elements: the physical and the mathematical. Traditionally, much time and effort and money have been spent on constructing triangulation pillars and ground marks that will stand the test of time. As Wright has suggested:[6]

a good permanent mark, like an iceberg, has most of its volume below the surface, and it presents a pyramidal or rounded upper part to the accidental or malicious shocks it has to resist . . . It is more important to be certain of finding the marks after 30 years than to be able to find them easily at any time.

The physical maintenance of the fabric of a geodetic network is as important as the maintenance of the records which relate to it. As an illustration of what can happen, the case of Uganda provides a cautionary tale. When the secondary and tertiary networks of triangulation points were established—largely by traversing using electronic distance-measuring devices and theodolites—each point was marked with a 1.2-metre high cylindrical pillar made of reinforced concrete. Beneath each pillar a brass bolt was buried in case the pillars were destroyed, for instance by elephants finding that they made a suitable scratching post. The theory was that, in such an eventuality, the pillar could be rebuilt over the buried mark. Unfortunately, mistaking the nature of these buried marks, the word got round in the south-western part of the country that under every tenth pillar the expatriate surveyors who did the work had buried a gold bar. As a result, many of the pillars were systematically destroyed in the vain hunt for gold. They can no longer be rebuilt in the same place, even if the money were available to do so.

The pillars, when constructed, were painted black and white and were visible from a considerable distance. Their outer coating was a thin sheet of metal, which was sometimes stripped off by the local population and used in buildings or for the construction of implements of war. The principle of treating survey pillars like icebergs was, in the past, correct. Today there are two practical differences. The first is the availability of the satellite network, which in effect creates beacons in the sky. The second is that relatively cheap ($20 or so) 'earth anchors' are available which are light and portable and can be driven firmly into the ground. As this is done, they break open at the bottom and curve out like a sea anchor, making it extremely impractical for anyone to pull them out again. They are, of course, not visible from a distance and would need to have a beacon erected above them before any observations could be taken to them. But their low cost, compared with building a concrete pillar, and their portability so that many more can be emplaced in a day, makes them relatively cost effective.

With every form of survey mark, someone sometime will try to remove it—such is human nature. It is for this reason that, in most countries, survey marks are protected by legislation and vandals can be prosecuted. That does not, however, prevent some people from being mischievous. The advantage of GPS is that many more points can be established and coordinated so that there becomes safety in numbers. Existing local networks, for instance those based on local township control, can be brought into the national system and recomputed. Alternatively, new networks can be laid down by putting in the main framework by GPS and then infilling by conventional ground survey traversing or by photogrammetry.

5.10   Network densification

The traditional sequence for establishing control is to work from the whole to the part, observing and computing primary, then secondary, and then tertiary networks, and finally, where necessary, those of fourth order. In this hierarchy, each level must be observed more accurately and hence more painstakingly and more expensively than the level below it. To obtain a positional accuracy of 0.5 metres over a 50-kilometre range requires distances to be measured to 1 part in 100 000; over a range of 5 kilometres, 1 part in 10 000 is all that is necessary. With GPS it is possible to dispense with the 'breaking down' of higher-order networks and instead to obtain, by direct and independent methods, a set of points measured to a uniform standard. Increased relative accuracy is possible with the use of differential measurement techniques, thus effectively reducing the hierarchical approach to two stages.

The density of control points that is needed for a land information system depends in part upon whether the data are going to be linked graphically by plotting overlays on a map, or whether the linkage is to be achieved numerically. In the former case, the requirements for control are less stringent than the latter. In the view of the United States National Research Council:[7]

Monumented points of known position . . . should be so distributed throughout the area concerned as to permit their ready use in the collection of both cadastral and earth-science data. Typical recommendations range from 0.2 to 0.5 miles (0.3 to 0.8 km) between monuments in urban areas to 1 to 2 miles (1.6 to 3.2 km) in rural areas . . . Ideally, the entire area concerned should be covered at a uniform density with a simultaneously adjusted network of control survey stations. As a practical matter, however, the necessary survey work will have to be carried out over an extended period of time. To provide the required uniformity in such successive surveys, a higher-order control network may have to be established. The spacing of the higher-order stations can be up to 10 miles (16 km) but is usually 3 to 5 miles (5 to 8 km). In any case, the local survey network should be an integral part of regional, state, and national control nets.

5.11   The principle of accuracy and consistency

Specification of accuracy

The quality of surveys is in practice difficult to define. A common method is to quote the estimated error of distances between points (either in the form of '1/5000', meaning that there is an expected error of 1 metre in every 5 kilometres, or '1 part in 5000 plus or minus 5 mm', the latter term representing errors internal to the measuring instruments). Another is to quote the size of the error ellipse, which defines a general area around a point within which the true position can be expected to lie. The latter approach is more logical when dealing with coordinates, but is unsatisfactory in that it implies absolute values where relative values are more important. The use of proportional errors is, however, misleading. For the misclosure of a traverse, it indicates only the magnitude of the accumulated error and not necessarily the quality of the individual points or lines. The figures should be interpreted as guide-lines giving a general impression of the standards, and not as absolute qualitative statements.

The accuracy of the control needs to be greater than the positional accuracy with which final detail is required. For cadastral purposes, this is rarely greater than equivalent graphical standards. However, for engineering and monitoring purposes, greater precision is necessary. The principle underlying control surveys is that the primary framework is established to the highest standards possible, allowing for less rigorous methods to be used for secondary, tertiary, and lower-order control. A traverse that is adjusted to fit within an existing network of control cannot for example be more accurate than the control on which it is based. Since the cost of survey is in part dependent on the precision that is sought, it is logical to work to a standard no greater than that of the existing control. On the other hand, the technology of today allows for measurements to be made to much higher standards than in the past, with the consequence that good-quality measurements must be distorted in order to fit within that control. This is in breach of the principle of consistency.

Upgrading control networks

There are three possible solutions to the dilemma. The first is to up-grade all the higher-order control. Such an approach is expensive, time consuming, and, apart from purely scientific considerations, generally unnecessary. It may, however, be possible to introduce a number of new measurements into the original network and to recompute the original observations. Because of the difficulties in measuring long distances before the late 1950s, many triangulation networks have a good geometrical shape but poor, that is, inconsistent scale. This means that distances are, within any given area, systematically out of sympathy with the ground. By introducing Doppler Satellite or Global Positioning System measurements into the network, new values for the coordinates of the old control points can be computed. Such an up-grading would be substantially cheaper than fully reobserving all the old angles and distances.

Computer programs now exist for optimizing networks by identifying from a statistical analysis where additional measurements would have the most beneficial effect. Given the existence of a primary or secondary network and access to such analysis techniques and computers, significant improvements are possible at relatively little cost.

The second solution to the problem of inconsistency is to lower the standard of subsequent surveys. Modern technology can, however, provide one-centimetre accuracy for ranges of one kilometre or so for the same price, time, and effort as it would for one-metre accuracy. Hence there is often little to be gained by such an approach, unless the technology is abandoned and a return is made to outmoded systems. The third solution is in effect to ignore the problem and to carry on regardless. The new data may all be stored on magnetic disk or tape and perhaps used at some future date when the quality of the control has been improved.

Many surveys contain inconsistencies and are in reality less accurate than is claimed. The point is important to stress, for the development of land information systems is often held back on the grounds that a good-quality framework must first be put in place or the existing network up-graded. Yet many systems have proceeded adequately on the basis of what the purist would regard as inadequate control. Provided that the topology remains accurate so that the relative positions of points, lines, and areas remain correct, then little harm can come. It will always be possible, at some future date, to readjust the coordinates of points in the light of subsequent knowledge. Simple mathematical transformations can be applied to stretch or shrink the measurements, a process which is sometimes used in digital mapping to make graphical displays fit together. Points can then be brought, on average, nearer to the truth, at a cost which is substantially less than that of a full resurvey.

Two developments are helping to alleviate the problems—GPS as described above and electronic data processing. GPS makes it possible for a large number of points to be fixed in relatively short time and, excluding the basic investment in the technology, at relatively low cost. In reality, the high standards that are sometimes being asked for have never existed. For most practical purposes, it is relative, not absolute, positions that matter. There is little doubt that in due course the quality of the geometry from a Euclidean point of view will rise. In the mean time the development of land information systems can be expedited on the basis of accepting lower geometrical standards. This is not to argue that high standards are undesirable. It is undoubtedly necessary to build a reasonable degree of precision into the system. It is, however, also necessary to keep the need for precise geometry in perspective.

5.12   The principle of economy

The standards that are deemed acceptable for any task will limit the number of methods which may be used. For some tasks, such as for cadastral surveys and many engineering surveys carried out under contract terms, there are nationally agreed specifications that must be followed. In some cases —particularly in cadastral surveying—not only the standards but also the methods to be used are laid down. Where flexibility is allowed, the choice of method will normally be made on economic grounds. The survey should meet the necessary conditions in the way that is most economic in terms of time, effort, and cost.

With control surveys, this principle does not necessarily apply in the short term. At the level of national mapping, standards are often set that are higher than those needed for the job in hand. The immediate needs can generally be clearly defined, whilst those of the future are unknown. The history of surveying, however, shows that sooner or later there will be a need for higher standards of precision and accuracy. High technology is accelerating this process. For a small increase in present costs there can be significant improvements in the quality of surveys that will lead to substantial savings in the future. In a later chapter, the problems and techniques of cost–benefit analysis are considered. Attempts have been made to use these techniques in the evaluation of control surveys where many of the benefits lie in the longer term. Too high a standard will lead to unnecessary costs and delays and will seriously jeopardize the benefits that can come from developing a land information system. Too low a standard will achieve similar deleterious results.

The traditional approach has been to trust the technology that is currently available and to work to the standards that it dictates. For Third World countries where resources are limited, the answer must be to trust what is currently affordable. Since every system has managed with the technology of its day, and since in most cases the crucial problems are not technological but managerial, the need is not necessarily for high-precision surveys, but rather for the best value for money. The principle of working economically implies the acceptance of risk. At some future date every system, even that which is currently the best in the world, will need to be up-graded. In accordance with the principles of economy, present standards must be set that are reasonable but not excessive.

5.13   The principle of independent check

Errors in surveying are normally classified as gross errors, systematic errors, or random errors. Random errors are those small inconsistencies in measurement that obey a Gaussian distribution; their effect is overcome by repeated observations and statistical treatment so the probability is that they are averaged out. Systematic errors, on the other hand, tend to have an accumulative effect. They are errors that arise from physical phenomena such as the refraction of electromagnetic waves through the atmosphere, or a psychological tendency of an observer to bias his results by overestimating or underestimating the reading on a scale. Systematic errors can be eliminated by identifying their cause and taking appropriate remedial action. Thus a theodolite that is exposed to the sun may suffer from uneven expansion but the effect can be overcome by using a sun umbrella. An electromagnetic wave undergoes refraction through the air by an amount that can be mathematically modelled; by measuring the atmospheric conditions, the resulting errors can be calculated and corrected.

What must be avoided is gross error. Gross errors are blunders or mistakes that arise through human or mechanical failure. They are often large and, if not eliminated, can grossly distort the quality of the rest of a survey. They are identified by the process of independent check. Simple methods of checking field survey measurements include measuring the three angles of a triangle and checking that their sum is 180 degrees, starting and ending a traverse on known points, or repeating an observation using different methods or under different conditions. Repeated observations under the same conditions may not provide evidence that a gross error has occurred. In photogrammetry, for instance, the repeated measurement of a point on a photograph that is thought to be a ground mark may produce consistent results, but they might be measurements in relation to a point that has been completely wrongly identified.

Once gross errors have been made, they can be expensive to rectify. Returning to the field to reobserve a measurement that was in error can substantially increase the costs of a survey. In general, when machines go wrong, the consequences are immediately apparent; when humans make mistakes, which is relatively often, the consequences can pass unnoticed for some time.

5.14   The principle of maintenance

Control nets need to be maintained, for as soon as they are established they begin to decay. For a variety of reasons the ground marks will disappear, for instance through vandalism, misfortune, erosion, corrosion, or construction and development in and around the site. Even the records can decay either through neglect—the records being so inaccessible that few people know of their existence and they are not kept up to date—or through physical decay. The long-term prognosis for records kept on magnetic tape is uncertain and many organizations make repeated copies of all important files of information just in case of disaster. The problems are universal and are of particular significance to those responsible for maintaining archives (as discussed in Chapter 8).

The single most common defect in existing land information records has been the failure to maintain them in good condition and to keep them up to date. The problem is common, and not particular to control surveys. Scant attention has, for example, been paid to the problems of map revision as opposed to those of initial map creation. Most maps, especially those of large scale, are seriously out of date. Many cadastral systems are only partially coping with the day by day transactions that take place. It is substantially easier to attract funds to cover the considerable unit costs for establishing a control network than it is to retain funds for supporting its maintenance. Yet, in econometric terms, it has been shown that the benefits of such a network accrue only after a decade or so. If by that time the network is seriously reduced, the economic justification can no longer be made. The case for establishing control networks is only strong if they are going to be properly maintained. Governments need to invest in long-term maintenance as much as in the short-term creation of control networks.

References

1. Dowson, Sir E. and Sheppard, V. L. O. (1952). *Land registration*, Her Majesty's Stationery Office, London.
2. Angus-Lepan, P. V. (1967). Land systems reform in Canada and their possible application in Australia. *The Australian Surveyor*, Vol. 21, p. 216.
3. See, for example, Maling, D. H. (1973). *Coordinate systems and map projections*. George Philip, London.
4. National Research Council (1982). *Procedures and standards for a multipurpose cadastre*, pp. 32–3. National Academy Press, Washington.
5. See, for example, Burnside, C. D. (1985). *Mapping from aerial photographs*. Collins, London.
6. Wright, J. W. (1956). Reference marks in land settlement. *Journal of African Administration*, Vol. 8/1, p. 42.
7. National Research Council, *Op. cit.*, p. 24.

6. Surveys and mapping

In this chapter we review some of the methods used and problems arising in the collection of spatial data. We consider the surveying and mapping of points of detail both from a geometric and from a land information point of view.

6.1 Data acquisition

In the previous chapter we considered aspects of the question 'where is what?' by examining some of the issues relating to control surveys and geodetic networks. The principles that underlie the methods and execution of such surveys also extend to detail surveying. The differences lie in the great precision needed for control and the greater emphasis on the 'what' in detail surveys. In terms of quantity and quality they differ; in terms of measurement principle they do not.

In this chapter, three sets of techniques will be considered: field surveying, photogrammetry, and remote sensing. Each contains a set of tools that differ in measurement principle and in practice. Each, however, may be regarded as complementary, the circumstances dictating whether one or the other or some combination is appropriate. All three sets of techniques are concerned with the discovery, recording, and presentation of spatially referenced data. In a strict sense, photogrammetry is a form of remote sensing. Although the two subjects have been coming more closely together, there has traditionally been a difference in emphasis. The photogrammetrist has concentrated on the geometric aspects of the measurement process and the remote senser on the determination of the nature objects from a distance.

In the context of remote sensing, the term 'ground truth' is sometimes used, implying information collected on the ground as a control to verify and calibrate information gathered from air photographs or from remotely sensed imagery. In theory there should be no better way to determine what an object is than by inspection at close quarters. But, as Rhind and Hudson have pointed out, two observers in the field do not always come up with the same land use classification for an area even if they are working to the same specification. In one project they reported that:

Accuracy can only be checked indirectly, by repeating some or all of the field survey and this was also done periodically: even so, stringent re-survey only tests for

106

consistency rather than accuracy in a strict sense. 'Errors' detected by re-survey varied by land use class, from fewer than 1/1000 occurrences for detached and semi-detached houses to about 1/50 where complex, multi-floor use of space was carried out.[1]

6.2   Feature definition

The discrepancies referred to above stemmed as much from ambiguities in the specifications as from human error, although the latter inevitably has a part to play. In determining the nature of objects by field surveying, the basic problem is one of specification, defining unambiguously what is required. Within a land information system, data are stored about entities or features such as buildings or rivers. The data may consist of positional information or relationships with other features or attributes. An attribute is a property of an entity such as its size, shape, colour, class, or function. Objects are collections of entities which in turn form a higher level entity—for instance, a stream may be an entity with attributes of width, length, volume of water, quality of water, and so forth, each stream being part of the higher entity or object called a drainage network.

It is only recently that attempts have been made to produce feature dictionaries, defining objects and attributes so that map data held in digital form can be exchanged electronically without ambiguity or uncertainty as to what is meant.[2] The distinction between a stream and a river, or when a line of bushes constitutes a hedge, have in the past been left to the arbitrary discretion of the individual surveyor in the field. The traditional land surveyor has, however, been more concerned with the quality of the geometrical measurements, for instance, of the distance to the edge of a stream, rather than with defining whether the end of the line should be the edge of the marshy ground or the edge of flowing water. The surveyor may have observed and recorded the distance to the nearest millimetre but it hardly matters if there is ambiguity in the definition of the end points.

There have, however, been signs of change. It is no longer uncommon to find a technician surveyor operating an instrument such as a combined electronic angle- and distance-measuring device (the so-called total station or electronic tacheometer) whilst the professional surveyor selects and classifies the points to be measured. This is a complete reversal of traditional roles and is one symptom of the change in emphasis from measurement science to information science.

6.3   Field survey measurement techniques

The techniques of geometrical measurement used by the field surveyor may be classified as graphical or numerical, though some are in practice a combination of both. Numerical data can always be plotted on a map in graphical form and can be recorded and stored at one to one scale with the environment. Graphical data are restricted in accuracy to the scale of the map on which they were compiled. They can be converted to numerical form by the process known as digitizing but, although they can then be held in a computer to apparently high levels of precision, their actual geometrical accuracy can be no better than that of the source material. This is, at best, half the thickness of a line drawn on a map. However, when distortions in the map base and the imprecisions of draughtsmanship are taken into account, it is unlikely to be better than 0.2 to 0.3 millimetres on the map scale. This represents 20 to 30 centimetres on the ground for a map at a scale of 1/1000.

Plane tabling

Of the techniques which are still in use, especially for cadastral surveying, the oldest are plane tabling and chain survey. Both techniques are still

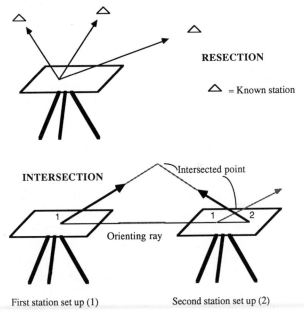

RESECTION

△ = Known station

INTERSECTION

Intersected point

Orienting ray

First station set up (1)   Second station set up (2)

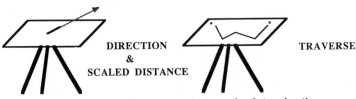

DIRECTION
&
SCALED DISTANCE

TRAVERSE

Fig. 6.1   *Detail Surveys: techniques for fixing detail*

employed in India and elsewhere. They depend on cheap, simple, and robust equipment. A plane table consists of a drawing board mounted on top of a tripod. The map, whether it is cadastral or topographic, is compiled in the field by direct plotting of the measurements taken. The surveyor sets up the plane table over a known control point, or in sight of known points, and aligns the map or plan to be in sympathy with the control using a sight rule or alidade (see Fig. 6.1). New detail is fixed by intersecting points from two set-up stations or by measuring the distance and direction to them. Successive points can be linked by traversing. If heights are needed, the vertical angle to any point can be measured with an inclinometer and the distance scaled off the map. The height difference is calculated by simple trigonometry.

Plane tabling requires very cheap equipment, a fairly low level of education, good draughtsmanship, and patience. In the hands of a craftsman, it is capable of producing accuracies to within the thickness of a pencil line. However, a high level of skill is essential especially in the initial compilation of a map. Once a basic map has been compiled, each point of detail can become a control point for all subsequent surveys and in consequence less skill is required. The Ordnance Survey of Great Britain has found that a combination of plane table and chain survey techniques is the most cost-effective way of conducting field revision on large-scale topographic maps. It has been used for many years to carry out map maintenance and the revision of the 1/1250 and 1/2500 large-scale map series, which form the basis for registration of title, utility mapping, and many land development projects.

Chain survey

Like plane tabling, chain survey makes use of cheap and simple equipment —essentially a chain and a linen or plastic tape. A point can be fixed by measuring one distance with a chain laid along a control line and one with a tape offset at right angles to it. The dimensions can be recorded for subsequent plotting at whatever scale is desired. Offset distances should be less than the length of the tape, which usually means a maximum of 30 metres. The control lines are configured in triangular shapes. Because no angles other than the right angular offsets are measured, the term trilateration rather than triangulation is preferred. The lengths of the control lines may be measured using the chain or by more sophisticated methods. Given good control, accuracies of a few centimetres can be maintained over short ranges. Less skill is needed than in plane tabling but more staff are required. With a plane table one person can work on his or her own or with one assistant: with chain surveying, it is advantageous to have several assistants. The exception is where there is sufficient existing detail already mapped for one person to be able to operate alone, as in the case of the Ordnance Survey's work in Great Britain.

It is tempting to advocate plane tabling combined with chain survey as a solution to many Third World mapping problems, particularly for day to day maintenance of cadastral and large-scale topographic maps. The equipment is cheap and can be manufactured or repaired locally, thus it does not draw on foreign exchange. The techniques do not require the surveyors to have high educational skills and therefore more people can be brought into employment. Provided that certain safeguards and independent checks are employed, the quality can be sufficient for most practical purposes. The rate of production of survey may be slow but, since the costs are low, the number of survey parties can be increased.

There are, however, two main objections. First, if advantage is to be taken of computer technology in the storage and retrieval of data, then there will be additional expense and complications in getting the data into the data base. Secondly, if more sophisticated techniques are already in use in a country, the suggestion that surveyors should revert to outmoded techniques and outdated technology may be considered insulting. When the objective is to move forward, the likelihood of willing agreement to step backwards is remote.

Angular measurements

The advantage of recording data in numerical rather than in graphical form is that they can be plotted at any scale and can be stored more easily in a data base. To produce the data in numerical form, two types of measurement are involved—angular and distance. A plane table is a graphical device for measuring angles. The simplest numerically oriented equivalent is the

Table 6.1   Measurement costs and accuracies: angle and distance measurements

	Accuracy	Complexity	Cost
Angles:			
Compass	Low	Low	Low
Optical square	Low	Low	Low
Plane table	Low	Low	Low
Theodolite	High	Medium	Medium
Electronic theodolite	High	High	High
Distances:			
Linen tape	Low	Low	Low
Chain	Low	Low	Low
Steel tape	Medium/High	Low	Low
Tacheometer	Medium	Medium	Medium
Subtense bar	Medium	Medium	Medium
Electromagnetic (EDM)	High	High	Medium
Electronic position fixing	High	High	High

surveyor's compass. This is capable of giving azimuth or direction readings relative to magnetic north but, owing to its inherent inaccuracies, it is rarely used today. The standard piece of equipment for measuring angles is the theodolite. Depending on its quality, the angle between two pointings of a theodolite can be measured to a precision of minutes or even seconds of arc. One second of arc represents the angle subtended by 1 centimetre at 2 kilometres, 1 minute by just under 3 centimetres at 100 metres. The higher the precision that the instrument is capable of achieving, the greater is its cost. Traditionally, the measured values have been read off a scale by eye and then written down in a field book. Increasingly, theodolites are becoming electronic so that the measured values can be automatically recorded. Errors may be introduced into a survey when writing observed quantities into a field book or when transferring these into a computer system. Electronic theodolites provide a means by which these may be avoided. In financial terms, they are currently more expensive though, as more manufacturers adopt the electronic approach, the price will fall (see Table 6.1).

Distance measurement

Distances may be measured in any one of three ways, the traditional methods being chaining or taping. With these, very precise measurements are possible if refined equipment is used and a variety of precautions are taken to eliminate systematic sources of error. In practice, accuracies of around a centimetre are possible by simple standard techniques. Similar accuracies, though over greater ranges, can be obtained by electronic distance measurement using microwave frequencies and measuring intervals of time. As with electronic theodolites, the measured quantities can be recorded automatically, though this is a more recent development. The equipment is expensive compared with taping but is reasonably robust. The most common cause of problems is the power source, notably flat batteries. On the other hand, if a tape breaks it can be repaired locally and the length of the tape recalibrated. However, if an electronic device breaks down then, unless it is a routine fault for which there is a replacement part readily available, the instrument will have to be sent to an electronic workshop for repair. In some cases this may mean sending it abroad, with a consequent drain on foreign exchange. Whereas with a broken tape work can proceed, if slowly, using the longest remaining section; with a broken electronic device all measurement work must stop.

Subtense Distances can also be measured optically by the techniques known as subtense and tacheometry. In subtense work, the angle subtended by a fixed-length bar is measured; over short ranges of up to 100 metres, accuracies of the order of 5 to 10 centimetres are possible. The technique has been successfully used in Malawi for traversing over property corner beacons. The equipment is relatively cheap, robust, and easy to use and sufficiently accurate for most practical purposes. It is labour intensive and hence only relevant where labour is cheap. But, given a good team trained in a routine way of operating, the productivity can be high. The measurement process does not compete in terms of speed with electronic methods, but it does not have the same technical problems.

Tacheometry   In tacheometry, the distances are deduced by measuring the distance on a graduated staff that subtends a fixed angle at the instrument station. Radial distances can be measured from a central point using a theodolite for both the angle and distance measurement. The modern version of this approach is the electronic tacheometer, or total station, referred to above. The analogue version is not capable of producing high precision and is more appropriate for the topographic mapping of 'soft' detail, such as hedge lines where the precise position is difficult to determine on the ground. The equipment is, however, robust and the maintenance costs are low.

Traversing

By far the most common method for carrying out detail surveys, for example of property boundaries or to record the positions of pipe lines, is to use a theodolite and either a steel band or an electronic distance-measuring (EDM) device. Traverses may be run from points on the control framework, either directly over the required points or nearby, leaving the final fixing to be done by measuring from the traverse points. Given that it is physically possible to set an instrument up over, for instance, a boundary beacon, then the technique is simple and straightforward; it also provides a mechanism for independently checking each measurement. The final quality of the survey is then indicated by the magnitude of the vector misclosure of the traverse. Traversing is much used for cadastral surveys throughout Africa where surveyors can be satisfactorily trained in the various techniques, in spite of relatively low levels of education. It is particularly relevant where boundaries must be described by metes, that is by bearing and distance, for such measures are a direct by-product of the method of survey. On the other hand, it is less suitable for setting out land parcels in conformity with an estate lay-out plan, or where the nature of the boundary monumentation makes the centring of a theodolite over a property corner beacon difficult or impossible. In such cases, the technique of measuring to points by direction and distance from some central control point is more appropriate.

Although the design work for estate lay-outs is increasingly being carried out on computers that produce numerical data for setting out, it is currently more common for the surveyor to start with a plan of the area with the dimensions to be set out marked upon it. It is possible to digitize the lay-out plan by methods indicated in the Chapter 7 and to use the resulting coordinates in the setting out process. Although this is a level of sophistication that is at present inappropriate to many societies, it is necessary to recognize the trend. It is one consequence of the modern technological approach. Ground surveying is as much concerned with putting designs on to the ground as it is with recording what is already there. Any savings that can be made in the setting-out stage of the development process should bring benefits later on.

6.4 Photogrammetric detail surveys

Setting out is a process which can be done only by ground methods. It cannot be done by photogrammetry or by remote sensing. Photogrammetry is a set of techniques for recording and measuring what is already on the ground by taking measurements on photographs. The techniques are only cost effective when economies of scale can be applied. They are relevant to topographic mapping and to the initial compilation of a land register, but rarely to its day to day maintenance.

Aerial photographs

An aerial photograph is essentially an historical document, which freezes the landscape at the instant at which the photograph was taken. It provides evidence of the conditions appertaining at that time. In addition, it provides some forms of evidence that cannot normally be perceived by inspection on the ground—for instance of archaeological sites from the patterns of disturbance in the soil. Evidence can be deduced about previous patterns of social behaviour, sometimes dating back many hundreds or even thousands of years. Evidence may also be gleaned on the current nature of the geology and soils, vegetation cover, land use, hydrology, and environmental conditions both in rural and urban areas (see Table 6.2). The quality of the harvest, the state of the traffic, and the condition of the housing stock may be analysed by a skilled photographic interpreter. However, photogrammetry has had its most far-reaching impact as a set of geometrical measurement tools. The overwhelming majority of topographic maps in use in the world today owe their quality and quantity to photogrammetric methods, particularly those as scales between 1/5000 and 1/75 000.

A photograph is a record of the rays of light that have passed from the ground through the camera lens to be recorded on film. Provided that the film is flat and stable, as most polyester-based photographic film has proved to be, and provided that the light-sensitive emulsion sticks firmly to that base and that high-quality lenses are used, then it is possible to put the process

Table 6.2   Aerial photographs for mapping data for
agriculture:

1. **Reconnaissance data**
   Spatial information and quality data about the
   land, its natural condition, forest cover,
   vegetation, crops, soil, and land use
2. **Semi-detailed qualitative information**
   Qualitative data about cultivated species, such as
   the vigour and health of crops, species of
   vegetation, etc.
3. **Detailed quantitative information**
   Potential crop production and timber yields,
   grazing capability, lost production after disaster,
   etc.

into reverse. As pointed out in Chapter 5, the relative positions of rays
entering the camera lens can be projected back outwards; this gives accurate
representation of the angles subtended at the lens by the objects photographed. Knowing that an object lies in a particular direction is, on its own,
insufficient to determine where that object is. A measure is needed from a
second direction; hence photographs for mapping purposes are normally
taken as overlapping 'stereo' pairs.

Types of aerial photography   Aerial photographs are classified in a variety
of ways. There are vertical photographs, which are usually taken from an
aeroplane with the axis of the camera pointing as near as possible vertically
downwards; there are high-oblique photographs taken with the camera
pointing so that the horizon can be seen; then there are low obliques taken in
between the two (see Fig. 6.2). The nearer the camera is to the horizontal,
the more the image will appear as it would to the human eye; the nearer it is
to the vertical, the less familiar will the object appear and hence the greater
will be the skill that is needed to interpret it. In general, photographs that are
not classifiable as 'vertical' are less relevant for mapping purposes, except of
course for mapping vertical surfaces such as the facades of buildings. In what
follows, vertical photography will be assumed.

Aerial photography may also be classified according to its scale; small
scale covers a large area, while large scale covers a small area but shows great
detail. It may also be classified in accordance with the type of camera lens
used, such as 'normal angle' (with a focal length of around 300 millimetres),
'wide angle' (about 150 millimetres), and 'super wide angle' (around 88
millimetres). It may further be classified according to the spectral sensitivity
and type of emulsion from which the film is made—such as panchromatic,
infrared, colour, or false colour. In the latter case, unfamiliar dyes are used
to colour the image so that green living vegetation might be represented by
the colour red, dead vegetation by blue.

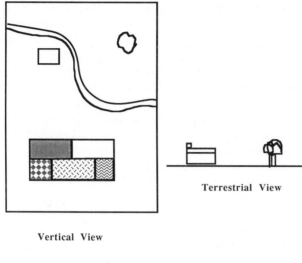

Vertical View

Terrestrial View

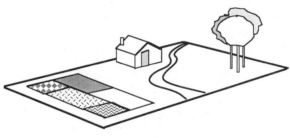

Oblique View

Fig. 6.2 *Oblique and vertical aerial views*

For topographic mapping purposes, vertical photography taken with a wide angle lens using black and white film is most common. Different types of film may, however, be used if the emphasis is to be on photo interpretation rather than basic mapping. For cadastral purposes, longer focal length lenses have certain advantages. Wide angle lenses improve the quality of height measurement and are used where contours are to be recorded. In cadastral mapping, the third dimension is of lesser importance. However, it is essential to be able to see on to the ground in between vegetation or buildings so as to be able to identify property corner beacons. This can be achieved by flying higher, relatively speaking, and using a longer focal length lens camera. A normal angle lens and a flying height of 4000 metres gives the same scale of photography as a wide angle lens at a flying height of 2000 metres.

Photo maps　A vertical aerial photograph has a number of the qualities that make it similar to a map. The imagery is obviously different and not all parts of the ground can be seen. Parts of a building may be obscured by overhanging trees, also the further away that a tall object is from the centre of the photograph, the more it will appear to lean over and obscure its own rear side. None the less, what are known as 'photomaps' are often produced as a substitute or underlying base for the abstract symbols of a conventional map. If the photograph were truly vertical, and if the ground and all things on it were absolutely flat, then any measurements taken off the photograph would be to a consistent scale of $F/(H-h)$. (In this expression, 'F' is the focal length of the camera, 'H' is the flying height, 'h' is the ground height; hence '$(H-h)$' is the height above the ground (Fig. 6.3)).

Two factors normally prevent such a simple relationship. First, it is never possible, especially in an aircraft, to ensure that the camera is pointing precisely in line with the vertical. The criterion for a photograph to be deemed to be vertical is that the camera is pointing straight downwards to within 3 degrees of the plumb-line. The result of this small displacement from the vertical is to appear to tilt the ground with, in consequence, a

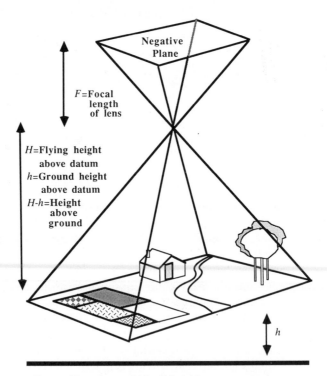

Datum Plane from which all heights are measured

Fig. 6.3　*Scale of a vertical aerial photograph* $= F/(H-h)$

uniform change of scale across the photograph. The second factor is that the ground and all upon it are not flat. The fact that a tall building appears to lean over when it is away from the centre of the photograph means that the top of the building has been displaced relative to the bottom. The effect is identical with variations of ground height. To put it another way, the scale of the photograph is different at every point of different height.

Height measurements

Measurements of the difference in displacement of a point on two overlapping aerial photographs permit the photogrammetrist to determine the heights of objects. Such heights can be measured to an accuracy of 1 part in 10 000 of the flying height, or thereabouts, depending upon the equipment used and the nature of the object being measured. Thus wide angle photographs taken from a flying height of 1000 metres, and hence at a scale of 1/6700, give the heights of specific points to an accuracy of 10 centimetres and contours can be traced with 0.5-metre vertical intervals.

The details of how this may be done are discussed in standard textbooks on photogrammetry.[3] To achieve such results there must be good ground control, good equipment, and skilled photogrammetric operators. Beyond that, the systems used are strictly routine. There has been much sterile debate about the relative merits of ground survey and photogrammetry, particularly in relation to the cadastre and property boundary surveys. Cadastral surveyors have seen what happened to their topographic counterparts and have raised a number of objections to further encroachment by the photogrammetrists. In many countries, they have ensured that the survey regulations specifically require that all boundaries must be measured on the ground with tapes or electronic distance-measuring devices, which must carry a certificate of calibration. Before examining the ways in which photogrammetry can be used for land title work, some other objections will be considered.

Air survey versus ground survey

The most serious objection is that photogrammetry cannot be used for setting out. That of course is undeniable. Topographic maps produced by photogrammetric methods can, however, form the basis of the design for a new layout (for example, of a new road, an estate of buildings, or an agricultural development project). In Malawi, for instance, a major land reform programme in the area around Lilongwe involved setting out new roads, drainage channels, and land parcels. The design for these was based on topographic maps produced photogrammetrically and plotted in pencil so that cheap dyeline copies could be printed. The boundaries of the parcels were then marked on the ground with concrete beacons, then their positions were fixed by field survey, using subtense bar traversing methods.

Air survey and ground survey are complementary techniques and a combination of the two is often the ideal. When existing land parcel boundaries are mapped, some points will inevitably not be visible on aerial photographs. This is either because the ground mark is too small for it to be seen from the height of an aircraft in the sky, or because the marks are obscured by overhanging buildings or vegetation. Some of the problems that result from this may be overcome by premarking, either by painting the boundary markers white if they are of sufficient size, or by laying white strips in the shape of a 'Y' or an 'X' centred around the mark. Others may be overcome by flying higher, and hence looking down more vertically, whilst using a camera with a longer focal length lens to produce larger-scale photography. Such a solution requires more photographs and hence more time and cost for the overall mapping process. But where the roof-line of a building overhangs the plinth line, only the former can be seen on the photographs. In such cases the most economic way of survey may still be photogrammetric, but in combination with a subsequent ground survey to plot the correct position of the walls in relation to the roof-outline, should this be necessary.

Questions of relative accuracy always bedevil the comparison between photogrammetry and ground survey. Such questions are, however, largely esoteric. What matters is what can be achieved for a given price in the given environmental circumstances. Different circumstances favour different techniques (see Table 6.3). Unfortunately this is rarely reflected in the regulations that govern the choice of cadastral survey methods. If the premise is made that graphical standards of accuracy are all that are required, then there is little need for debate since both sets of techniques are

Table 6.3   Boundary survey sources: capture of boundary information (based on Barnes[4])

	Options						
	Sketch map	Aerial photo (35 mm)	Aerial photo (format)	Semi-rectified photo	Ortho photo	Map from photo	Field survey diagram
Criteria:							
Accuracy	L	L	M	M	H	H	H
Simplicity	H	H	M	M-L	L	L	L
Cost	L	L	M	M-H	H	H	H
Efficiency	H	H	M	M	L	L	L
Utility	L	H	H	H	H	M-L	L
Flexibility	H	H	M	M	M	L	L

High(H);   Medium(M);   Low(L).

equally satisfactory. When contours are to be surveyed, the general standards achieved by photogrammetry are superior. When, however, it comes to numerical precision on the ground, for instance in measuring a plot frontage to within a few centimetres, ground survey prevails. This is not so much because photogrammetry is unable to achieve such accuracies, but because the cost of doing so is generally higher.

Problems of consistency can, however, arise if two different techniques are used and the absolute standard of one is significantly different from the other. If, for example, the corners of a land parcel are measured photogrammetrically to produce coordinates that are accurate to within 20 centimetres and if, later, the parcel is subdivided by ground methods that have a relative accuracy of 1 centimetre, then there will be a conflict of evidence. If the data are stored in a computer, then some way of reconciling the apparent conflict will need to be programmed into the system.

More difficult questions relate to the legal validity of photogrammetric evidence and the degree of responsibility for the accuracy of the data. Photogrammetric measurements may not be acceptable as evidence before a court because of a lack of confidence and familiarity with them. There may be further difficulty in persuading learned counsel that measurements that were taken indirectly from evidence gathered a mile above the site in question, can be compared with that on the ground. There is additional opposition to photogrammetry in countries where it is customary for the licensed surveyor to claim responsibility for the quality of work carried out either personally or under his or her direct personal supervision. In Kenya, for example, it is necessary for a private licensed surveyor to sign on each land title survey that 'I hereby certify that I, in person made . . . and completed the survey represented by this plan, on which are written the bearings and lengths of the lines surveyed by me . . .'. Where this is the case, then neither the photogrammetrist in overall control nor the technician who actually carries out the work is likely to be licensed.

With a ground survey, it is easy to provide independent checks on the quality of all the measurements, for example by traversing between known points. The quality of photogrammetric measurement for any point of detail, such as a property corner beacon, depends upon the correct measurement being taken to it by the photogrammetric operator. This is done by placing a black dot, known as a floating mark, over the point to be measured. Each measure is independent; therefore if the floating mark is incorrectly placed, through either carelessness or misidentification of the ground point, then the coordinate record will be incorrect. There is no immediate means of identifying when this has happened. To this extent the technique breaks a basic principle of survey as quality control for photogrammetric surveys is much more difficult than for ground. The quality can only be checked by sampling, comparing a limited number of points with their value as observed by ground survey methods. Few cadastral systems are operated on such a random checking process; managers prefer to check the quality of each and every point of detail.

Photographs as a data store

The objections raised above need to be kept in perspective. Aerial photography has been successfully used in the compilation of land records in a number of different ways. Of these, by far the easiest is simply to retain the photographs as a graphic data base. Though geometrically inaccurate, the photographs will allow future investigators to go back in history to the instant when each photograph was taken. Subject to the stability of the photographic material over time, the basic photograph can always be used, if the need ever arises, for both measurement and interpretation. It is a basic data store. Such a solution is rarely adopted and aerial photographs, though priceless historical and archival material, are rarely carefully stored. Conversely, much cadastral ground survey data are stored but the measurements involved will never be referred to again. An increasing number of the more developed countries are becoming aware that the aerial photograph is a record of their heritage that is being thrown away. They are endeavouring to establish archives to store the photographs for posterity. Few Third World countries, however, have the necessary resources to establish a central repository for aerial photography and thus to preserve such a record of their past.

Rectified photographs   Contact prints of aerial photographs are usually at too small a scale for simple measurements to be made directly from them. Enlarged aerial photographs are therefore more useful. In Kenya, extensive use has been made of such enlargements as a base for tracing off parcel boundaries. These, although topologically accurate, can contain errors of up to 10 per cent or more in the measured size of parcels because of the tilt and height displacement. Improved accuracy can be achieved by rectifying the photographs. A rectifier is a photographic enlarger that is capable of projecting the photographic image on to a tilted surface. If the slope of this surface is adjusted to equalize the effect of the camera's tilt, then the displacements can be compensated for. On level ground, the geometrical quality of the resulting print is as good as that of a map, and distances such as parcel dimensions can then be measured using a graduated scale.

Orthophotography   Further refinements can produce an orthophotograph. Here, stereo pairs of photographs are mounted in a special machine and profiles of the ground are measured in strips. New photographs are then compiled, strip by strip, placing each part of the photo image in its correct planimetric position. The result is a photograph that looks very much like the original but has improved measurement potential. A mosaic of such orthophotographs can be compiled and printed by lithographic methods as an orthophotomap. The equipment can cost up to $150 000 per machine and ground control is needed, but, apart from the level of amortization, the resulting map is cheaper to produce than an ordinary line map. It is, however, more difficult to revise and update, for that necessitates new photography. The occasional line can always be added to or deleted from an ordinary line map at relatively little expense.

Line maps   Line maps can be produced from aerial photographs by stereo restitution. Here, pairs of photographs are set up in a machine and their relative positions within the machine are adjusted. This can be done either manually, in the case of analogue machines, or mathematically, in the case of analytical plotters. The latter machines are significantly more expensive than the former and cost in the range of $50 000–150 000. Both machines are capable of producing digital data, although, for the former, additional equipment has to be attached to a standard machine. One of the advantages of using stereo-plotters is that contours and heights can be obtained during the restitution process. The cost of mapping, including ground control, is of the order of $50–100 per hectare, depending on how much detail is plotted and the type of the terrain.

Comparators   Where very precise measurements of individual points are needed, comparators may be used. Comparators may be 'mono', viewing a single photograph, or 'stereo', viewing stereoscopic pairs. They are designed to give very accurate measurements of the position of clearly defined points on the photographs. With a good machine, it is possible to measure to a precision of around a micrometre. The instruments can cost up $150 000 each. The measurements can then be mathematically transformed to give the equivalent ground positions of points. The technique is relevant where there is a need to produce precise coordinates, for example for densifying ground control or for some cadastral purposes if there is a need to record the coordinates of property beacons. So long as various precautions are taken, accuracies comparable with field survey methods are possible. The technique is, however, only cost effective if a large number of clearly identifiable points have to be measured.

6.5   Remote sensing

Remote sensing constitutes a set of techniques that extend the range of human perception beyond the visible spectrum. It is the science of analysing objects from the radiation they emit or reflect, each object having a characteristic 'fingerprint' or 'spectral signature' that gives clues to its identity. Certain objects become distinctive and detectable when viewed by means of radiation invisible to the human eye. Even within the visible spectrum, the images viewed from satellites give a more holistic view of the earth; much of the reputation of remote sensing in the mind of most people stems from the impressive way in which the earth appears when photographed from space. Table 6.4 shows the resolution that is possible with publicly available technology. When very fine detail can be revealed by satellites that have been launched largely for military purposes, then an impression is created that the techniques offer a cheap and easy solution to the problems of acquiring data for a land information system. They have a particular role to play in particular circumstances; they are, however, a far from universal solution.

Remote sensing has been closely associated with satellite technology and images from space. Although satellites have obvious advantages for monitoring the whole of the earth's surface, a satellite is only one platform from which remote sensing may be conducted: aircraft, balloons, or even hand-

Table 6.4   Resolution characteristics of weather and resource satellites

Satellite	Spatial resolution	Spectral resolution	Radiometric resolution	Temporal resolution
GOES	1 km × 1 km	0.66–0.7 µm 10.5–12.6		30 min
NOAA	1 km × 1 km	0.58–0.68 µm 0.725–1.1 3.55–3.93 10.5–11.5 11.5–12.5		12 hrs
Landsat MSS	60 m × 80 m	0.5–0.6 µm 0.6–0.7 0.7–0.8 0.8–1.1	64 radiance levels	16 days
Landsat TM	30 m × 30 m	0.45–0.52 µm 0.52–0.60 0.63–0.69 0.76–0.90 1.55–1.75 10.4–12.5 2.08–2.35	256 radiance levels	16 days
SPOT Multi-spectral	20 m × 20 m	0.50–0.59 µm 0.61–0.69 0.79–0.89	256 radiance levels	26 days
SPOT Pan-chromatic	10 m × 10 m	0.51–0.73 µm		
Seasat	25 m × 25 m	23.5 cm (L-band)		152 days

held cameras may be used to gather information. Most remote sensing is based upon electromagnetic radiation at frequencies that extend from gamma rays, through visible radiation to microwaves and radio waves. The radiation most commonly detected is that reflected by objects on the earth illuminated by the sun. Some of the radiation from the sun is absorbed by the atmosphere, some is absorbed by the objects themselves, and some is reflected and hence is capable of detection (for instance by the human eye or the light-sensitive film in a camera). Other wavelengths, such as heat, are radiated by a body. In thermal imagery remote sensing, measurements record the level of the heat radiated by objects on the ground. This is, for example, helpful in determining certain properties of rocks, the existence of pollution, or the lack of good insulation in buildings. Radiation such as radar may also be transmitted from a source and the level of its reflection then recorded. For example, as an aircraft flies along, the transmitter on board can scan the ground and a sensor can measure the strength of the return signal.

The pictures that result from remote sensing may represent near-instantaneous views as in conventional photography. From the black and white or colour negatives obtained it is possible to make straight contact prints or enlargements. Different types of film (such as panchromatic or infrared) can be used and different filters can be placed in front of the camera lens to get different effects, some of which may be emphasized by using false colours. One such system is that used to view the 'near infra-red'; this is a part of the spectrum just beyond that visible to the human eye but none the less able to be recorded on 'light'-sensitive film.

Pixel scanning

Alternatively, the imagery may be the result of scanning in which case the average reflectance from small areas known as picture elements or 'pixels' is recorded. These pixels are scanned in strips and the total picture is built up from successive scans. The data are recorded electronically as a measure of the strength of the reflected signal received, normally using an '8-bit binary code' (in binary $1 = 1$ in decimal, $10 = 2$ in decimal, $100 = 4$ in decimal, $1000 = 8$ in decimal, etc. so that the 8-bit number $11111111 = 255$ in decimal). Thus, in decimal terms, the reflectance for each pixel is measured as a number in the range from 0 to 255. The process then entails the interpretation of these values, given the wavelength at which they have been measured. As a simple example, consider the set of numbers in Table 6.5. If all the numbers between 70 and 79 in the left-hand matrix were printed in red (here xx) and the remainder in blue (here 00), the image of a question mark (?) would appear. In essence, that is all there is to much of remote sensing, and many patterns are discovered by using image analysis devices to

Table 6.5   Remote sensing data pixel values

68 69 75 74 73 66 62	00 00 xx xx xx 00 00
61 71 81 80 83 74 69	00 xx 00 00 00 xx 00
53 60 58 52 58 76 67	00 00 00 00 00 xx 00
55 58 65 64 65 71 69	00 00 00 00 00 xx 00
55 55 58 66 70 69 68	00 00 00 00 xx 00 00
50 55 60 73 69 65 60	00 00 00 xx 00 00 00
44 48 48 70 68 64 60	00 00 00 xx 00 00 00
40 46 55 70 66 62 58	00 00 00 xx 00 00 00
40 45 49 68 63 59 54	00 00 00 00 00 00 00
38 46 55 79 68 65 65	00 00 00 xx 00 00 00

experiment with different colours and different ranges and combinations of selected numbers.

Wave bands

In addition to different combinations of reflectance numbers, different wave bands can be used. In Landsat satellite imagery there are four such bands, numbered 4, 5, 6, and 7, so that various combinations and permutations of the numbers can be tried. For instance, at a simple level, if a pixel has a value N4 in band 4 and N5 in band 5, then the pattern of values (N4 − N5) or of (N4 + N5)/2 can be mapped. In the image analysis machine, appropriate mechanical levers are moved or buttons pressed to select or emphasize different levels of reflectance (that is, different groups of the numbers) until a pattern appears that seems to be meaningful to the interpreter. With experience, certain combinations become known as likely to produce meaningful results. Alternatively, from 'ground truth' it may be found that, for a particular data set, an object or feature such as a rock type has a certain combination of numbers. Using this as a key all similar combinations can be sought, thus indicating those areas where that rock type is likely to occur. This can greatly reduce the time spent on reconnaissance and exploration.

Accuracy and cost-effectiveness

Research continues in an effort to find more precise ways of determining objects. Current methods for interpreting crop types can have accuracies as high as 85 per cent of the cases, which, put another way, means at least every seventh piece of information is wrong. The validity of the technique depends upon an acceptance of a high level of 'noise' in the system, making the results unreliable to an indeterminate degree. For broad-brush pictures of the environment this may be perfectly acceptable, but for a detailed picture with a one to one relationship with the ground it may not. If accuracy is not vital, then cost considerations may bring remote sensing into a more favourable light. One study of land use classification for an area covering a number of counties in Illinois showed costs of $100 000 for three counties mapped from a motor car, $25 000 for six drainage basins mapped from aerial photographs, and $15 000 for seven counties using Landsat imagery.[5] The cost-effectiveness of using satellite imagery for remote sensing depends upon the charges made for the data, much of which has until recently been provided at substantially less than commercial production costs by the American National Space Agency. This has distorted the market and made a fair economic assessment of the techniques impossible.

Image resolution

Part of the unsuitability of remote-sensing imagery for most conventional mapping purposes, and some of the inaccuracies in the interpretation, have stemmed from the low level of resolution of the scanning systems. For the Landsat series of satellites, the pixels were of an average size of approximately 80 metres square. Improvements on this have been taking place; the most recent imagery from a French commercial organization is called SPOT and has a resolution of around 10 metres. Whereas, at the very best, Landsat can be used for 1/100 000 mapping (though 1/500 000 is preferable), SPOT provides data that can be used on maps at scales of 1/25 000 and possibly larger. Governments or private organizations can contract for imagery of specified areas at an appropriate price. No scanning system can, however, compete in terms of geometrical accuracy with straightforward photographic methods. The quality of scanned data is improving and imagery such as that from SPOT is a significant improvement on anything that was commercially available before 1986.

6.6   What to choose

The survey and mapping of detailed information has two components: the classification and coding of the features, and the determination of their positions. The techniques referred to above provide mechanisms by which these objectives may be achieved. For continuous maintenance of individual elements in a land data bank, such as small subdivision work for land titles, field methods of survey are essential. Photogrammetric methods are often preferable if the data are of the type that can be brought up to date periodically, as with small-scale maps, or if mass production methods are needed, as in the initial compilation of a land register. The legal and administrative objections to photogrammetry given above can be overcome by government either carrying out the work itself, or subcontracting it to the private sector. In either case, government should take direct responsibility for the results. If geophysical data are to be recorded, or if a generalized level of measurement is sufficient (for instance in detecting the extent of urban expansion into the rural environment) then remote sensing may have a role to play.

Within the management of the data base, a major problem lies in reconciling data from different sources to different standards of accuracy and precision. The problem referred to above concerned the reconciling of the length of a plot frontage measured to 1 centimetre by ground methods with coordinates of the corner pegs measured to the nearest 20 centimetres by photogrammetry. This can be resolved by associating with each value an attribute indicating its reliability or origin. For the purposes of graphic display, the differences are insignificant. In drawing a deed plan, the line work can be plotted from the coordinate data and the dimensions, being attributes, can be written on the plan in accordance with their field-measured values. In this, there is no effective difference from traditional procedures in which the coordinates were held more precisely but plotted as if they were less so. As long as the relevant information is held in attribute form within the data base, appropriate action can be taken when necessary.

It is a spurious argument to maintain that, because some measures can be taken to a high standard of accuracy and precision, then all measures must be taken to these standards. Measures have always been taken to differing standards and the economic consequences of pursuing policies that adopt this argument are proving unacceptable. The point has to be stressed, for progress towards the development of unified land information systems is being seriously retarded by a failure to determine what, in the overwhelming majority of cases, are the minimum standards that are both necessary and sufficient for almost all practical purposes. There are, of course, certain circumstances under which precise measurements for detail surveys are right and proper. To argue that all surveys must therefore be to this standard is illogical and leads to a serious waste of resources and lack of productivity. For each task, the most appropriate technique should be used. That may necessitate changes in the cadastral law but, if progress is to be made, this must happen. There are many circumstances under which relatively low levels of precision are satisfactory and should be pursued.

References

1. Rhind, D. W. and Hudson, R. (1980). *Land use*, pp. 92–4. Methuen, London and New York.
2. For instance, Canadian Council on Surveying and Mapping (1982). *National standards for the exchange of digital topographic data*, EMR, Ottawa.
3. See, for example, Burnside, C. D. (1985). *Mapping from aerial photographs.* Collins, London.
4. Barnes, G. (1985). Unpublished paper, University of Wisconsin.
5. Rowley, R. L. (1978). Remote sensing and information. *European Seminar on Regional Planning and Remote Sensing*, Council of Europe. p. 106.

7. Digital mapping

In this chapter we examine several of the operations involved in digital mapping and describe some of the methods used in handling digital map data.

7.1 Digital mapping and LIS

Digital mapping is the process of producing maps from spatial data held in numerical rather than in graphical form. The concepts of digital mapping are inherently simple, but the practice tends to be more complex. The greater the range of demands that are put upon the data, the greater the complexity of the processing becomes. Essentially, digital mapping comprises three operations:

(1) data capture or data acquisition, which involves converting the data into digital form;
(2) data processing, in which the data are transformed into different structures to serve different functions;
(3) data presentation, using either computer graphic techniques for visual display or electronic methods for transmitting the data to other users.

A more detailed list of digital-mapping activities is given in Table 7.1.

Some land information systems have grown out of digital mapping and some people have tended to equate the two. Traditional line-drawn maps

Table 7.1 Components of digital mapping

Action	Examples
1. Data acquisition	Line digitizing
2. Data classification	Allocating feature codes
3. Data structuring	Vector, raster, and topological
4. Data restructuring	Raster to vector conversions
5. Data editing	Corrections, squaring buildings
6. Data transformations	Map projections
7. Data selection	Feature overlays
8. Data generalization	Small-scale map compilation
9. Data enhancement	Graphic displays, symbolization
10. Data analysis	Calculating areas

answer the questions 'what is where?' and 'where is what?' and constitute a simple land information system. The digital version of this process does the same. But whereas digital mapping can constitute a land information system, it is not a necessary component of one. The Swedish Real Estate Data Base is an example where, within the data base, there are coordinate values that provide a spatial reference for each land parcel. These coordinates are an attribute of the parcel and can be used for choropleth mapping and for the graphic display of patterns and distributions. The system is not, however, dependent on digital map data and is primarily concerned with non-graphic attributes of the land.

In the early days of digital mapping, there were some who saw the process as no more than an extension to the armoury of tools already available to the map producer. An analogy was drawn with the technique of scribing, which had allowed clear-cut lines of even thickness to be drawn on a map base with less skill and greater speed than before. Digital mapping was regarded as a similar process in which the machine could draw the lines, thus removing the need for skilled draughtsmen. Additional benefits were seen to lie in the increased ability to:

(1)   redraw maps at a changed scale or on a different projection;
(2)   delete and add revision data and thus to speed up the process of keeping maps up to date;
(3)   overlay specialist data;
(4)   store the material in a way that, over time, would not result in the data becoming distorted. Existing reprographic map material can stretch or shrink over the years but the coordinate value of a point remains the same.

Feature selection

It soon became clear that, once each feature on a map was given an appropriate code, it was possible to make selections of features either by type or by area. A feature or entity is something about which data are stored in a data base—such as a building or a tree. Thus a machine could be made to draw only the road network, or only those buildings within a particular area with a particular assessed value. It also became possible to overlay different distributions, for instance where one particular land use type coincided with a specified soil type. Gradually, it was realized that users require only certain types and categories of information and have no use for others. In traditional mapping systems, the cartographer chooses what is to be revealed; the map user has to accept all or nothing. Increasingly, the user began to demand data in a form which could be more easily exploited, thus linking digital mapping with land information systems.

7.2   Data acquisition

Digital map data are normally held in one of two forms, called vector or raster (see Fig. 7.1). Data structures exist that combine the two forms, but these will not be considered here. In a vector data structure, points may be held as numbers representing their coordinate values, lines as sequences or strings of coordinates, and areas either as the strings representing their perimeter or as points giving a reference to the whole area or sections of it. In raster data, source material such as a map or aerial photograph is scanned in a series of pixels as if the map or photograph were made up from the squares of a very fine grid. In Chapter 6, raster data acquired by remote sensing was described, each pixel being given a numerical value between 0 and 255. This can be used to represent a scale of tones from black through to white. For a black and white line map, only two values are need: 0 and 1. Where a line covers a pixel, a '1' is recorded; where the pixel is empty a '0' is registered

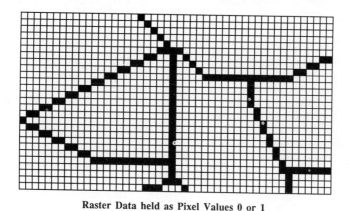

Raster Data held as Pixel Values 0 or 1

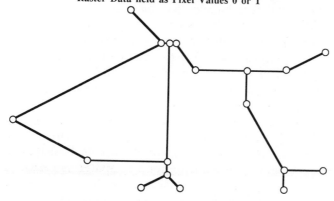

Vector Data held as Co-ordinate Pairs
for each start, turning and intersection point

Fig. 7.1   *Raster and vector line forms*

(Fig. 7.1). The map is then represented as series of rows of the numbers 0 or 1.

The advantage of raster scanning is that it is quick, automatic, and produces data in a form most suitable for certain types of processing, such as when determining the area of intersection between two polygons (Table 7.2 and Fig. 7.2). The disadvantage is that certain other types of processing are more complex and the volume of data generated is very large. Vector data are not easy to acquire automatically but are more closely related to normal field survey techniques. The vector approach results in substantially less data being generated and can for many operations be more easily handled than raster. For instance, it is much easier and more accurate to determine the length of the perimeter of an irregular polygon, or the direction and distance between two points, by vector methods than by raster.

Table 7.2 Rasters and vectors

	Raster	Vector
Data capture	Fast	Slow
Data volumes	Large	Small
Graphics	Medium	Good
Data structure	Simple	Complex
Geometrical accuracy	Low	High
Linear network analysis	Poor	Good
Area/polygon analysis	Good	Poor
Combining data layers	Good	Poor
Generalization	Simple	Complex

One of the analytical techniques that can be used in digital mapping is to compare and contrast distributions by overlaying polygons representing different phenomena. Given two polygons, each defined as a string of coordinates, the problem is to isolate those areas that belong to one polygon and not the other, or vice versa; or else to find the area that is common between the two. With a raster-based system, the problem is simple, for each polygon will be formed by a set of pixels that can be examined in turn to see if they lie within one polygon or the other, or both. Given a vector format, the problem is more difficult to solve, for it necessitates computing intersections between the sides of one polygon and the next. In complicated cases this can be time consuming and tedious even for a computer. Although there are many programs that will do this,[1] tests such as whether a given point is within a defined polygon (commonly called the point in polygon (PiP) test), or whether one polygon overlaps another, are more easily carried out with data in raster format.

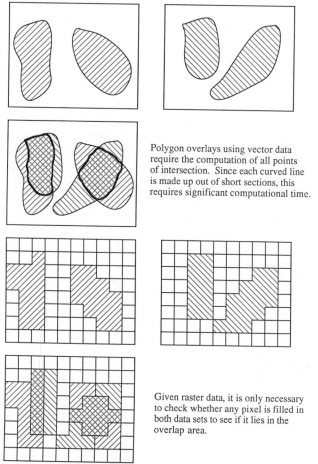

Polygon overlays using vector data require the computation of all points of intersection. Since each curved line is made up out of short sections, this requires significant computational time.

Given raster data, it is only necessary to check whether any pixel is filled in both data sets to see if it lies in the overlap area.

Fig. 7.2 *Raster versus vector overlays*

7.3 Vector data acquisition by manual methods

Spatial data may be acquired from primary sources (such as by direct survey in the field) or as a by-product when mapping from aerial photographs. The coordinates of all point and line features are a common form of output from such surveys. The majority of the spatial data for digital mapping are at present coming from the conversion of existing maps into vector form. Some data are being scanned in raster form, then converted into vector form. The direct capture of the data in vector form is, however, more usual and is mostly undertaken by manual methods using digitizing tables. These usually have an orthogonal net of embedded wires, which is sensed by a cursor as it passes overhead. The resulting electrical pulses are converted into a measurement of the position of the cursor on the board. Alternative systems work in a polar form, measuring the angle and distance from a point of origin.

Point and stream modes

Features may be digitized either in 'point mode', in which a button pressed on the cursor gives a coordinate pair, or in 'stream mode', in which coordinates are generated continuously when the cursor button is depressed (Fig. 7.3). The stream mode can operate either on a distance interval, recording a point whenever the cursor has been moved a preset distance in the 'x' or 'y' direction, or on a time interval, so that a preset number of coordinates are generated every second. Stream-mode digitizing is used to record points along curved lines such as along a river or contour. For the purposes of subsequent plotting, each curve is defined by a series of straight-line sections between successive pairs of coordinated points. If the system is set to stream digitize on a time basis, then the length of these small sections will depend on the time interval and the speed with which the operator traces the line. The faster the operator moves, the greater is the productivity but the less accurate the work is likely to be; conversely the

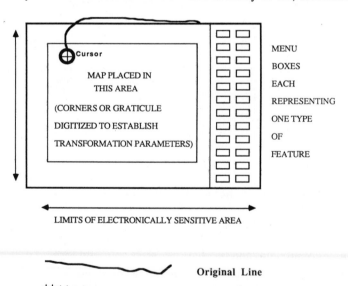

Fig. 7.3 *Digitizing table, menu, and line digitizing*

slower the movement, the greater is the number of coordinates generated, but many of these will be redundant and have to be filtered out at the editing stage.

Digitizing

The values recorded by the operator will be dependent upon the characteristics of the digitizing table. In order to transform them into the map reference system, known points such as the intersection of grid lines or the corners of the map must be digitized. Comparisons can then be made between the values as coordinated on the digitizing table and their known ground or map values. Using mathematical transformations, the coordinates of any subsequent point that is digitized can then be transposed to the map reference system.

In their simplest form, these transformations are:

$$X = ax + by + c$$
$$Y = dx + ey + f$$

where (X, Y) are the coordinates of the points in the ground or map reference system and (x, y) are those in the digitizer table system. a, b, c, d, e, and f are simple numbers whose values must be calculated. Given three pairs of corresponding points, then there will be six equations for the six unknown values a–f. These can therefore be solved. If more than three pairs of corresponding points are known then, not only is there an independent check on the transformation, but also a best-fit solution can be derived using the statistical technique of 'least squares'. From then on, the required values (X, Y) can be calculated from the corresponding observed values (x, y) as recorded by the digitizing system.

Before any point on a feature is digitized, the classification of the feature concerned will need to be recorded. This may be done either by typing the information in manually, or by using a cursor with a number of buttons, each of which should be allocated a special meaning (for example, button 1 = building, 2 = road, etc.). Alternatively, a 'menu' can be used, which is an area of the digitizing table set aside specially for coded messages. A series of boxes may be drawn up in which each point within each box has a specific meaning, such as 'major road', 'minor road', 'borehole', etc. By digitizing a point within the menu box, the computer knows it must record the next feature to be digitized as that predetermined type.

Digitizers for manual use are relatively cheap. Their price depends upon their size and the precision with which they were designed. Precision of the order of 0.01 millimetres or 0.001 inches can be built into the instruments, though attainable accuracies are not as high as that. This is in part due to human factors. Manual digitizing is an extremely tedious and boring task that requires steady concentration by the operator; two to three hours concentrated effort is as much as most people can manage without a break. Two approaches are adopted; one is known as 'blind digitizing' and the other as 'interactive'. In interactive digitizing, the results of each operation are immediately shown on a graphic screen so that the extent of progress and the incidence of error can be checked. The disadvantage of it is that progress is slowed down as the operator has to watch the screen continually. In blind digitizing, the operator traces the features but sees no immediate results. A check plot may not be seen for several days and therefore a progress record has to be kept by marking up a spare copy of the map that is being digitized. The approach is suited to a flow line though the relative advantages of one approach over the other are not entirely clear cut.[2]

7.4   Vector data capture by non-manual methods

Some of the mental and physical stress and strain associated with manual digitizing can be relieved by using automatic line-following devices. Once such a device is pointed at and locked on to a line, it scans across it and picks up the alignment. At nodal points such as line junctions, the operator may have to intervene but otherwise most of the tedious work is taken care of. The devices are relatively expensive but they have a high accuracy and good rates of productivity. This is particularly so where, as in following contour lines, there are few if any junction points.

If the source material is a pair of stereo photographs mounted in a photogrammetric plotting machine, then the coordinates of points can be obtained either from encoders on the plotting table or by attaching encoders to parts of the stereo-plotting machine. These generate electronic phases, which may be processed to give coordinate values. As with manual digitizing, a method of entering feature codes is required. This may be done from a keyboard.

Automatic field survey data capture

Digital data in vector form may be captured directly by field survey. Many computer programs exist to help in this process and almost all the leading manufacturers of field survey and photogrammetric equipment offer such packages. In some systems, the automatic recording of the field survey measurements is built into the measuring device; in others an electronic notebook or data logger may be required. Such a device has a small keyboard, as is found on any pocket calculator, through which data may be entered and temporarily stored. Usually the data are then transferred into a larger computer for permanent storage and subsequent processing. With the increasing efficiency and power of microcomputers, it is now possible to take such a machine, complete with a sophisticated program, into the field and use it directly in the process of data gathering.

Unfortunately, many such programs restrict the options open to the surveyor in the field, forcing the survey to be carried out in a way that suits the program but increases the time and cost of field work. Flexibility is lost in the cause of making the program less complicated and more easy to handle—what is euphemistically referred to as making it 'user friendly'. Such packages can greatly expedite the production of clearly defined and routine topographic and cadastral mapping. But they do not solve all of the technical problems and can create difficulties for the person in the field. Not all aspects of human behaviour and the environment can be satisfactorily modelled.

7.5 Raster data capture

An alternative approach to digital mapping is to use raster data. If only a coarse level of generalization is needed, the raster map can be compiled longhand. A simple grid can be overlain on the map and the classification of each grid square determined by eye (Fig. 7.4). The value can then be entered on an alpha-numeric keyboard. Given a grid that is 100 by 100 unit squares, then 10 000 values would have to be entered so the process quickly becomes tedious.

Fortunately it is easy to capture raster data by automatic means. To do so, a source document is placed in a scanning machine, which then measures the

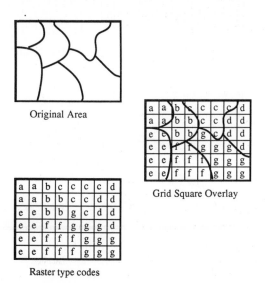

Original Area

Grid Square Overlay

Raster type codes

Fig. 7.4 *Raster equivalent of areas*

reflectance of each pixel. The size of these pixels can be altered to suit the task in hand. The larger the pixel, the quicker is the scan and the less data there is to process; conversely, the smaller the pixel size, the higher is the resolution but the slower the scanning process and the greater is the volume of data. If a black and white line map measuring 50 centimetres square with a pixel size of 50 micrometres (0.05 millimetres) were scanned it would generate 100 million bits; with a 25-micrometre scan this would become 400 million bits of data. If the latter were stored on magnetic tape at a packing density of 1600 bits to the inch, then nine magnetic tapes each 2400 feet long would be needed to store all the data for that one map.

Data compression techniques

Much of a black and white map is blank (up to 80 per cent or more in some cases). There are techniques for reducing the volume of data stored using, for example, either 'run length encoding' or a 'quad tree' structure (Fig. 7.5). The former records the number of like occurrences of a code so that the binary string 000000111110000 can become 605140. In the quad tree structure, the map is broken up into groups or blocks of squares that are recorded

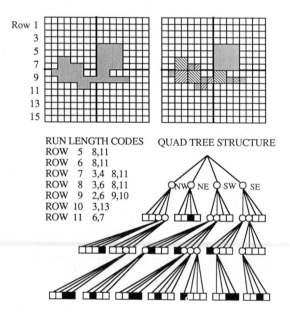

RUN LENGTH CODES
ROW 5   8,11
ROW 6   8,11
ROW 7   3,4 8,11
ROW 8   3,6 8,11
ROW 9   2,6 9,10
ROW 10   3,13
ROW 11   6,7

QUAD TREE STRUCTURE

The Quad Tree Structure reduces the shape to a series of quadrants which are represented by zero if nothing is in them. This significantly reduces the amount of data that has to be stored.

Fig. 7.5   *Run lengths and quad trees*

as zero if the whole block is blank. Thus if it so happened that the top left quarter of a map contained no detail at all, all that area could be set to zero in one record, thus reducing the data storage by a quarter. Each quarter of a map can be subdivided into four quarter-quarters, which in turn may be subdivided into quarter-quarter-quarters, and so on until a fully blank subsquare is identified.

Raster data recording

When raster scanning a document, everything that appears darker than a certain threshold level will be recorded as black or '1'. By adjusting the sensitivity of the instrument, lightly toned areas of a map, such as where there is a fine stipple, can be ignored. If this were not done then, depending on the size of the stipple and the size of the pixels used in the scanning process, every dot of the stipple would be recorded. Everything above the threshold will be captured, for instance small blemishes on the map, squashed flies, coffee stains, and damage to the source material. A certain amount of post-processing is therefore needed to clean up the data.

Raster data plotting

Once the data have been captured, the process can be reversed to produce an exact facsimile copy (exact, of course, within the geometrical tolerances of both the scanning and plotting instruments). With reasonably good instruments costing in the range of $300 000–$500 000 for scanners, depending on the system, and $150 000–$250 000 for plotters, it is possible to lay the results of scanned and plotted data over the original source material and to obtain a level of agreement that satisfies the human eye. Prices are beginning to come down and the quality is generally improving.

Although the basic capture of raster data is strictly routine, there is as yet no foolproof way to determine the nature and classification of each object whose shape has been recorded as a series of 0s and 1s. Image analysis techniques have been developed that recognize the patterns formed by numbers and letters of the alphabet, though these techniques are as yet far from perfect. Some progress has been made in the automatic interpretation of line features on a map[3], but there is need for further research and development before a system will become commercially available. Human intervention is still often required if the data that have been recorded relatively quickly and cheaply by raster methods are to be converted into a form suitable for a land information system.

In the case of remote sensing, the scanned data will be captured in digital form, but without any associated classification. The spatial location of each pixel within the reference frame can be determined provided that some points are identified whose ground values can be related to their position in the raster scan. Transformation parameters can then be computed. Because of geometrical distortions in many remote-sensing scanning devices, the planimetric accuracy of the transformed values is not very high. The classification of the features is, as indicated in Chapter 6, even more uncertain.

7.6   Converting between rasters and vectors

Data are interchangeable between raster and vector formats. Vector to raster conversion is relatively straightforward, raster to vector less so. Conversion from vector to raster inevitably loses a small amount of information because pixels close to the true mathematical line defined by the vector coordinate values will inevitably be slightly off-line. The amount of displacement will depend upon the size of the pixels and the degree of sinuosity of any line being followed. Algorithms for this conversion have been discussed by a number of authors.[4]

Raster to vector conversion is more complicated. In practice, if the data are derived from raster scanning, the lines will be several pixels thick. The first stage is to thin the lines down to an equivalent width of one pixel; then the best-fit vectors must be found, during which process each bend in the line and each nodal point should be detected. The process can give rise to wrong junction points and an excessive number of short vectors (Fig. 7.6), though recent algorithms have tended to sort these out. Overall, in terms of

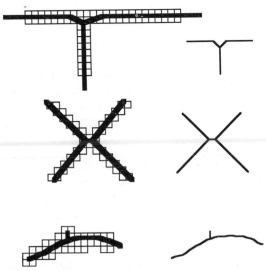

Fig. 7.6   *Raster to vector conversion problems*

processing, raster to vector conversion still remains a relatively expensive exercise.

7.7 Data processing and structure

Data editing

Once the data have been entered into the system, they must be processed. The first stage in data processing is data editing. Since the process of locating digitized lines and points in the data files is fundamental to systems for editing vector data, suitable data structures must be adopted. The coordinates and attributes of strings and points need to be retrieved from the computer so that the whole or part of features and single points can be deleted, their feature codes changed, or their positions altered. Some of these corrections are needed to remove digitizing errors or to revise the map data; others are needed for cosmetic purposes.

The edit facility should permit any feature to be added, deleted, changed, or simply retrieved for display either graphically or in its alpha-numeric form. This can be done at what is known as a 'workstation', which normally is made up of two screens, one alpha-numeric and one graphic, together with a keyboard and digitizing tablet, all linked to the computer. A feature such as a piece of text may be plotted on the graphic screen and details of its classification, size, and style given on the other screen. Changes may then be applied as appropriate.

The graphic screen can be used to help locate features. By moving the cursor on the digitizing tablet, a pointer on the graphic screen can be directed close to a feature. The coordinates of the pointer can then be determined and used to match up with the data in the graphics files. Computer instructions can then be issued so that identified points that are unconnected can, if desired, be joined up. Pairs of lines that do not quite meet can be extended to their point of intersection, or a point can be connected or 'snapped' on to a nearby line by the shortest distance.

For example, a place name on the map may look better in a different position so the data relating to it must be retrieved and revised. It must be possible to draw a name or piece of text in any selected position, at any orientation, and in any available style and size of lettering. Thus the attributes of a name must include not only the text but also a coordinate of where it is to be written (normally the bottom left-hand corner of a rectangle that would just cover that text) and codes to indicate its orientation, size, style, and classification. The latter would indicate whether the text related to the name of a building, a road, a river, land use, and so on. Thus it should be possible for all river names to be retrieved by testing, first, whether the feature had been classified as a name and, if so, whether its code was that for a water feature.

Data structures

Data codes may be alphabetic or numeric, depending on the design of the system. There are many ways in which these data might be structured. As one example of how a name might be held in a data file, consider:

−6012204550902181River Thames83451286

This would be read by the computer in predetermined groups of numbers as:

/−6/0122/0455/09/02/18/12/River Thames/8345/1286/

which represents a format with groups of numbers in 2, 4, 4, 2, 2, 2, 2, n, 4, 4 columns, the 'n' being the number of characters in the name. Here $n = 12$, the space between 'River' and 'Thames' counting as one character.

In the above example:

−6 means the start (−) of a piece of text (6);
0122 means it is the 122 feature; this is used for identification purposes only;
0455 means it is to be drawn at an angle of 45.5 degrees;
09 means the text represents a water feature;
02 means it should be written in text style 2; the style of lettering will be constrained by the number of fonts available in the plotting system;
18 means it should be in letters 1.8 mm high;
12 means there are 12 characters to follow;
8345 means the eastings coordinate 8345 where the text is to be placed;
1286 means at northings coordinate 1286.

A symbol might appear as

−521340000002623754681

and be decoded as:

/−5/2134/0000/0026/2375/4681

Or:

−5 meaning start of a symbol (5);
2134 being the feature serial number;
0000 meaning zero orientation (horizontal)
0026 meaning its feature code was 26, which might for instance mean a bench mark;
2375 4681 being its coordinates.

A line feature could appear as:

−433120031512145855181 4702 . . . etc.

decoded as:

/−4/3312/0031/5121/4585/5181/4702/. . .

or as the start of a line feature (−4) identified by the feature serial number 3312, having feature code 0031 (= a fence), and running from coordinate (5121, 4585) to (5181, 4702) (etc.).

Anyone who embarks upon the development of a land information system will need to make decisions on what data to include, how those data are classified, and what codes should be attached to them. The examples above are not standard but illustrate a principle. Although attempts are being made in Australia, Canada, the United States, and a number of European countries to standardize on formats, feature codes, and classifications,[5] there are as yet no international agreements. At the national level, each organization tends to adopt its own procedures. The system of coding and classification in every 'turnkey' system (that is, a system bought 'off the shelf' as a standard set of packages for general use) is currently different. Although this is mainly an internal matter and of concern only to the computing system, problems arise when there is a need to exchange data between different systems.

Error correction

Data cannot be collected without errors, some of which are human and some electrical or mechanical. Some items of data need to be deleted, some modified, and some additions added where information has been left out. For example, a variety of editing problems may arise for line features:

(1) The operator may have incorrectly placed the cursor when digitizing some points on a section of a line; the whole section, once located in the file, would need to be removed and the section redigitized and added to the file.
(2) One coordinate might be out of place; here the single value can be corrected without disturbing the length of the records.
(3) A feature might have been incorrectly coded; for instance as a road instead of as a river; the amended feature code would need to be entered and the string refiled.
(4) A point feature, such as the location of a sampling point, the centre point for a symbol, or the start position for a piece of text, may have the wrong coordinate; this would need to be amended and the corrected value refiled.

Cosmetic actions, such as making sure that all angles of a building are rectangular, can also be carried out. The eye is particularly sensitive to squareness and alignments, and a failure to take account of this can lead to a lack of confidence in the overall quality of the information. In the case of rectangularity, adjustments can be carried out by locating the string that represents the relevant building and by mathematically adjusting the co-ordinates using an appropriate algorithm. For example, the coordinates of the longest straight side can be fixed and the remaining sides can be adjusted to be parallel or at right angles to it.

'Spaghetti' files

The techniques that are used depend upon the structure of the data and how it has been sorted and stored in the computer. One of the simplest structures is based on what is commonly referred to as the 'spaghetti file'. In this, the line data are just a series of strings of coordinates, where each string

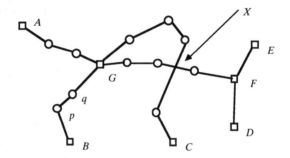

□	= NODE - A,B,C,D,E are Nodes of VALENCY 1
	F is a Node of VALENCY 3
	G is a Node of VALENCY 4

A NODE is an end of a LINE or LINK

A LINE and a LINK are series of consecutive line segments which share the same attribute

O	= Coordinated Points

$BpqG$ is a LINK. AG, BG, DF and EF are all LINKS

Bp, pq, pG are LINE SEGMENTS

X	is uncoordinated. If such points are allowed, then the sequence of line segments between G and C and between G and F would be called LINES not LINKS.

LINKS DO NOT INTERSECT — LINES MAY DO SO

Fig. 7.7   *Links, lines, and nodes*

represents some coded and classified feature. In order to alter any of the points held in the file, it is first necessary to locate the appropriate point or string. Such files are normally read sequentially, so that each coordinated point in turn has to be considered to see if it is the required one.

There is, in practice, a limit to the amount of editing that can be done on 'spaghetti-type' files before heavy time penalties are incurred through trying to locate the appropriate section of the data set. There might, for example, be a series of polygons representing land parcels, soil patterns, or census data boundaries. Every junction point in such a set of polygons will have been manually digitized more than once, each time probably with a slightly different value. It is immensely time consuming to search through a spaghetti file to see if there are any common points between strings. With other types of feature, such as buildings, the lines may actually cross over but the intersection points may never have been digitized (Fig. 7.7). Thus nodal points may exist on the graphic but not in the digitized data set. However, if the data are compiled in a 'links and nodes' format then the search can be conducted very much more quickly.

Links and nodes

A link is a series of consecutive, non-intersecting line segments with common attributes and with no connection to any other link except at its start or end. It is represented in a digital map by one or more attribute codes, together with the 'string' or list of coordinate pairs that make up each line segment. A node is the start or end of a link; it can be shared by several links. The coordinates of the nodes can be listed in a separate file and can be cross-referenced to any links that start or end at them. An example of a link and node file is given in Fig. 7.8 and Tables 7.3 and 7.4.

If the nodes are sorted into order, then searching for nearby links becomes easier. If a link is to be found in the bottom right-hand corner of the map, then its nodal points are likely to be in that area. By searching through the list of nodes, a few possible choices of links can be identified and each can be checked to see if it is the one required. When starting to digitize a new line, the start and end points can be checked to see if they are very close to any node that already exists; if a node is found, then the new link can be made to share its value. Under the spaghetti system, all links would have to be checked from the start of the file until the appropriate one was found—a process which, even with the speed of modern computers, costs time and money.

Topology

Links and nodes structures also permit the handling of topological features. By referring to the features to the left and right of a link, adjacency and

144   *Digital mapping*

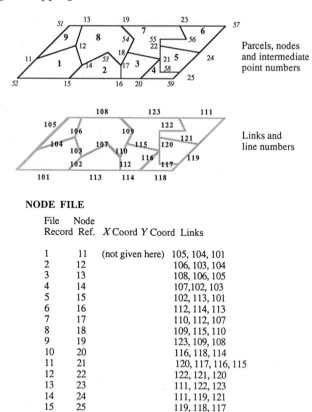

Parcels, nodes and intermediate point numbers

Links and line numbers

NODE FILE

File Record	Node Ref.	X Coord Y Coord	Links
1	11	(not given here)	105, 104, 101
2	12		106, 103, 104
3	13		108, 106, 105
4	14		107,102, 103
5	15		102, 113, 101
6	16		112, 114, 113
7	17		110, 112, 107
8	18		109, 115, 110
9	19		123, 109, 108
10	20		116, 118, 114
11	21		120, 117, 116, 115
12	22		122, 121, 120
13	23		111, 122, 123
14	24		111, 119, 121
15	25		119, 118, 117

The node file contains node references, coordinates of nodes and lists of associated links.

Fig. 7.8   *Links and nodes data structure—NODES file*

context can be added to the data set. Topology is concerned with establishing the location of objects, identified by points, lines, polygons, and surfaces, with respect to each other in a non-metric relational structure. It is based on a branch of geometry that deals, not with the Euclidian shapes of surfaces and the directions of lines, but rather with those properties of geometric figures that remain unchanged even under distortion, so long as no links are broken or surfaces are torn. It is thus concerned with connectivity, adjacency, and containment (see Fig. 7.9). It is used in:

(1) network analysis, where the inclusion of sequences or connectivity of segments allows the selection of such details as shortest paths, or emergency access;

(2) neighbour relations, by knowing the neighbours of a given polygon such as a land parcel;

Table 7.3 Links and nodes data structure—links file

File record	Line	Area Left	Area Right	Nodes From	Nodes To	No. of points	X, Y coords
1	103	1	8	14	12	0	
2	123	7	0	23	19	0	
3	111	0	6	23	24	1	(pt. 57)
4	101	0	1	15	11	1	(pt. 52)
5	117	5	4	21	25	1	(pt. 58)
6	122	7	6	22	23	2	(pts. 55, 56)
7	107	8	2	14	17	1	(pt. 53)
8	113	0	2	16	15	0	
9	102	1	2	15	14	0	
10	116	4	3	21	20	0	
11	112	2	3	16	17	0	
12	108	0	8	13	19	0	
13	120	7	5	21	22	0	
14	115	3	7	21	18	0	
15	106	9	8	12	13	0	
16	105	0	9	11	13	1	(pt. 51)
17	121	6	5	22	24	0	
18	109	7	8	19	18	1	(pt. 54)
19	118	0	4	25	20	1	(pt. 59)
20	114	0	3	20	16	0	
21	110	3	8	18	17	0	
22	119	5	0	25	24	0	
23	104	1	9	12	11	0	

The links file contains a record of each line, giving its reference (here the alpha-numeric values 101–23) the reference to the parcels to the left and right of the line, the node reference numbers at the start and end of the link, the number of coordinated points on the line, other than the nodes and the coordinates of these points (not shown here).

(3) overlay processing, where new polygons can be created from the overlaying of existing polygons, such as soils over land use.

7.8 Basic trigonometric operations

All editing and analytical operations are based on computations using simple trigonometry. A common requirement in data processing is to compute distances, angles, bearings, shapes, areas, and volumes. Distances between two points may be computed using Pythagoras' theorem, namely from the square root of the sum of the squares of the difference in eastings and the difference in northings:

$$\text{distance} = \text{SQRT}((X_2 - X_1)^2 + (Y_2 - Y_1)^2)$$

Similarly the tangent of the bearing is given by:

$$\text{tangent value} = (X_2 - X_1)/(Y_2 - Y_1)$$

Table 7.4 Links and nodes data structure—areas file

Areas files			Tuples file					
File record	Area	Tuples pointer	Record	Numbers		Pointers		Link
1	0	61	52	53	54	76	95	1
2	1	62	55	56	57	67	58	2
3	2	77	58	59	60	116	−6	3
4	3	83	61	62	63	97	118	4
5	4	79	64	65	66	89	107	5
6	5	64	67	68	69	88	59	6
7	6	100	70	71	72	53	82	7
8	7	55	73	74	75	0	−2	8
9	8	86	76	77	78	−1	71	9
10	9	94	79	80	81	65	110	10
			82	83	84	74	112	11
			85	86	87	56	104	12
			88	89	90	92	101	13
			91	92	93	80	103	14
			94	95	96	119	−8	15
			97	98	99	85	−9	16
			100	101	102	68	115	17
			103	104	105	−7	113	18
			106	107	108	109	−4	19
			109	110	111	73	−3	20
			112	113	114	91	70	21
			115	116	117	−5	106	22
			118	119	120	52	98	23 etc.

The record in the *Areas* file points to a record in the *Tuples* file, thus for *area* 3, start at *Tuple* record 83.
Tuple record 83 is on line with *links* file record 11
It also shows the value 112
Tuble record 112 is on line with *links* file record 21
It also shows the value 91
Tuple record 91 is on line with *links* file record 14
It also shows the value 80
Tuple record 80 is on line with *links* file record 10
It also shows the value 110
Tuple record 110 is on line with *links* file record 20
It also shows −3 to mark the end of area 3 which is formed by
links file records 11 – 21 – 14 – 10 – 20
or *links* 112 – 110 – 115 – 116 – 114

The junction angle of a stream or the rectangularity of a building corner can then be computed from the difference in bearing between two lines.

Shapes have no agreed mathematical definition unless specified by some simple relationship such as a triangle, rectangle, circle, or ellipse. Parameters to define irregular shapes are more arbitrary—a problem which arises in pattern recognition. Areas can, however, be calculated

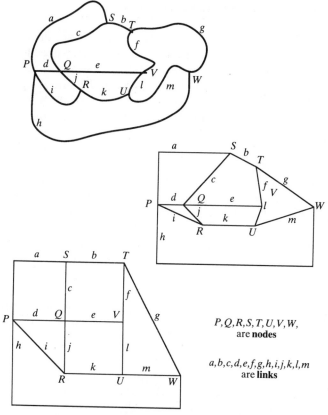

Fig. 7.9 *Topologically similar shapes*

from the coordinates; the area enclosed by the points 1, 2, 3, and 4 is given by:

$$2*\text{area} = X_1{}^*Y_2 + X_2{}^*Y_3 + X_3{}^*Y_4 + X_4{}^*Y_1 - Y_1{}^*X_2 - Y_2{}^*X_3 - Y_3{}^*X_4 - Y_4{}^*X_1$$

Similar equations exist for calculating volumes.

The equation of the line joining the points (X_1, Y_1) to (X_2, Y_2) is:

$$(Y - Y_1)^*(X_2 - X_1) = (X - X_1)^*(Y_2 - Y_1)$$

or $Y = M^*X + C$ where M is the slope of the line and C is a constant.

Two points (X_3, Y_3) and (X_4, Y_4) are the same side of the line if $Y_3 - M^* X_3 - C$ and $Y_4 - M^* X_4 - C$ are both the same sign, that is, either both values are positive or both values are negative. If the signs are opposite, the points are on different sides of the line.

7.9   Filtering and curve fitting

Assuming that the actual data are free from error, then a number of operations may be carried out. Redundant points may need to be removed, either because they are unnecessary and therefore take up valuable storage space and computer time when processed and plotted, or as part of a generalization process. The filtering of data is particularly important when using small and less powerful microcomputers. Simple redundancies can be removed by checking how close a point coordinate is to the previous value in the string; if it is less than a specified value then it can be deleted. Points may also be checked to see if they are, within a given tolerance, on line with the points either side of them; in this case, provided they are not junction points, they can be removed. In cleaning up the data, essential points that define the overall shape of the feature or which form nodes for other strings must be retained.

More refined methods of filtering exist, particularly for dealing with points along a curve. Curves do not necessarily have to be digitized by manual, longhand methods. Many mathematical curve-fitting routines exist in which all the points along a smooth curve can be computed and made to fit through a series of datum points, either exactly or in the best-fit form of a predefined curve. The most commonly used curve is the third-degree

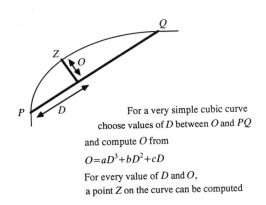

For a very simple cubic curve
choose values of D between O and PQ
and compute O from

$$O = aD^3 + bD^2 + cD$$

For every value of D and O,
a point Z on the curve can be computed

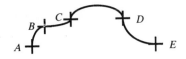

Curves can then be built up in sections "piecewise"
fitting a cubic to AB, then BC, etc., ensuring continuity
at each junction point

Fig. 7.10   *Cubic curves*

polynomial or cubic, fitted in the form of a spline (that is, each section of the curve has a cubic form and is made to blend smoothly in with the sections either side of it). Given a series of points 1, 2, 3, 4, 5, 6, etc. the section from point 2 to point 3 must start smoothly with section 1–2 and finish smoothly with 3–4.

Various algorithms exist to do this.[6] The simplest solution (Fig. 7.10) is to calculate the offset 'O' from the distance 'D' along the line from P to Q in the form:

$$O = a*D^3 + b*D^2 + c*D$$

where a, b, and c are constants that depend on the length PQ and the slope of the curve at P and at Q. If the coordinates of P and Q are known, then for every value of D the value of O can be calculated. From these values, the coordinates for any point on the curve can be derived. The problem, though simple to define and mathematically easy to solve, can result in solutions where the curve either looks bad or in some circumstances loops over on itself. Although fulfilling all the defined mathematical properties, it does not behave as a contour line should. As a result, some packages for contouring produce lines that are either straight or, at best, are not as a conventional draughtsman would have drawn them by manual methods.

7.10 Cartographic generalization

Curve- and surface-fitting techniques, using polynomial functions and other mathematical transformations such as the Fourier series, can be used to smooth multidimensional data. Graphic data in two and three dimensions and complex statistical data can all be treated in the same way. For the cartographer, however, the results may not always be satisfactory. One of the outstanding problems of cartography is that of developing suitable algorithms for generalizing cartographic data so that small-scale map data can be derived from larger scales. Simple methods exist for generalizing a feature such as a coast line, by selecting fewer and fewer points as the scale decreases. However, depending on which points are selected, the shape of the feature can be seriously distorted and the resulting impression can be most misleading.

A similar problem arises when reducing the number of places shown on a map. There are no agreed criteria for determining which features to select and which to reject. Visual criteria may play as important a part as population size or economic significance. Until such time as better mathematical models can be developed to simulate the processes of generalization, land information managers will have to rely on the interactive editing facilities in their systems as much as upon mathematical algorithms to solve the problem.

7.11 Forming digital terrain models

Digital terrain models

The processing and display of three-dimensional information pose particular problems in a land information system. The term digital terrain model (DTM) is normally used where the data are measured on an 'interval' scale, that is, where there is a quantifiable third dimension. The third dimension may be some geophysical measure such as gravity, or the strength of the earth's magnetic field, or it may represent socio-economic data such as land values or population density. Where the third dimension is not quantifiable (such as where the data are classified as 'nominal', that is, by name only) then the data are said to be in layers, levels, strata, or sometimes views. Examples of layers are all buildings, all vegetation, land use, or roads. Each layer may be made up of sublayers (major roads, minor roads, tracks, footpaths) where there is some hierarchy, in which case the data may be classified as 'ordinal'. The sublayers may, on the other hand, be classified as 'nominal' and have no hierarchy (apple orchards, cherry orchards, coniferous trees, etc.).

Digital elevation models

Where the third dimension in a DTM is related to the height above sea level, the term digital ground model or, more appropriately, digital elevation model (DEM) is used (Table 7.5). DEMs are more closely associated with field surveying and photogrammetry, and DTMs with remote sensing and other physical and social sciences. DEMs may be surveyed and held on the computer as a set of spatially random points.[7] They are in general not truly random, for if they were the result of a field survey then they would most probably be at the tops and bottoms of hills and at breaks of slope. For the purposes of statistical analysis they may, however, be chosen on a totally random basis; this is done by generating random numbers to define coordinates of points at which the height is measured. DEMs may also be based on a regular grid of points covering the area in question. When photogrammetric methods are used, it is easy to measure on such a basis. However, a regular grid is more costly to set out by ground survey; this method is rarely used except for engineering purposes and in certain types of terrain for seismic work. The advantage of a regular grid is that the data can be stored in sequence; if the size and location of the grid are known, then only the height values need be recorded. This reduces the data storage to a third. With an irregular distribution of points, all three coordinates must be recorded for each heighted point. However, fewer points may be needed.

Digital elevation models may be observed and recorded in other ways. They may be based on two-dimensional strings, for example by digitizing the

Table 7.5 Digital elevation models

Models may be used for:
- Topographic mapping and deriving contours
- Engineering design and calculations
- Computing slopes, transects and intervisibility
- Three-dimensional display of townscapes and landscapes
- Route planning
- Statistical analysis
- Background display for thematic maps

Models may be formed from:
- Regular grid corner values
- Irregular (random) distribution of points
- Two-dimensional strings such as contours
- Three-dimensional strings such as profiles

---

line of a contour, or by surveying its planimetric position on the ground and storing the resulting coordinates. They may also be formed as three-dimensional strings, as in cross-sections along a transect or profiles along a road. In surveying the sea bed, for example, the position of the boat from which the profiles are measured would need to be fixed; the depth measures would be taken separately but instantaneously with the horizontal position fix, thus producing a three-dimensional 'string'.

Delaunay triangles and Thiessen polygons

Contouring from random points may be done by joining each point to its neighbours, thus forming a set of triangles. Alternatively an estimate can be made from the randomly distributed points of what the height should be at the intersections of an overlaid rectangular grid (Fig. 7.11). In the former case, a number of algorithms exist for selecting the points that should be joined to form the triangles. Many of these achieve the same effect by different means and create what are known as Delaunay triangles, from which Thiessen polygons can be formed. A Thiessen polygon surrounds each point in such a way that all places within that polygon are nearer to the controlling point than to any other. The Delaunay triangles are formed by the lines that are perpendiculary bisected by the sides of the polygons. It can be shown that they are, according to various criteria, the best-shaped triangles to use for contouring and other forms of spatial analysis.

Contouring

Once the triangles have been formed, heights can be linearly interpolated along their sides. These determine points along the contours, which can then be joined up either by straight lines or by curves. In the latter case, a suitable

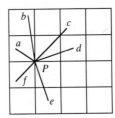

A Digital Elevation Model may be based on a regular grid either by observing heights at grid intersection points or by taking a weighted mean of nearby randomly distributed points

Thus the height at P might be a weighted average of the heights at points a,b,c,d,e,f. Contours can then be interpolated within the regular grid.

The advantage of a regular grid is that only the height values need be stored as long as they are in sequence and the position of the grid is known.

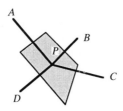

Randomly distributed height points may be formed into triangles and contours threaded through them by linear interpolation of heights along the sides of the triangles.

A Thiessen Polygon is one in which all points within it are nearer to its seed point (*P*) than any other seed point (such as *A, B, C*, and *D*).

The sides of a set of Thiessen Polygons perpendicularly bisect the sides of a set of Delaunay triangles. These are judged to be the best set of triangles for contouring from a D.E.M.

Fig. 7.11   *D E Ms and contour interpolation*

curve-fitting algorithm must be used to prevent adjacent contour lines from crossing over each other.

Height determination

The random points can be used to generate heights on a regular grid by taking a weighted mean of the surrounding values. If the distance from a grid intersection point to the nearby random points is d_i and the height of the ith random point is h_i, then the height of the grid point could be computed as:

$$h_g = (h_1/d_1 + h_2/d_2 + \ldots) / (1/d_1 + 1/d_2 + \ldots)$$

or more generally:

$$h_g = \text{sum of } (w_i{}^*h_i) / (\text{sum of } w_i)$$

where w is some weighting factor, which in the so-called gravity model would be the inverse square of the distance. For contouring, a great variety of weighting systems have been tried, details of which are given elsewhere.[7] Contouring from a regular grid can be undertaken either by linear interpolation or by fitting a mathematically smooth surface.

7.12 Displaying digital elevation models

A DEM can be used to calculate heights, slopes, and volumes. It can be displayed in a variety of ways. Data from the regular-grid DEM can be used to calculate the average height of each grid square, which in turn can be mapped as colour or grey-scale values. The third dimension can also be displayed on block diagrams that can be viewed from any angle. To do so requires two separate operations: the first is to make a perspective transformation of the surface; the second is to remove the 'hidden lines'. In addition, it may be necessary to display only part of the model or picture, in which case a process known as 'windowing' is involved.

For most practical purposes, the rotation, translation, and projection of an object such as a DEM on to a graphic screen can be achieved in one mathematical operation. If the coordinates of any point in three-dimensional space are (x, y, z) then the coordinates on the screen (X, Y) can be found by applying a linear transformation, multiplying the homogeneous coordinates $(x, y, z, 1)$ by the 4×4 matrix:

$$\begin{bmatrix} a & b & c & p \\ d & e & f & q \\ h & i & j & r \\ l & m & n & s \end{bmatrix}$$

The numbers 'a, b, c, d, e, f', when applied to the coordinates by simple multiplication, produce changes in scale, shearing, and rotation. This changes the object's size, angularity, and the direction in which it is facing. The terms 'l, m, n' produce translation, that is, they bodily shift the whole object in space. The 's' term alters the whole scale, whilst the 'p, q, r' terms produce a perspective translation. The actual values of the numbers to be used depend upon the effect that is desired.[8] The technique is ideal for handling by computer since such machines are efficient at multiplying numbers together. Elements of the matrix can be used to reposition objects, change their scale, rotate them, and distort them in predetermined ways.

Hidden line removal

In displaying objects in three-dimensional form on a two-dimensional screen, it is necessary to remove 'hidden lines' or 'hidden surfaces' (Fig. 7.12). A variety of algorithms exist to achieve this effect.[9] Most rank the surfaces or lines in the order in which they will appear to the observer, either

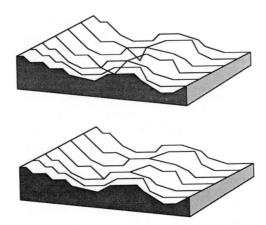

Fig. 7.12   *Profiles with and without hidden lines*

near to far, or vice versa. Each line or part of the line or surface must be tested to see if it will be in the perspective field of view. The process is slow, especially with less powerful machines.

Windowing

The process of selecting part of the area of a digital map for display or analysis is known as windowing. In the case of raster data, the picture is made up of elements that are based on a rectangular grid. Windowing into an area aligned with that grid is then simple; pixels are plotted only if they are within the defined perimeter or window. Raster data are ideally suited for 'zooming in' and 'zooming out'—a process which entails enlarging or reducing the scale of a selected window. For vector data, the processes are more complex. In the case of windowing into a convex shape, each line segment has to be tested to see if it is within the area. If both ends of the line are within it, then the whole of the segment must be within it and should be plotted. If one end is inside it and one end is outside, then the intersection between the line and the polygon boundary must be computed—a process known as clipping. If both ends are outside, then the line element may still cross the window, so additional tests must be carried out.

In any map series, each map sheet is in effect a window in a very large map. Individual map sheets are often surveyed and compiled separately and are certainly digitized separately. As a result, the features that cross from one map sheet to another may not form a continuous whole. There may be differences in classification, either through error or through disagreement between the data gatherers. For instance, field scientists working on adjoining map sheets may not agree on the soil or geological classification in the abutting areas. Such disagreements can be settled only by negotiation.

Edge matching

Spatial disagreement may also arise through deficiencies in the mapping process or distortions that have taken place in the materials on which the digitized maps are based. As a result, there is an 'edge-matching' problem. If the adjoining features are close together then a simple smoothing of the line across the edge may suffice. In more complex cases, with vector data, it may be necessary to stretch or compress the space at the edges of the map using mathematical transformations. These techniques, known as 'rubber sheeting', are not relevant to raster data, for that is based upon regular squares whereas these transformations are designed to distort such shapes. Solutions to the edge-matching problem are important, for one of the advantages of digital map data is in the ability to select a complete data set within any defined area. The traditional problem of every battle being fought or every town being located at the corners of four map sheets need not arise with digital data if they have been compiled as a unified whole. It should be possible to window in to any part of the data base and find a consistent set of data.

7.13 Data output

Printers and plotters

Digital map data may relate to points, lines, or areas (Table 7.6). They may be output in various ways. Line printers, especially those with a dot-matrix print-out, can be programmed to provide low-resolution graphics. Some of the early systems such as SYMAP[10] made use of the standard characters on a typewriter to produce coarse but effective graphics. Dot-matrix printers and the more recent ink-jet plotters work in a raster mode, printing a map scan line by scan line. By and large they are quick, cheap, and give relatively low-quality line work, but are good for certain graphics effects such as shading different layers or levels. Drum plotters and flat-bed plotters use pens to draw the lines. They work off vector data and produce good-quality line work reasonably quickly and with a resolution that is largely dependent on the price that has been paid for the equipment. They can produce good-quality so-called 'hard copy' on paper or plastics materials, but are generally slower than matrix plotters.

VDUs and graphic terminals

Ephemeral data is produced on visual display units (VDUs) or graphics terminals. These may be connected to thermal-printing or ink-jet-printing devices to give a semi-permanent hardcopy of the image on the screen. The

Table 7.6   Point, line and area data

	Points	Lines	Areas
Features	Property beacons	Roads or rivers	Planning zones
Areas	Centroids	Boundaries	Polygon intersections
Networks	Parcel corners	Pipelines	Enumeration districts
Frequency	Sampling points	Isarithms	Choropleth maps
Surfaces	Spot heights	Contours	Proximal maps
Text	House numbers	Street names	District names
Symbols	Survey marks	Roads or railways	Polygon infills

screens come in two forms: storage tubes and refresh type. A storage tube retains the image on the screen once a line has been drawn upon it. Additional lines can be added, but deletions can be achieved only by clearing the whole screen and replotting every remaining feature a second time. With refresh tubes, the picture has to be redrawn repeatedly at least 25 times per second, as on a television screen. The resolution of black and white screens is currently superior to that of colour, though improvements in the latter are taking place. The advantage of colour is in the greater variety of layers that can be displayed and analysed by eye at any one time.

Many of the display systems and plotters have used their own sets of commands to control their operations. Some degree of standardization was achieved through the lead given on the one hand by Calcomp for pen plotters and on the other by Tektronix for graphics screens. Although there still remains no agreed international standard, there are moves to support the Graphic Kernal System,[11] which has been developed primarily through the efforts of the German Standardization Institute (DIN). If accepted, it will make many more computer programmes transportable from one system to another and give greater flexibility of choice in the selection of hardware systems.

References

1. Baxter, R. S. (1976). *Computer and statistical techniques for planners*, Methuen & Co, London.
2. Thompson, C. N. (1984). *Test of digitizing methods*, OEEPE Official Publication No. 14, IFAG, Frankfurt.
3. De Simone, M. (1986). Automatic structuring and feature recognition for large scale digital mapping. *Auto Carto London*, Vol. 1, pp. 86–95. London.
4. Pavlidis, T. (1982). *Algorithms for graphics and image processing*, Springer-Verlag, Berlin.
5. See *Proceedings of Auto Carto London*, Vol. 1, (1986). pp. 282–401. London.
6. See, for example, Rogers, D. F. and Adams, J. A. (1976). *Mathematical elements for computer graphics*, McGraw-Hill, New York.

7. For a general review of DEMs see Petrie, G.and Kennie, T. J. M. (1986). Terrain modelling in surveying and civil engineering. Conference on 'State of the Art in Stereo and Terrain Modelling', British Computer Society, London.
8. See Rogers, D. F. and Adams, J. A. *Op. cit.*
9. For example, Newman, W. M. and Sproull, R. F. (1979). *Principles of interactive computer graphics*. McGraw-Hill, New York.
10. For a review of early developments and many matters relating to digital mapping in general, see Burrough, P. A. (1986). *Principles of geographical information systems for land resources assessment*, Clarendon Press, Oxford.
11. Burrough, P. A. *Op. cit.*, p. 76.

8. Data management

In this chapter we examine some of the issues and problems that arise in the storage and management of land-related data. Data may be held in manual or computer compatible form; we discuss both in this chapter.

8.1 The functions of data management

Data management is the process of looking after the data. It begins with a set of procedures for entering the data into the system and to check, sort, and classify them. The data must be stored in a secure way so as to minimize any chance of physical destruction by accident, by malicious persons, or by the ravages of time. It should not be possible for unauthorized persons to alter the logical content of the data. The form of the data should enable their analysis and processing to produce whatever type of information is desired. It must be possible to extract, reproduce, transfer, or display the data in a variety of ways.

Types of data

Three broad categories of data must be managed within a land information system. They are:

(1) alpha-numeric data, such as lists of landowners or the site characteristics of properties;
(2) graphical data on maps, photomaps, and aerial photographs;
(3) numerical spatial data in either vector or raster form.

Each poses its own type of management problem, whose solution will differ in each case.

Alpha-numeric data may be held in paper files and filing cabinets or within a computer system; graphical data may be stored within map chests; numerical data may be kept on punched paper tape or, more commonly, on magnetic tape or disk. The manner in which the data are stored and managed depends upon whether they are held in manual or computer form. In general, computers provide for the compact storage and rapid retrieval of large volumes of data. Manual methods are slower and require more storage space.

Problems with computerization

The technological revolution has given rise to a number of new problems. These have been identified by Glenn Morgan of the World Bank as including (Table 8.1):[1]

(1) *The ability to handle very large volumes of data.* Users are asking for a much greater range of data types, formats, map sheet sizes, spatial cover, map content, symbolization, and attribute coding. Although storage of data is no longer a great problem, their analysis is affected by the volume of data to be processed. Doubling the size of the data set may exponentially increase the duration of processing. There are also significant constraints associated with the processing of the very large quantities of data acquired through the use of automatic scanning devices. The conversion of hard-copy maps, images, records, and tabular data into digital form remains a serious bottleneck.

(2) *The ability to reduce hardware and software dependence.* The proliferation of hardware, software, and data structures means that data exchange can be cumbersome and expensive. Although national standards for the exchange of data are beginning to emerge, there is as yet no universal agreement as to their use.

(3) *The ability to manage technological change.* The rapid change in technology creates problems for long-range planning. Resources may become committed to one system, and then a newer and better system may emerge. Technologies can become obsolete before they are fully operational.

(4) *The ability to sustain administrative and financial commitments.* Because of the uncertainties arising from technological change, there is a need to demonstrate that investment has a favourable benefit to cost ratio. Yet because of the unpredictable nature of those very changes, such assessments are open to justifiable criticism. There is need to account for the initial capital costs, the maintenance of the equipment over time, replacement with new and more efficient equipment, and other overhead costs. These must be calculated over an agreed time scale. Inevitably, the benefits do not arise immediately. Funds must therefore be committed for a period during which there is no overall financial return.

Table 8.1   Obstacles to computerization

1. Difficulty of handling large volumes of data
2. Dependence on hardware and software systems
3. Rapidity of technological change
4. Difficulty of sustaining commitments
5. Requirements for institutional reform
6. Shortage of skilled workers

(5) *The ability to effect institutional reform.* New technologies often re-
     quire major changes in the supporting organizational structure. The
     experience to date in the development of land information systems is
     that the institutional problems are by far the most difficult to deal with.
(6) *The ability to develop a skilled workforce.* There is a major shortage of
     skilled and experienced staff at all levels but particularly amongst
     production managers. Decisions on systems and systems develop-
     ment are often made, by default, by those unqualified to make them.
     There is a major challenge to develop more technically literate
     managers.

8.2   Data files and records

Data are the raw material from which every land information system is built.
They are gathered and assembled into records and files. These may be
considered as physical or logical.

Physical and logical records

The physical records and files are the bits of paper, such as pages of a book,
or sections of a magnetic tape or disk on which the data are recorded. The
logical record or file is the abstract content of what is physically stored. In
order to gain access to the data, both the physical and the logical records and
files must be structured in an appropriate way.

A logical record has two parts: a key, which identifies the record, and the
data to be stored. Unlike the physical record, the logical record need not
necessarily occupy the same contiguous space in a storage system. It is,
however, common to store one logical record to one physical record. In
addition to the data items, the logical record may also contain additional
information such as its size and a pointer to the next record in the sequence.
A physical record may consist of any fraction or multiple of the logical record
size. Normally it is an integer multiple, so that several logical records can be
read from or written to a storage device as a result of a single input or output
command.

Files

A file is a collection of records, such as all the parcels on a map sheet. A
collection of related data records is known as a logical file or data set. A
particular record may belong to only one physical file but be cross-
referenced to several logical files. In general, logical files are categorized as:

(1) serial access files, in which the data are in no particular order; they must
     therefore be read through from the start to find a particular record;

(2) sequential access files, in which there is some order (for example, an alphabetical list of names);

(3) index files, which have an index table containing a list of the keys and addresses of the corresponding records, (for example, a land parcel reference to the volume and folio on which the data are stored (see Chapter 2));

(4) direct access files, in which the address of the record can be calculated without first having to look it up in an index table (a process known as hashing or address-generation);

(5) inverted files, in which there are multiple keys linking different data items;

(6) list structured files, where each record contains a pointer to some other record.

For electronic data processing (EDP), the data in structures (1) and (2) above can be stored on magnetic tape. For (2) to (6), there must be direct access, as can occur when storing data on magnetic disk. With sequential files, it is helpful to have the data on disk since it is then possible to gain quicker access by jumping backwards and forewords through the file. Magnetic tapes have to be rewound to move back to an earlier record, which is time consuming.

8.3   Data bases

A data base is a collection of data that can be shared by different users. It is a group of records and files that are organized so that there is little or no redundancy. In a simple filing system, there might be one file containing a list of property owners in alphabetical order, and beside each their postal address. Thus, given the name of an owner, one could quickly find out where he or she lives, just as in a telephone directory. Given the name of a property, it would, however, be necessary to read through the file, record by record, until the name of the postal address was found. Then the name of the owner would be revealed. To speed up the search for owners, it would be possible to have a second file listed in alphabetical order of the names of the postal addresses, and beside each would appear the name of the owner. This second file would contain all the same information as the first but in a different order. Everything would need to be duplicated. In a data base, however, there would be only one file so that an inquirer could ask either for the name of the owner of a particular property or for details of the property that a particular person owns. The file of names would contain pointers to the address file, and vice versa.

One problem with a simple filing system is that there tends to be a high level of redundancy, different versions of the same data being stored in different places. Such systems are relatively inflexible, and are expensive to modify. If, in the above example, the name of an owner changed then the correction would have to be entered in two different places. The objectives in creating a data base include (Table 8.2):

Table 8.2   Objectives of data base management

1. Permits various methods of access
2. Stores data independent of applications
3. Controls access to data
4. Facilitates data modification
5. Minimizes data redundancy

(1) the structuring of the data to permit various methods of access;
(2) the storing of the data in formats that are independent of current and potential applications;
(3) the control of access to the data, including who is allowed to use or alter any data entry;
(4) the facilitation of record updating, changing, or modification, including the insertion of new records and deletion of old;
(5) the minimizing of data redundancy.

Creating a data base

The development of a data base usually follows a series of processes such as:[2]

(1) Data investigation, which is a fact-finding process. The types and qualities of data that are to be incorporated into the data base need to be identified. Data consist of entities and attributes. An entity is a feature that exists and about which there is specific interest. The data associated with it may consist of relationships, attributes, and other characteristics. An attribute is a quality of an entity. However, the distinction may not always be clear. Thus the soil type may, to one person, be an attribute of a land parcel, but to a soil scientist it may be an item of particular interest and therefore an entity in its own right.
(2) Data modelling, which involves the formation of a conceptual model of the data, taking into account all the basic facts and constraints under which the data base will have to operate. In particular, it will be concerned with relationships between different entities and their attributes.
(3) Data base design, in which a practical design is created for the data base management system.
(4) Data base implementation, in which detailed decisions are made on such matters as file sizes and organization and on physical matters, including the creation of the data base.
(5) Data base monitoring, in which the system can be fine tuned and additions and deletions to the proposed design can be implemented.

8.4 Data base management systems

Within a computer environment, a specialized computer program called a data base management system may be used to control the storage, retrieval, and modification of the data. One of its functions is file handling and file management. A file management system does not necessarily need a structured data base, although some of the more sophisticated file-handling systems verge on data base management systems. The latter have highly structured data, handle both data input and retrieval in response to user enquiries and may undertake general purpose data manipulation. They may also perform a variety of 'housekeeping' functions, for example protecting the integrity of the data by allowing only certain persons the right to change the data entries. In addition, data base management systems may keep records of each time a user has access to the system and provide checks on certain operations that may be carried out only by those who know a key password. They may also provide back-up and recovery procedures if, for example, there is a power failure or some electronic or mechanical breakdown—though often, in such circumstances, some data may be lost.

Processing structures

The primary objective of a data base management system is to permit a user to deal with the data without needing to understand how the data are physically structured and stored in the computer. Such systems employ different processing structures, such as (Fig. 8.1):

(1) Hierarchical structures, in which the records are divided into logically related fields, which are connected to other fields in a tree-like arrangement. In each group of records, one field is designated the master. Groups of records are then arranged in a serial order and data is retrieved by searching through the various levels according to a prearranged path.

(2) Network structures, which are similar to the hierarchical arrangement, except that multiple connections between the files are introduced. This enables the user to gain access to a particular file without searching the entire hierarchy above that file.

(3) Relational structures, in which flexibility is achieved by abolishing the hierarchy of fields. All fields may be used as keys to retrieve information. A record is no longer thought of as a set of discrete entities with one item being designated the master field. Instead, each record is conceived as a row in a two-dimensional table, and each field becomes a column in the table.

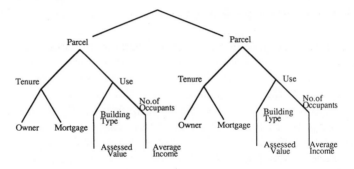

HIERARCHICAL STRUCTURE

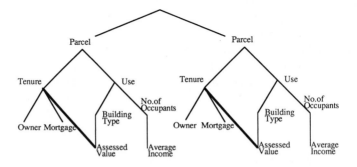

NETWORK STRUCTURE

Fig. 8.1   *Data base types*

Advantages of a data base

According to Palmer, the advantages of a data base management system are:[3]

(1) flexibility, for the system permits existing data to be used for purposes that were not envisaged when it was collected;

(2) simplicity, in that the data base gives those with permitted access a global view of the data within an enterprise;

(3) fewer restrictions on what users can do with the data, compared to fixed file structures;

(4) centralized data control, which ensures that all users operate on the same data and that they have an identical meaning to all users;

(5) easier implementation of new applications, especially where some of the data already exist;

(6) easier program writing, since validation routines and other data base procedures reduce the amount of programming effort;

(7) data independence, which allows the data base to be modified to meet

the requirements of new applications without impairing existing operational programs;

(8) standardization, which simplifies the meaning and usage of data.

Disadvantages of a data base

Conversely, there are a number of disadvantages, namely:[4]

(1) Additional hardware may be required, especially to cope with the increase in processing activities.

(2) Because of the additional work carried out by the data base management system, individual tasks may take longer to carry out than on a directly dedicated system.

(3) The collection, correction, and reconciliation of the data alone may be a major and expensive project.

(4) All those concerned with the operation of the system, from senior management to users, will need some degree of education in how to get the best out of the data base system.

(5) The system can permit very inefficient application programs still to operate.

8.5 Networks

Data bases may be centralized or distributed within a network (see Fig. 8.1). The latter may cover a wide area or may be a local area network. A centralized, time-sharing system permits users to share data and peripheral equipment such as plotters, thus reducing some costs and the duplication of resources. Procedures can be standardized and there should be efficient communication amongst users. One disadvantage, however, is that each user must wait in a queue until the central processor completes other tasks. The resulting unpredictability of response time, especially for those with low priority in the system, means that interactive use may not be available to everybody. In many municipal authorities, for example, the demands of those working with digital mapping almost certainly take lower priority than those handling financial matters, yet these often require more time dedicated to input and output from the system. This discourages some development and applications. Further disadvantages to centralized systems are that they require high initial cost, and if the system breaks down then everybody is affected.

With a computerized land information system there are likely to be many potential users working in different geographical locations with different computer equipment at their disposal. In distributed network systems such different devices and processors are linked together electronically, thus allowing communication between them. According to Palmer there are three general classifications:[5]

(1) Distributed data processing (DDP), where many devices in different locations are linked by real-time communication to a centralized data base. Each organization can use its own processing capabilities and software.
(2) Distributed data bases (DDB), where portions of the data base are stored at several sites linked by real-time communication; each site has sufficient processing power to manipulate the data base.
(3) Distributed operating systems (DOS), which allow for the provision of a data communication system through the distribution of data base processing and network control.

The degree of sophistication in a network can vary in accordance with the needs of those responsible for its implementation. The advantages of using computer networks are that:[6]

(1) each user can have a dedicated workstation, providing a much faster response time;
(2) their modular structure allows for incremental expansion; one part of the overall system can be up-graded without disrupting the rest of the network, thus allowing for a faster response to technological improvements;
(3) if one machine fails or needs maintenance, the rest of those involved need not suffer;
(4) lower total organizational costs.

On the other hand, automatic back-up and recovery in case of some disaster is more complicated because data may be anywhere around the network. It is also difficult to prevent unauthorized access to data because of the proliferation of users and information.

8.6   Data storage media

Land data may be stored on paper, on microfilm, or electronically. The traditional physical record base is paper, stored in a variety of filing systems. The most appropriate system will depend on the size and type of the records, how often they are to be referred to, the type of building in which they are to be housed, and the extent of the need for security. It will also depend on the estimated rate of growth in the volume of records. Options include the use of vertical filing cabinets, open-shelf files, compactable files (which are a variation of open-shelf filing designed for use where space is at a premium), and automated files, where the record is brought to the user instead of the user having to go to the record.[7] Particular problems arise with the storage of maps, not only because of their physical size but also because of their dimensional stability must be retained.

Microfilm

Microfilm techniques provide a valuable storage medium for a variety of land-related records. Micrographics, a silver halide method of photocopying document originals, permits reduction ratios of up to 50:1. It is a very low-cost medium that saves considerable space; for example, more than 20 000 A4 pages can be recorded on a single role of 16-millimetre film. It is relatively permanent and can be linked to computers. Duplicate filmed copies of important records can be stored off-site at a minimal cost. These act as 'disaster copies' in case of some catastrophe. A wide variety of microfilm products is available for records managers. Such products include serialized microforms (so named because records are accessed sequentially), and unitized microforms, in which records can be directly accessed (for example, aperture cards, card jackets, and microfiche). During the 1970s a form of microfiche that could be updated became available. This permitted additional documents to be filmed on the master copy. The system has certain attractions for land registration systems. This is reported in a study from Newfoundland.[8]

Electronic storage

Within a computer environment, there are a variety of magnetic and optical storage technologies available. Magnetic disk technology, for example, uses magnetic particles or rigid support substrates to produce a binary code. It is a relatively low-cost medium with significant compaction capabilities; a 5¼-inch (133 millimetres) disk, for example, can store more than 3 million bytes of data. The data can be easily erased and entries rewritten. Optical disks are similar, except that they are coated with light-sensitive materials exposed by laser light. Optical disk technology provides unparallelled data compaction capabilities. A 12-inch (305 millimetres) disk can store at least one gigabyte of data on each side, which is equivalent to more than 400 high-density magnetic disks, or the contents of 600 five-drawer filing cabinets. They are capable of storing textual, numeric, and image data, provide high-speed random access retrieval capabilities, and are especially rugged and durable. Currently, however, the technology is relatively expensive and has only recently enabled data to be erased and rewritten. It has a reported error rate of about one error per million characters,[9] which may still be too high in practice.

Archiving

The storage of data in archives is of special concern when dealing with land-related data. There is often a statutory requirement to maintain records for some period of time. This may be from 5 to 15 years for sales and valuation data, and often indefinitely for land titles and cadastral survey data. Archival legislation regulates the 'maintenance, security, transfer, disposal, and selection of records worthy of preservation'.[10] Several methods are available for storing archival records. For example, there are well-established standards for archival quality microfilm, and recommended procedures for microform storage that include guidelines for a temperature- and humidity-controlled atmosphere. Optical disks, which currently can be written only once but read many times, have significant archival potential. However, at present they are rated as being satisfactory for only up to 10 years and have not yet been given formal recognition.

8.7   Data security

Security is a matter of particular concern for land information managers, because of the nature and legal significance of the records with which they deal. Security measures include the use of fireproof vaults, the preparation of microfilmed duplicates, or the regular creation of back-up copies for all computer files, and controlled access to sensitive areas. Security entails:

(1)   protection of resources from damage so that the data can always be recreated if they become corrupted or are lost;
(2)   use of passwords and authorization rules to protect data against accidental or intentional disclosure to unauthorized persons, or their unauthorized modification or destruction.

The requirements for security in a computer environment can be described in terms of four layers of control.[11] The first layer consists of controls that are built into the computer hardware and software. These may include privacy locks and authorization schemes, password keys, message authentication, and cryptography. The second layer is that of physical security, and may include fire precautions, locks on doors, alarms, and guards. Administrative controls form the third layer. These could include regulations concerning the activities of data-processing staff, and auditing and monitoring procedures. The outer layer consists of the legal framework required to deal with the broader social issues related to security and privacy.

References

1. Morgan, G. (1985). Presentation to the World Bank seminar of land information systems, St Michaels, Maryland, March.

2. Oxborrow, E. (1986). *Databases and database systems*, Chartwell-Bratt. Lund.
3. Palmer, D. (1984). *A land information network for New Brunswick*, Technical report No. 111, Department of Surveying Engineering, University of New Brunswick, Fredericton, N B.
4. Palmer, D. *Op. cit.*
5. Palmer, D. (1984). *A review of recent computer and telecommunication developments*, Occasional paper No. 14, Department of Surveying Engineering, University of New Brunswick, Fredericton, N B.
6. Masry, S. E. and Lee, Y. C. (1984). Lecture Note Number 56—Digital mapping. Department of Surveying Engineering, University of New Brunswick, Fredericton, N B.
7. Diamond, S. (1983). *Records management*, American Management Associations, New York.
8. Decision Dynamics Corporation (1978). *Land registration study for Newfoundland*, Study prepared for the Government of Newfoundland, St John's, Newfoundland.
9. Moody, H. G. (1986). Optical storage: mass storage with mass appeal?. *Information Strategy*, Vol. 2, No. 4, p. 44.
10. Hunter, G. (1985). Archival data and land information systems. University of Melbourne, Dept. of Surveying technical report, Parkville, Australia.
11. Martin, J. (1983). *Managing the data-base environment*, Prentice-Hall, Englewood Cliffs, N J.

9. The economics of LIS

In this chapter we consider the nature of information and the extent to which the costs and benefits associated with it can be quantified. Only limited examples are as yet available where the proved benefits of a land information system exceed the costs. There is, however, evidence for this in the longer term.

9.1 Information as a resource

Information is a basic resource. Like any other resource, some people are in possession of it or have access to it and others need it but do not have it. Those who have it can use it, waste it, market it, or else give it away. Information has, however, special characteristics that distinguish it from material goods (Table 9.1). It is not consumable and hence remains however much it is used; yet it can be destroyed or corrupted. It can be transferred; yet it remains with the transferrer. It is indivisible; yet it can be accumulated. It has social and cultural value but, on its own, it has very little material use—its value is tangible only when it is used in conjunction with other tangible products.

Information is used on a day to day basis by every citizen. Many jobs are concerned specifically with the transfer or processing of information. All

Table 9.1 Four inherent properties of information that distinguish it from material goods

1. **Not consumable**—goods are consumed by being used, but information remains no matter how much it is used
2. **Non-transferable**—in the transfer of goods from A to B, they are physically moved, but in the transfer of information, it remains with A
3. **Indivisible**—materials, such as electricity and water, are divided for use, but information can only be used as a 'set'
4. **Accumulative**—Goods accumulate when they are not used, but information cannot be consumed or transferred, so it is accumulated by being used repeatedly

Table 9.2 Role of information in the development and
management of resources

1. Monitoring the environment for conditions
   requiring a decision (monitoring phase)
2. Developing models that permit the analysis of
   alternative courses of action (planning phase)
3. Selecting a particular course of action
   (policy-making phase)
4. Administering the course of action (operations
   phase)

communication, for example, is information exchange; even money has
been described as information in transit. Few jobs, however, are concerned
with the creation of information, even in such information-intensive
businesses as insurance, commercial credit, and law.[1] All are concerned with
using it.

Land-related information is a particular subset of information. Spatial
data may relate to specific sites or points of detail, or may be generalized and
have global applications. There is a hierarchy of needs for such information,
from sovereignty, defence, and public safety, through resource management to basic intellectual curiosity. The focus of this chapter is on the value
of such information for land management (Table 9.2).

9.2 The value of land information

The economic value of land information can be measured, at least concep-
tually, in terms of the extent to which it reduces uncertainty. Given a specific
land-related task, there will be a need to expend a certain amount of time,

Table 9.3 Economic issues

Costs:
- Overhead costs
- Maintenance costs
- Life-cycle costs
- Time costs
- Trade-offs
- Externalities

Benefits:
- Tangible benefits (dollars, time)
- Intangible benefits (social indicators)
- Employment

Revenue:
- Grants
- Taxes
- Pricing strategies

money, and energy on collecting the information necessary to accomplish it. Energy has a price, whilst time can be converted to cost by applying the hourly rates of pay of those involved. Hence the cost of producing land information can, in theory, be derived. The cost of production is not, however, necessarily the same as its value. The benefits that arise from the use of a product may be less than, or may substantially exceed, the cost of its manufacture. In the particular case of land information, (Table 9.3) experience shows that many unforeseen uses of the information arise subsequent to the inclusion of the data in a land information system.

The value of land information also lies in the avoidance of cost. The savings in time, money and energy that arise from the use of spatial information are extremely difficult to assess and yet are none the less real. Thus it is usually impossible to determine by how much a map may save a motorist when, without it, a longer route might be taken. Similarly, an efficient land registry system may expedite the transfer of property, enabling new development to proceed sooner than would otherwise be the case. The delay of even one day may be costly to a developer who is paying interest on a development loan or property taxes before revenue has started to come in. The quantification of such benefits is, however, impossible where the costs that would have arisen without the system are a matter of conjecture.

Some determination of the value of land information is, however, desirable if investment in land information systems is to be more than just an act of faith. The level of investment needed in the development of such systems needs to be justified. As Bernstein has observed:

In most developing countries, the inadequacy of land information poses a severe constraint on land transactions, land consolidation, property taxation and public planning of all kinds. Due to intensifying pressures on land for development as well as the need to mobilize increased revenues from the property tax, governments are investing in programs to clarify land ownership and boundaries, value property, and in some cases, establish computerized multipurpose land data banks. Unfortunately, the investments are often not appropriate to the limited resources available on a continuing basis and not consistent with prevailing levels of expertise, institutional capacity and economic development.[2]

9.3 Benefit–cost analysis

One technique for determining whether an investment is worth while is benefit–cost analysis. This may be described as a quantitative comparison of the outputs (that is, the benefits) with the inputs (that is, the costs) of a particular course of action. It is a general economic tool for organizing and assisting in the evaluation of information required in the decision-making process. It is designed to assist policy makers by:

(1) helping them to understand the nature and scope of the projects upon which they are required to make investment decisions;

(2) helping them to identify and understand the nature of the costs and benefits associated with these projects;

(3) measuring the costs and benefits which are quantifiable or tangible and identifying those which are not;

(4) providing an indication of the distribution of project costs and benefits among different groups in society;

(5) providing a coherent and consistent framework for evaluating the projects.[3]

Discounting

The development costs of creating a land information system arise from the very start of such a project; the benefits, however, do not arise until later. In order to equate the two, the effects of inflation must be taken into account. In discounting, all projected future benefits and costs are converted to a present-day value. This assumes that consumers prefer present consumption to future consumption and that the uncertainty of predicting costs and benefits increases over time. For example, if there were a 7 per cent discount rate, then:

(1) a cost of $50 000 incurred at the end of two years would be discounted to $43 671;

(2) benefits of $50 000 incurred at the end of 10 years would be discounted to $23 764.

The derived benefit to cost ratios, together with a subjective analysis of the unquantifiable and intangible benefits and costs, are compared for each alternative proposal considered. Those programme proposals where the quantifiable benefits are less than the costs will normally be eliminated from further consideration, unless there are overriding social or political concerns. The remaining alternatives are then ranked according to their relative benefit to cost utility. From then on, any decision on whether to go ahead with a project will take these rankings into account. The final decision will incorporate these with many other factors that may be of a political or social nature.

In reviewing the technique of benefit to cost analysis, Epstein and Duchesneau noted that it:

is often seen as an attempt to substitute mechanical methods for reasoning in administrative decision-making. Benefit cost analysis makes no decisions, nor is it an algorithm which produces a number that solves all decision-making problems . . . The contribution of the benefit cost approach to public expenditure analysis is that decision makers are forced to consider all factors—the quantifiable and nonquantifiable—in making decisions. As a result, implicit factors often become explicit. The decision process tends to focus more directly on critical elements, and orderliness and structure are imposed on the decision-making process.[4]

9.4   Assessing benefits

Benefits come from satisfying needs. In attempting to quantify the benefits, the initial task is to identify applications of land information and to ascertain the level of need for each. Land information applications may be manifest in specific products or services. The need for these may be very general (such as the need for improved land use planning), more specific (as in a requirement to complete the conveyance of property within an average of so many days), or very specific (such as the relationship between the soil of a particular quality and the topography in a certain region).

Time savings

One of the potential benefits is greater efficiency through prevention of time-wasting duplication of work. If it is possible to establish the level of duplication that takes place within or between organizations, then it may be possible to calculate the savings that arise from preventing it. In some cases, benefits can be measured from market studies and the analysis of question-naires issued to consumer groups picked to represent different levels of need and expertise. The interviewee can be asked how much he or she would pay to obtain a particular piece of information if a particular product were not available. In a project initiated in 1982 by the Royal Norwegian Council for Technical and Industrial Research, an attempt was made to compute the community benefit from the total production of maps and spatial data in Norway. The primary method for measuring benefits of land information systems was based upon the time saved among the users of the products. Around 100 different people were interviewed in order to determine who were the principle users of the system and what use they made of it.[5]

Cost savings

Alternatively, it may be possible to establish in direct cash terms how much would have to be paid for a particular item (for example, a map) if no similar product existed. Such an approach may, however, be oversimplistic. A national mapping agency may raise the price of its maps and thereby increase its revenue even though the number of sales declines. The value of a map lies in the extent of its use, because with it the user will operate more efficiently. Thus if the use declines, the value to the nation as a whole declines, even though the revenue to the map producer goes up. Measuring the savings that are made by users of maps is in any case difficult or impossible. Some of the benefits are tangible, such as in route planning; others are intangible, such as the increased security of tenure that arises through having a sound cadastral map.

In Australia, several attempts have been made to quantify the value of information. But, as reported in one particular study:

In practice, it is a formidable task to try to measure the value of information to ultimate users. It is difficult to identify all the types of decisions in which land information is used. It is even more difficult to establish the ways in which individual decision makers process the information. And, it is extremely difficult to specify how changes in the form of the information will alter the individual decisions made.[6]

Effects of land titling

One positive approach is to consider the increases in productivity and land values that come from the improved information. Economic theory suggests that farmers lacking secure ownership will have less incentive to invest in capital formation and land improvement. Furthermore, such farmers do not have a viable land collateral, and as a consequence their access to institutional credit is limited. Theory predicts that land not held legally will be less productive and will fetch a lower market price. In Thailand, studies have shown that squatters have less access to institutional credit than titled farmers.[7] As a result, titled land is significantly more valuable than illegally occupied land, although the latter is freely traded. Farmers who own titled land, accumulate more capital and undertake more improvements to the land. A Thai farmer with a secure title is more likely to buy equipment, erect more substantial buildings, and invest in irrigation and land conservation measures. Unfortunately, there is also evidence that the incidence of land disputes and land grabbing by larger or more powerful farmers increases as the potential return on land increases.

Since ownership of titled land implies better benefits than ownership of untitled land, the value of titled land is higher. The converse of this is that the provision of a secure title to squatters tends to increase the productivity of their land (see Fig. 9.1).[8]

Examples of benefits

In a study on the computerization of a land titles office in Canada, four categories of benefit were identified: tangible internal and external, and intangible internal and external. The tangible internal benefits included savings in hours spent on searching for, handling, and processing documents, reduction in equipment, stationery, and storage requirements, and increase in overall efficiency. There were also a number of tasks that would no longer need to be carried out manually and that constituted cost avoidance. Tangible external benefits arose from the better service

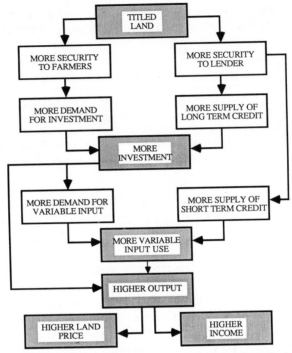

Fig. 9.1   *Ownership security and farm productivity (from Feder, G.*[8]*)*

provided, allowing others to reduce their costs. Intangible benefits were essentially in the estimated improvements in productivity, notably by:

(1)   reducing file search, access, and refiling times;
(2)   increased physical and access security for the titles and general register;
(3)   increased efficiency in the examination and registration process;
(4)   elimination of errors in fee calculations and billing;
(5)   improvements in accounting;
(6)   improved services to clients;
(7)   fewer claims against the assurance fund;
(8)   improved communications;
(9)   automated tax arrears notifications.

9.5   Assessing costs

In theory it should be relatively straightforward to measure costs, given proper accounting procedures. For example, detailed cost estimates for acquiring the hardware and software necessary for computer-assisted mapping have been published.[9] In practice, particularly in the context of comprehensive land information systems, they are not so easy to establish. Some costs are relatively fixed, for instance building and equipment maintenance, which can be put out to contract. Some are relatively variable, for instance those that depend on the volume of dealings, such as the number of registrations, queries, or sales; and those that depend on alternative methods of operation.

Problems in assessing costs

In theory, costs should be well documented and therefore easy to assess. This, however, is often not the case because:

(1) There are variations between different parts of a country, for instance in the terrain and vegetation leading to different accuracy requirements, variations in the nature and complexity of land tenure arrangements, availability of pre-existing information, and institutional arrangements.
(2) There is often a lack of adequate reporting of time and expenditure.
(3) There is often a failure to separate out information costs from overall operating costs.
(4) There are difficulties in reconciling costs shared between different government departments.
(5) Figures are often available only for initial production costs and do not include updating, maintenance, overheads, and training costs.

Documented costs

Specific data on costs were collected by Bernstein from a number of sources.[10] Two examples were:

(1) For a comprehensive cadastral survey and registration project carried out in the Caribbean in the early 1970s, the unit cost per parcel was $75 (based on the value of the United States dollar in 1974). The percentage breakdowns showed that 12 per cent went on administrative overheads, 28 per cent on demarcation, 14 per cent on recording, 40 per cent on survey, and 6 per cent on settling disputes and petitions.[11]

(2) The north-east Brazil land tenure improvement project was designed to secure land ownership for up to 700 000 small farmers and to provide an information base for formulating land policy throughout an area covering 1.5 million square kilometres. The project was to provide mapping through the use of aerial photography and ground survey control. Also, land tenure rights and ownership were to be identified and relevant geographic information digitized. Finally, there was to be

institutional strengthening through the provision of buildings, equipment, and staff training. The estimated total cost of the project was $US 250 million at a unit cost of about $8 per hectare. The average land parcel size is 30 hectares; thus the per-parcel cost would be approximately $240.[12]

Probably the most rigorous documentation of costs has been that associated with the development of the Land Registration and Information Service in the Maritime Provinces of Canada. For the period 1973–1983, the costs for each parcel ranged from $19.82 to $50.32 (Canadian), which on an area basis worked out to between $2.20 and $5.60 per hectare.[13]

Software costs

Costs for writing software are an additional element. Over a hundred person-years were spent on software development for the Swedish real property data base.[14] Software writing is an expensive process. Using a compiler language such as COBOL, it can cost $40 per line to prepare a major program. A COBOL program of 50 pages is not uncommon, and with 60 lines per page, the average COBOL program costs $120 000.[15] Additional costs and benefits of computerization are highlighted in Table 9.4.

Principles of costing

Research into the modelling of costs specifically relating to photogrammetric operations has been carried out on behalf of the European Organization

Table 9.4   Costs and benefits of computerization

Costs:
1. Institutional change
2. Costs and problems of data conversion
3. Human and financial resources required
4. High costs of initial investment in systems
5. Marginal benefit–cost advantage for some operations

Benefits:
1. Physical compaction of data
2. More efficient data handling
3. Capability for data manipulation
4. Capability for spatial and temporal data analysis
5. Merging of graphic and attribute data
6. Integration of data bases

for Experimental Photogrammetric Research[16] A more general attempt to develop a unit cost methodology for any land information product has been made by Hamilton.[17] His method is based on four principles:

(1) For each product, two unit costs are essential: the cost of initial production and the cost of maintenance.
(2) An inflation factor must be incorporated and all figures must be translated to a base year;
(3) To accommodate fluctuations in exchange rates, every effort should be made to convert unit costs into person-hours;
(4) All person-hours should be normalized with the skill level of the norm clearly stated.

9.6 Pricing LIS products

Land information creates marketable products and services. One way to assess the value of information is to determine its market price. Such a policy does not work well within the public sector. Some services can be subject to interdepartmental accounting, for instance where maintenance services are provided or printed maps are sold through a paper transaction, debiting one department and crediting another. There are three general strategies for determining the price to charge:

(1) cost-based pricing, where prices are set largely on the basis of the fixed and variable costs of production and handling;
(2) demand-based pricing, where the price is based on what people are actually prepared to pay or what is perceived as the value of the product;
(3) competition-based pricing, which depends on what other producers of the same product or service are charging. This of course, does not apply when one organization has a monopoly.

Traditionally, public goods have been provided at a token price. Nationally produced maps and surveys have been marketed at a price well below their true cost of production. Cadastral surveying has had direct or hidden subsidies; for example, the true cost of checking surveys undertaken by the private sector is almost never passed on. Where surveys are done by government surveyors, the scale of fees is almost always below the over-headed costs. In moving away from this approach, it is necessary to establish:

(1) who should pay for the land information products and how much;
(2) whether all front-end costs, such as the establishment of geodetic control, should be recovered through fees;

(3)   what should be the contribution from general revenues and what from special taxes;

(4)   what is the case, if any, for price discrimination between different users and different products.

Such questions have been asked in the recent controversy in the United States with respect to the pricing of remote-sensing products.[18] The answers will depend very much upon the economic and political climate in which the questions are posed. Around the world, there is a continuum that begins with products and services of a purely public sector function; it passes through those that are primarily public sector to those that are primarily private sector; it ends in areas that legitimately and wholly belong to the private sector.

Throughout many Third World and ex-colonial territories, the provision of a national geodetic framework and the subsequent mapping at small, medium, and large scales have traditionally been the exclusive preserve of the national survey organizations. The private sector has, in many cases, been allowed to carry out only property surveys and surveying for engineering purposes.[19] It has been assumed that the resources and experience available to the private sector preclude them from undertaking more major projects, which have therefore been let to contractors from overseas. Scales of fees, particularly for cadastral surveys, have tended to be laid down by government. In practice, however, private surveys have often been charged at a more realistic rate.

The balance of work between the public and private sectors is partly social and educational, and partly economic. Many of the related issues are political and are not peculiar to land information. They none the less have a major effect on the determination of costs and benefits that arise from land information products and services.

9.7   Conclusions

Benefit–cost analysis allows comparisons to be made between different approaches to the solution of a problem. It is not a technique that can readily be applied to the evaluation of new products. It has to be tempered by the existing constraints. Improvements in a system may be restricted where the use of high technology is impractical or socially unacceptable. Certain courses of action may be politically undesirable or legally impossible within the present legislative framework. Seed capital to get a project started may not be forthcoming because of its limited availability. In many circumstances, immediate gain comes from adopting approaches that are cost effective rather than financially beneficial.

A substantial amount of work needs to be done if reliable estimates of benefits and costs are to be secured. All programmes should be subject to frequent monitoring and re-evaluation to ensure continuing efficiency and the relevance of their goals in the light of changing circumstances. From such studies, a more certain picture should emerge. Every attempt that has so far been made to obtain reliable figures has been open to criticism. Tentative evidence from a number of quarters suggests that the return on investment in land information products and services can run at between two and three to one, provided that a critical level of investment is reached. As such, land information management is a wealth-creating activity in which almost everybody gains. The only losers are those who profit from misinformation.

References

1. Edwards, C. (1986). Organizational resources. *Information Strategy*, Vol. 2, No. 4, pp. 41–2.
2. Bernstein, J. (1985). The costs of land information systems. Paper presented to the World Bank Seminar on Land Information Systems, St Michaels, Md.
3. Weir, C. (1986). *D.G.S. cost-benefit procedure*, Report produced by Stewart, Weir and Co., Edmonton.
4. Epstein, E. and Duchesneau, T. (1984). *The use and value of a geodetic reference system*, Report prepared for the Federal Geodetic Control Committee, April, Rockville, Md.
5. Bernhardsen, T. (1986). A cost-benefit study of a LIS—methodology and result. Paper presented to the FIG International Congress, Toronto, June.
6. Angus-Leppan, P. (1983). Economic costs and benefits of land information. *Proceedings of the XVII Congress of the International Federation of Surveyors*, Vol. 3, Sophia.
7. Feder, G. (1986). The economic implications of land ownership security in rural Thailand. Paper prepared for the World Bank Seminar on Land Information Management, Annapolis, Md.
8. Feder, G. *Op. cit.*
9. Hansen, D. (1984). An overview of the organization, costs and benefits of computer assisted mapping and records activity systems, *Computers, Environment and Urban Systems* Vol. 9, No. 2/3.
10. Bernstein, J. *Op. cit.*
11. Howells, L. J. (1974). The cadastral survey and registration project in the Caribbean. *Chartered Surveyor, Land, Hydrographic and Minerals Quarterly* Vol. 1/4, p. 57.
12. Bernstein, J. *Op. cit.*
13. Council of Maritime Premiers (1981). *LRIS Planning Document*. Fredericton.
14. Andersson, S. (1986). The Swedish Land Data Bank. *Proceedings of Auto Carto London* Vol. 2, pp. 122–8.
15. Gorman, M. (1984). *Managing databases: four critical factors*. Wellesley, Mass.: QED Publications.

16. Jerie, H. and Holland, E. (1983). Cost model project for photogrammetric processes. *ITC Journal* Vol. 2.
17. Hamilton, A., *et al.* (1985). Unit cost principles and their application to property mapping in New Brunswick. *The Canadian Surveyor* Vol. 39/1, pp. 11–22.
18. Aronoff, S. (1985). Political implications of full cost recovery for land remote sensing systems. *Photogrammetric Engineering and Remote Sensing* Vol. 551/1.
19. Ayinde, B. (1983). Changing Times: A Case for the Private Sector. *Proceedings of the Conference of Commonwealth Surveyors*, Cambridge.

10. Institutional arrangements

In this chapter we review some of the fundamental needs, values, and priorities of a society that will be instrumental in determining when and in what manner a land information system is developed.

10.1 The institutional perspective

The operation of a land information system entails two separate sets of issues, the technical and the institutional. The term 'institution', as used here, refers to the established laws and customs and the administrative structure needed to support them. It includes various aspects of organizational behaviour that influence and control the freedom of the individual, particularly in the context of what is allowed to be done with the land. Organizational structures differ widely from country to country and hence only issues of broad policy will be considered.

The importance of examining institutional problems was highlighted by the UN Ad Hoc Group of Experts on Cadastral Surveying and Mapping:

Institutional problems are among the most difficult to resolve in the establishment and maintenance of a cadastre; the lack of recognition and adequate resolution of such problems are probably the most common causes for the ineffective functioning of a cadastre. The effective implementation of a cadastre is a complex operation involving the establishing of a functional system of relationships among several institutions for its establishment, maintenance, effective use and continuing development.[1]

The underlying weakness of many of the cadastral systems currently operating in less developed countries is that their administrative costs are excessively high, whilst the tangible benefits are low. They appear to divert scarce resources that could arguably be better used on other, more socially justifiable, tasks such as building and running hospitals and schools. They have often been based on techniques, laws, and practices that were copied from elsewhere and are unsuited to local conditions. Many have been unable to respond to changing social and economic conditions. Yet land remains a fundamental resource that must be properly administered. In order to respond to the present challenge, it is necessary to formulate improved land information policies, to build the necessary institutional arrangements for implementing these policies, and to develop effective and efficient

183

Table 10.1 Matters for policy review

- Human resource analysis—determination of technical and professional skills available
- Economic analyses—determination of national and international economic policies
- Institutional analyses—assessment of organizational arrangements and alternatives
- Determining requirements for LIS

systems for their implementation, subject to institutional and other constraints.

Before embarking on any reform of institutional arrangements, attention needs to be focused on understanding (Table 10.1):

(1) the social environment within which a land information management programme is to be developed, especially the human resources available and the levels of technical and professional skills;

(2) the economic environment and, where applicable, the policies and priorities of donor agencies and countries;

(3) the current government structure and policies, especially with regard to land, capital, and labour;

(4) the current and evolving requirements for land information management and the constraints which deter its progress.

10.2 Policies for information

Every organization requires an information-handling policy that covers its creation, availability, and value. Such policies may be implicit or explicit. Information policy should start with the recognition that information is a major corporate resource. As Diebold has remarked:

Effective information resource management means treating information like other corporate resources—such as labor, capital, plant and equipment—and integrating technological capabilities with human resources. As advances in information technology bring the business community into a new era, the strategic management of information will be pivotal, and the organization will be affected at every level.[2]

Policy issues

If land information is to be managed as an economic commodity that can be bought and sold, then certain policy issues arise (Table 10.2). For proper management, each element of information must be:

(1) identified, measured and costed at each stage of its life cycle;

(2) anticipated and planned for, to ensure that the information is

Table 10.2 Land information policy issues

- Responsibility for developing and co-ordinating
  LIS activities
  Centralized ← → Decentralized
  (Data bank)   (Networks)
- Pricing mechanisms and procedures for budgeting,
  accounting, and auditing the handling of land
  information products
- Data definitions, codification, standards
- Access to data, privacy, security

genuinely required and its existence is brought to the attention of potential users and decision makers;

(3) budgeted for, to ensure that the cost of land information is properly balanced against other resource costs;

(4) managed, so that the value arising from the use of the information is properly assessed against the cost of its collection;

(5) accounted for and audited, to ensure that costs are kept under control and that designated information management personnel are held responsible for the proper and efficient use of the information.

Documenting costs

A first step in developing a policy for the management of land information is to document the costs entailed in collecting and maintaining that information. A Government of Canada study team, for example, has found that:

Federal major surveys cost the Canadian taxpayer over three-quarters of a billion dollars each year and employ slightly more than 10 000 persons. They collect basic information about the country, its people, its economy, its natural resources and its environment . . . No one has been paying much attention to the federal surveys as a system. In the view of the study team someone should! There are major opportunities to make survey taking more efficient, to make access to surveying information easier, and to save Canadian taxpayers tens of millions of dollars annually. Federal information needs must be clearly defined. More harmony and program integration should come about in our survey-taking and information-sharing with provinces. We need to make more effective use of new technology. How do you decide what basic information is the right information to run a country? Ideally you decide what needs to be done, who is responsible for what, and which organizations should gather the information required to get those jobs done.[3]

Determining factors

Factors that determine the form and content of any policy for land information management include:

(1) the resources available to develop land information products and services;

(2)   the relative responsibilities and institutional arrangements within the public sector;
(3)   the role of the private sector and the professions;
(4)   the role of the educational and training institutions;
(5)   the problems associated with technology transfer;
(6)   the perception and legal status of social issues such as accessibility to the data, security of the data, and privacy of the individual;
(7)   the identifiable needs and priorities for land information;
(8)   the impact that such information may have on society.

A policy for information is as important as a policy for the land itself. It is often relatively straightforward to demonstrate that benefits come from improved land information procedures and techniques. To obtain a consensus that this needs to happen is, however, another matter. In the competition for scarce resources, the necessity for improvements in land information systems must be weighed against the necessity for very different forms of investment. The need for and economic advantages of surveying and mapping in development has, however, been gaining recognition. For example, in 1980, the African Heads of States and Government agreed in Lagos, Nigeria, and re-affirmed at their meeting in Addis Ababa, Ethiopia in 1985, the need:

To recognize the importance of their national mapping and surveying institutions and to rate them high amongst their national priorities and to provide sufficient budget for them to take steps to establish them where none exists.[4]

10.3   The social and economic environment

Different policies for land information management are needed to reflect the differing needs of the urban and rural environments. The urban community is involved in a wide range of land use activities from commercial and industrial activities, through transport and social services such as schools and hospitals, to residential and recreational activities. Within the urban areas, particularly the cities, population levels are growing rapidly. This is in part due to high birth rates and the lengthening period of life expectancy resulting from better sanitation and health care. Population numbers are also growing through migration from the rural areas. In the rural areas the predominant uses of land information are in resource management, including agriculture, forestry, and mineral exploitation.

National and international economics

The provision of both urban and rural land information systems needs to be seen within the broader context of national economic development. The extent of this development in many Third World countries has, over the last few decades, often been dependent on forces beyond their control. Economic success and failure have to be seen against a background of varying demands and prices in the world commodity markets, fluctuations in currency exchange rates, and the overall internal political stability in the region. As Wood has pointed out in the context of Thailand:

A nation experiencing disruptions in its political base, either through the democratic vote of 'no confidence', or from the more radical process of revolutionary overthrow, suffers economically. Traditionally, investors, both internal and external, are reluctant to back large capital projects until a level of stability returns . . . The implementation of an urban land information system in Bangkok requires long term planning, substantial capital investment, and above all, political commitment to the project. A lack of political cohesiveness and stability to strategically plan futures can severely jeopardize the success of implementing an integrated urban land information system . . . Certain types of information which appear worthwhile to one power base, such as a civilian government, may become a security issue to another political group, while program funding over extended periods of time may be subjected to change.[5]

Land tenure

One matter of major institutional concern is land tenure. The relationship between people and land is essentially dynamic. In many communities, there is a transition from communal and customary tenure to more formalized arrangements in which the individual or family has recognized rights. This trend is most apparent in African countries where there is a general move towards individualized land holdings. As Barnes has observed:

Exposure to western concepts of land ownership and a widespread move from subsistence farming to cash cropping has strengthened the man–land relationship. As individuals cultivate fields for longer periods of time, so the association between the cultivator (man) and the parcel of land becomes more entrenched. This contributes to the perception of land being 'attached' to individuals and simultaneously weakens the man–man relationship and the role of society in the allocation and determination of land rights.[6]

It is a trend that does not necessarily meet with universal support. At the United Nations Habitat Conference, the view was expressed that:

Land, because of its unique nature and the crucial role it plays in human settlements, cannot be treated as an ordinary asset, controlled by individuals and subject to the pressures and inefficiencies of the market. Private land ownership is also a principal instrument of accumulation and concentration of wealth and therefore contributes to social injustice; if unchecked, it may become a major obstacle in the planning and implementation of development schemes. Social justice, urban renewal and development, the provision of decent dwellings and health conditions for the people can only be achieved if land is used in the interests of society as a whole. Instead, the pattern of land use should be determined by the long-term interests of the community, especially since decisions on location of activities and therefore of specific land uses have long-lasting effect on the pattern and structure of human settlements. Land is also a primary element of the natural and man-made environment and a crucial link in an often delicate balance. Public control of land use is therefore indispensable to its protection as an asset and the achievement of the long-term objectives of human settlement policies and strategies.[7]

Social impact of land information

Land is both a social and an economic factor in society. So too is land information. The social impact of information is through the decision-making process and in the extent to which private and confidential information, maintained within a system, is available to the public. Where there is freedom of access to information held in the public domain, the privacy of the individual is under threat.

Economic impact of land information

The economic impact of land information is measured in part by the revenue it generates and the costs involved in its creation. The fundamental economic problem is that the return on capital invested in the development of land information systems is neither immediate nor guaranteed. The costs of survey in particular can be high. Modern mapping techniques are pre-

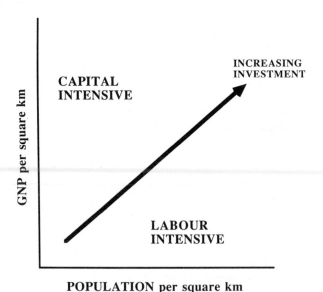

Fig. 10.1   *Population density and GNP: capital and labour*

dominantly capital rather than labour intensive, and require substantial investment in equipment and skilled labour. Many Third World countries, on the other hand, have an abundance of unskilled or semi-skilled labour but a lack of capital. The choice between a capital- or a labour-intensive system will depend to a large extent on the ratio in between a country's Gross National Product per unit area and the density of its population. Where the ratio is high, capital-intensive methods may be more appropriate; however, where a relatively low GNP per unit are is combined with a high population density, labour intensive methods may be more suitable (see Fig. 10.1).

10.4   The role of the public and private sectors

In the development of any land information system there will be contrasting interests between the public and private sectors, in both the formulation of any land information policy and its implementation. A United Nations Ad Hoc Group of Experts have argued that Governments should assume the responsibility for developing land information systems since:

(a)   the output of a land information system can and should contribute to many governmental policy decisions;

(b)   its output can mean success or failure in the implementation of many major government decisions, e.g. resource exploration and exploitation, industrialization and land reform;

(c)   its effective operation may require new legislation or modifications to existing legislation affecting many ministries.[8]

Policy implementation

While there is little disagreement that government should play the major role in formulating policy, albeit in consultation with the community, there are various approaches to its implementation, including:

(1)   total responsibility within government with no input from the private sector, as is the case for example in the Indian subcontinent;

(2)   a system of licensed professionals who can carry out private work for individuals or on contract to government, as is the case with surveyors throughout much of Africa;

(3)   privately operated systems, as in the United States where title companies provide an insurance and information service;

(4)   quasi-government and large private sector bodies such as the utilities who input data into the national or local system or who operate their own system, exchanging data for a fee.

In Australia, for example:

One of the critical factors which ensured the success of the textual LIS system in the Northern Territory and which is being extended to other areas . . . is the concept of corporate data and its associated management advantages . . . each contributing user has a responsibility to input and maintain those items of data which may be useful to other users or to the general public.[9]

Public and private institutions

The balance of responsibilities between the public and private sectors ultimately depends upon:

(1)   the nature and traditions of the particular jurisdiction;
(2)   specific information needs and priorities;
(3)   the available funding;
(4)   questions of access to the data and the need for privacy;
(5)   the initiative shown by the private sector.

In some countries, there is strong pressure for privatization. Such is the case in Canada, where a recent government task force recommended that the government concentrate on providing the leadership and co-ordinating role necessary 'to create an efficient and forward-looking National Survey System within which the private sector should be encouraged to assume a key role.'[10]

Government administration

Within all governments, there is a need to define the agencies that will be responsible for policy formulation and for day to day operations. There also needs to be a body that is responsible for co-ordination. In Australia, in New South Wales, a State Land Information Council has been formed. It consists of nominees of a wide range of Ministers who can ensure that land information issues receive appropriate attention within their portfolios. The Council reports through the Minister for Natural Resources to a Cabinet sub-committee where any outstanding issues relating to priorities or funding and resources can be decided.[11] At the national level, a National Co-ordination Committee on Land Information Exchange has been formed to investigate such things as a single data exchange standard for all digital land-related data.

Many present systems suffer from overlapping responsibilities leading to the duplication of data recording. This amongst other things, makes the maintenance and update of the records extremely complex. The problems that beset reform are as much administrative as technical. There is rarely one institution which is the clear leader with the power to co-ordinate the work of other ministries and agencies. The relationships and exchange of information between those responsible for handling land data is often complex and compartmentalized. Figs. 10.2 to 10.4 show the models developed for the province of Alberta,[12] and the states of South Australia[13] and Western Australia.[14] Globally, there is no set pattern as to which ministries and departments are responsible for forming and implementing land policies. The administration of land is a multidisciplinary affair. As a result many departments may be involved—in Indonesia, for example, several government ministries have a direct interest in the cadastre and land reform. Often, the people responsible for planning the urban environment and those responsible for the rural environment may work in different ministries; the administration of private land may be divorced from the administration of state land; agriculture and public works will almost certainly fall under different departmental control, even though both shape the rural environment; and the revenue earners such as the Lands Departments may be divorced from the revenue spenders, including the Survey Departments, who provide a service for which they are unable to recover the true costs.

It is often difficult to determine what land policies are officially in force, either in the urban or in the rural environments. This in part stems from the

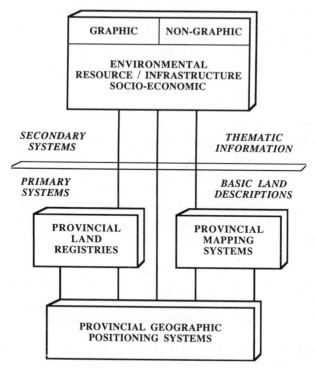

Fig. 10.2 *ALBERTA network (from McKay and Walker*[12]*)*

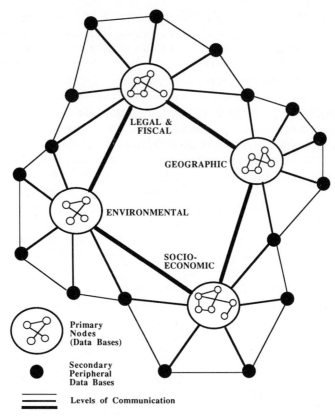

LEGAL &
FISCAL

GEOGRAPHIC

ENVIRONMENTAL

SOCIO-
ECONOMIC

Primary
Nodes
(Data Bases)

Secondary
Peripheral
Data Bases

Levels of Communication

Fig. 10.3   *LOTS—South Australia (from Sedunary[13])*

generally low level of expertise amongst administrators whose task it is to formulate such policies. It is common to find that those responsible for forming land policy are untrained in matters of the land. In many countries, the standard of education in 'land economy' is very low. As an academic discipline, the subject embraces land administration, land management, land development, land valuation, land acquisition, and the implementation of land reforms. 'Land information management' is a separate but related discipline requiring a knowledge of land economy and resource management as well as an understanding of technology.

Monitoring policies

Even where clear land policies exist, there may be limited mechanisms for monitoring their consequences. In countries such as Bangladesh, a new national development plan is implemented every five years. Work on a new five-year plan begins almost as soon as the latest one is launched and there is little opportunity for analysing what has gone wrong with the current one. If

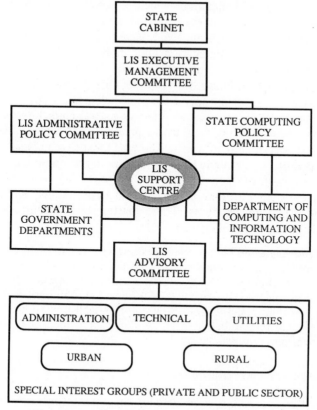

Fig. 10.4 *LIS organization—Western Australia*[14]

policies for land and land information management are to be revised, then mechanisms for monitoring their effects must be established so that appropriate action to rectify faults can be discussed and taken if needs arise. The model from Australia referred to above provides one such solution to the problem.

Co-ordination of land information

Many different government departments handle land-related data. The control and exchange of these data require interdepartmental co-operation and some degree of surrender of departmental autonomy. Two possible candidates for the role of overall co-ordinator are the lands and the surveys departments. Historically, in many countries, these were one department, but their diverging interests and aspirations led to their separation. Lands departments usually have a limited mandate and understanding of the fundamental nature of land. They concentrate on valuation and buying, selling, and leasing land for government. They are not, for example, concerned with physical planning, which is usually the responsibility of another ministry. Their role in government has tended to have a low profile. Survey departments, on the other hand, have traditionally been concerned with the handling of land information, though not with the breadth needed for a multipurpose cadastre. But they have not shown the flexibility needed to undertake the task and have, for example, failed to respond to the needs of the cadastre with sufficient speed and at sufficiently low cost.

Experience so far has suggested that any central co-ordination of land information is best undertaken by an independent body responsible directly to the highest government authority. The staff for such a body should come mainly from those who already have experience in government but with the additional support of technical experts. Their tasks will involve co-ordination between different ministries and departments, and between central and urban governments. These matters often require a delicate and tactful approach. For instance:

The major problem to be faced in New Zealand is that as the LIS development extends beyond the departmental activity into the area of local government and beyond, the rationalization in these sectors is going to be a huge task. For a country of 3.2 million people, New Zealand has 232 territorial local authorities, 22 regional authorities, 160 utility authorities and in excess of 200 ad hoc authorities. There are many overlapping responsibilities with the duplications of data recording and maintenance being a considerable problem.[15]

Centralization and decentralization

Administrative operations, as reflected in the relationship between central and local government, may be centralized or decentralized. Centralization can lead to economies in administrative procedures, standardization in documentation and the exchange of information between users, and economies of scale in which large and powerful systems can be used along with what are effectively mass production techniques. In the context of land registration, on the other hand:

Decentralization of land registry offices appears to offer many advantages, especially in a country where distances are great or travel is inconvenient. As a means of bringing government closer to the people, decentralization has considerable political appeal, but this may be partially offset by the reluctance of the bureaucracy to relinquish its central control . . . If only a central office is maintained, care must be taken to accommodate the needs of landowners in outlying areas by providing them with appropriate searching and registration services by mail or perhaps even by telephone.[16]

Both the land registration and land survey functions should ideally be performed under the overall control of a single agency. Such an arrangement should guarantee the best possible co-ordination between the various parts of the whole operation. In reality, many countries already have separate institutions, and in practice it is difficult to alter arrangements that may be well established politically and historically. In Nepal, for example, registration, survey, revenue, land reform, and land administration are all conducted through the district land administration offices. This leads to a degree of cohesion and consistency. On the other hand, the implementation of the compulsory cadastral programme in Tunisia in 1964 suffered because the operation involved three separate agencies, namely the Land Court, the Surveys and Mapping Office, and the Land Registry, each of which was organized in a different way, with different resources. Some argue that it appears logical to combine the entire cadastral process, from boundary survey through adjudication to final registration, in a single institution with a separate administrative status. However, the crucial element is the extent of co-operation and co-ordination between the separate parties that would be involved.

10.5   Education and training

Education and training have a crucial role to play in the development of a land information system. The establishment of land information systems requires a large number of specialists with broad experience and knowledge to advise and supervise the formulation of nationally compatible systems. The problems are wide and diverse, and at present there are relatively few people with such qualifications. In 1972 the United Nations ad hoc Group of Experts recommended that:

Training requirements are so varied from country to country that little useful information of a general nature can be given. Nevertheless, there are some demands for training, common to developing countries, to which international bodies and countries having technical assistance programmes could address their attention:

(a)   High-level policy-makers in developing countries sometimes require short-term intensive training in the fundamental aspects of cadastres, particularly when a country is about to initiate a cadastral programme. This demand could best be satisfied by periodical regional seminars;

(b)   High-level administrative and professional staff could benefit by observation of cadastral programmes in effective operations in other countries in order to adapt procedures and techniques to their own local circumstances;

(c)   Professional personnel should also have the opportunity to receive mid-career training for the purpose of broadening their outlook and keeping up to date on modern developments in their fields by means of periodical seminars in particular disciplines;

(d)   The general public must, of course, be reached through mass media. Such information programmes are particularly important in countries where customary rights prevail or where a segment of the population fears that the cadastre threatens its property rights. While simple in concept, these information programmes are frequently exceedingly difficult to administer and require knowledge of mass media techniques.[17]

Three separate layers of education and training give rise to concern: the training of technicians in the field of appropriate technology, the training and education of managers in production techniques so that they may operate an efficient flowline, and the education of the public in what is going on. De Hennsler, commenting on the importance of the technician and skilled worker, has observed that:

A disturbing trend has been observed lately: in many countries, too much emphasis is placed on the formation of top echelon personnel at the graduate engineer or equivalent level, and too little on the training of technicians and skilled workers, who still constitute the core of the cartographic work force. In addition to the obvious effect of not providing sufficient personnel to actually perform most of the tasks, this development directly favours an unhealthy engineer/technician worker ratio, which tends to downgrade the position of the engineer and is, therefore, counterproductive *per se*. This problem, however, is not limited to number and quality of training. It goes much deeper and has its roots in the civil service structures of countries, where technicians and skilled workers may not receive adequate remuneration or promotion possibilities. The direct consequences are a high turnover rate and brain drain to the private sector and expatriation, all highly detrimental to the national mapping potentials of the countries affected. Institutions, which are in the forefront of cartographic teaching and education, have a golden opportunity to exercise their considerable influence to rectify this situation and to foster awareness of the importance of a strong class of technicians and skilled workers.[18]

Training should wherever possible take place within the country and hence the environment in which the technician will operate. Trainees, particularly those from Third World countries, who study abroad and hence in an alien environment invariably suffer from a degree of culture shock. They have to absorb far more than the technological issues and frequently take much longer than indigenous people to settle down and be able to concentrate on and absorb technical matters. They also find difficulty in relating the many new things that they learn to the traditional background from which they have come. Further, if they have lived abroad for an extended period, they suffer from a reverse form of culture shock when they return home and find it difficult to readjust to a less materially advanced environment.

Education is concerned with broadening the mind and opening up new ideas and opportunities. Advanced courses within the country of origin are more cost effective than attendance at courses overseas. But, in an area where the rate of development and change is so fast, there is a danger that such courses may be unable to compete with the pace of change. Even in the more advanced communities, the advantages of international co-operation and the exchange of ideas between peoples from different environments are considerable.

10.6 Transfer of technology

In addressing the general topic of land information systems for Third World countries, and speaking from experiences in the World Bank, Dunkerley referred to:

the delicate subject of well meaning aid for LIS. Frankly, much too much of it has been wasted. In a few cases, where a poorly functioning existing service has been replaced by a much more highly developed system that has subsequently failed due to lack of capacity to maintain it, the net result may even have been negative. More frequently, the effect has been to pre-empt a high proportion of the local resources available for a quite limited area or aspect with scant regard for the LIS needs of the rest of the country. The gap between the perception of needs by an individual agency or donor and the more general public or private sector has been too great. . . . Unfortunately, too, the compartmentalized training usually offered in donor countries is, despite some recent improvements, still strongly oriented towards the latest high technology frontiers appropriate to the host countries. Little attention is paid to the reality of the local resources and other constraints of the developing world which greatly narrow the appropriate choices and enhance the need for long term strategies of phased progressive improvements.[19]

Few would deny that aid in one form or another is needed. The problem is to determine which form is most suitable. Referring to the need for technical assistance, and speaking from experience in Zanzibar and Tanzania, Sulaiman has commented that:

In view of changing attitudes of donor countries to aid in general and to survey and mapping in particular, the recipients ought to review the whole concept of technical assistance. Is there a need for it? Could countries not just get on with using current techniques, which do produce results, if rather more slowly and less elegantly than with advanced technology. The answer must be 'yes'. The problems of developing nations are so acute that they must be solved in the short-term, before the gap between the 'haves' and the 'have-nots' becomes so large as to be unbridgeable . . . Technical assistance is needed because resources, either human or technical, of the recipient country are not adequate to carry out the task envisaged. The response to this by the donor should emphasize the assistance aspect, to help the recipient country to do the job itself; it should rely on external execution only when the task is clearly beyond the scope of the recipient, either now or in the foreseeable future. The trend of introducing recipient countries to techniques and equipment which, even if initially provided as a gift, will eventually eat up the limited supplies of foreign exchange with servicing and material requirements, should be examined by donor countries, towards a need for setting up a programme that provides in-country technical assistance and continuing supplies of consumable materials, as well as servicing of specialized equipment.[20]

While sophisticated technologies are extremely useful tools, their introduction in developing countries requires high capital investment and costly maintenance. Environmental conditions such as humidity and dust and uncertain electrical supply may cause frequent breakdowns. Lack of skilled engineers may result in long delays before the equipment is again operational. Manufacturers have a tendency to oversell their systems and to make claims which can only be substantiated in ideal circumstances. Lack of confidence in the systems may result in reverting to well-tried and trusted manual techniques and a failure to take advantage of all that modern technology has to offer.

10.7   Legal and political issues

Copyright

If information is to be treated as a resource then there must be access to it by interested parties. Two factors that may prevent the free exchange of data are copyright and security. Land information may be subject to copyright; therefore communicating land-related data to the public may cause legal or financial problems if the copyright laws are to be enforced. In the case of maps printed on paper, some measure of control can be exercised in the same manner as it is with books and other published material. In the case of digital maps, extracts can be made more easily and transferred between systems electronically, for example over telephone lines. The policing of copyright is much more difficult for digital maps than for paper copies. If government policy is to distribute land information freely then it will be missing an opportunity to recover its costs. If it charges for the data, then it will need to establish mechanisms to control its resale.

Security

In some countries, paper maps and aerial photographs carry a security classification and may in consequence be unavailable even to other government departments. Difficulties with the exchange of spatial data exist, for example, on the Indian subcontinent, where the ready availability of certain types of land information such as maps and aerial photographs may have military implications. There may be implicit or explicit regulations governing the access to government-held land-related data by other state authorities and by the public. Data Protection Acts may also impose constraints on what information may be held or divulged. In some countries, the public may have a degree of protection against the divulgence of personal information, whilst in others their rights to privacy may be set at nought.

Data base protection

Protection is needed for a land information data base itself. So-called 'hackers' must be prevented from entering the system and, for example, changing the name of the registered owner of a property. Although the problems are technical and differ more in kind than in principle from what has been the case in the past, they are more urgent because of the volumes of data that can be tampered with or destroyed.

The creation and management of land-related data bases also raise a number of legal and institutional concerns, few of which have as yet been dealt with satisfactorily. These include such questions as: 'who should have access to the information contained in the data bases?', 'who owns the information?', and 'who is responsible for loss of data or errors in the data bases?' In general there is little legal guidance to go by. Those legal rules that are often said to deal with information usually in fact deal only with the physical objects representing information. For example, intellectual property laws have traditionally focused on the medium rather than the message; it has not been possible to copyright or patent information as such. Similarly, legislation governing access to information, despite its title, is invariably framed in terms of access to documents, including microform and electronic records, rather than to information itself. It thus generally fails, for example, to consider the question of whether it is legal to disclose data held in a computer. In the United Kingdom, for example, the Data Protection Act allows individuals access to information about themselves if it is kept on a computer; if the information is kept on paper, their rights are different.

Accuracy of information

The laws of evidence, as they relate to the role of computer information and computer-generated information, need to be clarified. If an individual or organization contributes data to a centralized system then there needs to be agreement about the legal responsibility for the quality and accuracy of those data. Within most cadastral systems, the responsibility for the data, once entered into the system, lies with the organizer of the system. This is normally central government. Consequently, in order to protect itself, it insists that privately executed surveys may only be carried out by those licensed to do so. None the less the government carries out meticulous checks on the work of licensed surveys, which adds significantly to the cost and delay in their completion. If such a system is to be extended to all forms of data contributed by the private sector, the resulting land information system will probably become unworkable.

Commenting on the security, confidentiality, and privacy of the data held in South Australia, Williamson has reported that:

A comprehensive Land Information System of the type envisaged for the State will hold a considerable amount of data that might be considered socially or politically sensitive. Even at the current level of development where the only 'personal' data open to computerized access is already available on other media—concerns have been expressed relating to the removal of the 'difficulty' barrier . . . Considering the number of individual data elements, files, data bases and machines comprising the total system, and the variety and potential directions of access to that data, the protection of individual and corporate rights is seen as a major issue of the future . . . It is considered that data 'ownership' will need to be clearly defined in all future developments, and that any restrictions on the rights of access be vigorously protected.[21]

10.8   Data standards and exchange

Although administrative mechanisms may exist for the exchange of land-related data between government departments, they may not operate effectively. At a technical level, national standards for the exchange of data will almost certainly need to be established. These should cover data transfer formats, data classification, and accuracy standards.[22] Although such standards as already exist are directed towards the exchange of data rather than at internal procedures of operation, they inevitably change the way that things are done.

There is a need for co-operation between all producers and users of land information. Unfortunately, interdepartmental rivalry occurs in almost every country. Even within a land survey department the cadastral staff may not know or co-operate with what the topographic branch is doing. There is a conflict of interests and lack of co-operation between those maintaining land records, such as a register of titles, those keeping assessment records and those involved in land survey. Each, however, has a role to play in the team of land information managers. For example, the role of the land surveyor may be defined as that of providing the physical, social, and institutional information necessary for the allocation, development, and conservation of land resources. From this perspective, the functions of the surveyor may include the delimitation of human settlements, the delineation of the earth's natural and artificial features, and the measurement of people's social and economic impact on the land. The surveyor may be viewed as an information specialist and, in a more general sense, as a participant in the land resource management process. A similar perspective may be developed for the other land professions.

The management of any centralized land information system and the effective networking of that system with other organizations depend both on national policies and on continuing resource allocations. An individual department is unlikely to be able to develop a computerized land information system on its own. Systems often begin as minor technical improvements to what has always been done, introducing a limited amount of computer equipment to overcome clearly defined problems. Slowly and inevitably, relationships with external bodies begin to develop and then become more complex. It is therefore important to establish what computing facilities exist within other government departments and what maintenance facilities exist for the upkeep of computer hardware and software. With time, the interfacing of one system with another is becoming easier from a technical point of view, and national standards of data transfer are beginning to emerge. None the less, no single government department can operate a land information system without considering the national implications.

10.9 LINZ—a case history

New Zealand presents an interesting land information management case study from both an institutional and an organizational perspective. The national government has been concerned about the development of a modern land information system (LINZ) for several years, and has recently formed a new Department of Survey and Land Information.

New Zealand shares certain similarities with the Maritime Provinces of Canada (see Chapter 4) inasmuch as it is a relatively small, resource-based economy, with a land administrative structure based on the common-law tradition. It has an area of 268 046 square kilometres and a population of approximately 3.2 million, the vast majority of whom are located in urban areas. The economy of New Zealand is based largely on agriculture, the export of dairy, wool, and meat products being primary sources of income. Approximately a quarter of the country is forested, and timber and forest products are also major contributors to the national economy. Unlike the Maritimes, New Zealand has a well-established surveying and mapping framework and a national policy for land administration. Almost all of the title to land in private ownership is based on the Torrens land titles system.

The survey system

The Department of Lands and Survey manage an integrated survey system through the maintenance of a national survey control framework, the examination and approval of all subdivision survey plans, all of which are co-ordinated in terms of the survey control grid, and through the maintenance of a national cadastral record mapping series, which continuously reflects the latest subdivision of land parcels within the country. Cadastral record maps are maintained on a district office basis to show day to day changes in the cadastre at scales of 1 and 2 chains to an inch for urban areas and 10 chains to the inch for rural areas (metric conversion to 1:1000 and 1:10 000 was begun in 1973). The system identifies the boundaries of each land parcel, its survey plan number, appellation, area, and details of any gazetting.

Computerization

Of particular interest in New Zealand is the role that the national surveying and mapping organization has taken in attempting to form a co-ordinated approach to the introduction and application of computer technology to land-related fields. New Zealand was relatively late in introducing computers into public administration. Gradual development of computing into the line agencies of government became important only in the late 1970s. As elsewhere, computerization was largely based on *ad hoc* decisions by individual organizations who were setting up systems to meet their own requirements without concern for the broader community. This has led to considerable duplication of data recording (for example, the government has identified at least seven separate environmental data bases), the *ad hoc* growth of computerization of land-related records in various central government departments, and subsequently a call for wider access to data and minimization of duplication.

In 1983, following several years of study and recommendation, the New Zealand government issued a series of directives calling for a co-ordinated and co-operative approach to the development of computerized systems to be used in the collection, maintenance, and dissemination of land information within the public sector. It is estimated that the establishment of a national LIS for New Zealand may ultimately cost in excess of $30 million. Government has developed a policy of cost recovery on all electronic data-processing ventures; therefore the LINZ strategy involves concentrating on those data sets that can provide a positive return on investment over a relatively short period of time.

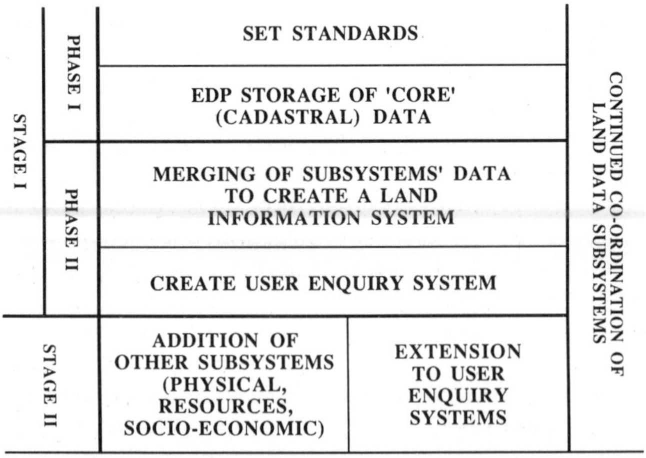

STAGE I	PHASE I	SET STANDARDS	CONTINUED CO-ORDINATION OF LAND DATA SUBSYSTEMS
		EDP STORAGE OF 'CORE' (CADASTRAL) DATA	
	PHASE II	MERGING OF SUBSYSTEMS' DATA TO CREATE A LAND INFORMATION SYSTEM	
		CREATE USER ENQUIRY SYSTEM	
STAGE II		ADDITION OF OTHER SUBSYSTEMS (PHYSICAL, RESOURCES, SOCIO-ECONOMIC)	EXTENSION TO USER ENQUIRY SYSTEMS

Fig. 10.5　*LINZ—New Zealand (from LINZNEWS No. 1)*

LINZ objectives

With this in mind, Cabinet approved the development of the first phase of a comprehensive land information system with the following objectives:

(1) the rationalization of data capture and maintenance of land-related data within the public service;
(2) the standardization of common access keys to land data (such as the appellation of land, street address, and geographic location);
(3) the establishment of a core LIS (see Fig. 10.5).

The core LIS

The development of a comprehensive national LIS is seen as a long-term project, of which the development of a legal/fiscal cadastre core system is a major initial step. This core system will require the capture of some 3.5 million cadastral parcels, with over 2 million titles and 25 000 Maori titles. By the end of 1986, only the valuation data were fully computerized. The core LIS is to be established by developing:

(1) a computerized cadastral data base;
(2) a computerized land transfer journal system and computerized index to titles;
(3) a computerized index to Maori land titles and ownership;
(4) the standardization of appellation and street address within the existing computerized valuation system;
(5) the development of a pilot model to illustrate possible linkages between land data systems and to demonstrate the LINZ concept.

In support of these objectives, the government had, by the end of 1986, awarded a joint tender for the supply of hardware and software for the department's Digital Cadastral Data Base. More than 40 VAX work-stations were being purchased to be distributed among the department's 12 district offices. The digital capture of the department's existing cadastral data, currently held on 15 000 manually drawn record maps, is expected to take four years to complete. The Department of Justice has computerized the land transfer journal. Since May 1986, this has been made available to the public in Auckland and New Plymouth offices in order to carry out user tests. Good progress has been reported and the system appears to be operating smoothly. Design work has now begun on the second computer project, which is to computerize the land transfer indices. The data conversion of the Maori Land Court records is also well under way.

The policy, development, and operation of the core LIS is being directed by a LINZ Board of Management, the final accountability being with the Surveyor-General and the Minister of Lands. An Inter-departmental Con-sultative Committee advises the Surveyor-General on the co-ordination and development of both existing and planned land information systems.

At the same time, a LINZ Support Group has been created to provide operation support for both the Board of Management and the Consultative Committee. Its responsibilities are to:

(1) advise and report to the Surveyor-General in his capacity as Chairman of the Board and Co-ordinator of the Committee on the core LIS project and the co-ordination of other land-related projects.
(2) co-ordinate, plan, and manage the departmental core subprojects.
(3) develop a small-scale pilot project to test linkages to other subsystems and to demonstrate the system.
(4) develop a reference directory of geographic data and standards for LIS development;
(5) analyse LIS user feedback to assist in determining future LIS development strategies.[23]

The Department of Survey and Land Information

Most recently the government has announced the creation of a separate Department of Survey and Land Information, comprising the Survey and Mapping Division of the Department of Lands and Survey and some advisory, statutory and regulatory functions in respect of Crown Land. This new department has the following objectives:

To administer, integrate and extend the survey and mapping systems supporting secure land tenure, communication, and efficient administrations of government.
To ensure the provision of topographic, cadastral and other land data bases to adequate standards for the efficient administration, enjoyment and development of the resources of New Zealand.
To provide survey, mapping and information services.
To promote and manage the generation, coordination, assessment and integration of data on land and associated resources.[24]

References

1. United Nations Ad Hoc Group of Experts (1973). Cadastral surveying and mapping. *Seventh United Nations Regional Cartographic Conference for Asia and the Far East*, Tokyo, Vol. II, Technical Papers (No. E.74.I.25).
2. Diebold, J. (1985). *Managing information: the challenge and the opportunity*; AMACOM.
3. *Major surveys: a study team report to the task force on program review* (1986). p. 11, 12. Supply and Services Canada, Ottawa.
4. *Plan of action for the economic development of Africa 1980–2000* (1980). para 87(i) of Chapter 111 on National Resources, Lagos.
5. Wood, A. (1986). Evaluating the viability of implementing an urban

land information system in the city of Bangkok, Thailand. Paper presented to the *XVIII International Congress of F.I.G.*, Toronto, paper 310.3, pp. 5, 6.

6. Barnes, G. (1986). Cultural dynamics and emerging land information needs in Africa. *Technical Papers of the ACSM-ASPRS Annual Convention*, Vol. 3, Washington.

7. United Nations (1976). *Report of habitat: United Nations Conference on Human Settlements*, (A/Conf. 70/15), p. 6. Stockholm.

8. *Report of the Meeting of the Ad Hoc Group of Experts on Cadastral Surveying and Land Information Systems* (1985), UN publication No. E/CONF.77/L.1, p. 19. Berlin.

9. Williamson, I. P. (1985). *Report of the Working Group on Statewide Parcel-based Land Information Systems in Australasia*, p. 35. AURISA, Technical Monograph No. 1, Sydney.

10. *Major surveys: a study team report to the task force on program review* (1986). p. 29. Supply and Services Canada, Ottawa.

11. Williamson, I. P. *Op. Cit.*, p. 23.

12. McKay, L. J. and Walker, W. J. (1985). Land-related systems in Alberta—an overview. In Hamilton, A. and McLaughlin, J. (eds) *The decision maker and land information systems*. Papers and Proceedings from the FIG International Symposium, Edmonton, 1984. p. 215. Canadian Institute of Surveying, Ottawa.

13. Sedunary, M. E. (1985). LOTS and the nodal approach to a total land information system. In Hamilton, A. and McLaughlin, J. (eds) *The decision maker and land information systems*. Papers and Proceedings from the FIG International Symposium, Edmonton, 1984. p. 77. Canadian Institute of Surveying, Ottawa.

14. *Western Australian land information system: management summary* (1982). Government of Western Australia, Perth.

15. Williamson, I. P. *Op. cit.*, p. 35.

16. McEwen, A. (1985). Institutional aspects of a cadastre. Paper presented to the World Bank Seminar on Land Information Systems, Annapolis, p. 10.

17. United Nations Ad Hoc Group of Experts (1973). Cadastral surveying and mapping. *Op. cit.*

18. De Hennsler, M. (1985). In *Proceedings of the United Nations Inter-Regional Seminar on the Role of Surveying, Mapping and Charting in Country Development Programming*. Aylmer, Quebec, 1985. p. 24. Surveys & Mapping Branch, EMR Canada.

19. Dunkerley, H. (1985). Land information systems for developing countries. Paper presented to the *Fifth General Assembly and Symposium*, Commonwealth Association of Surveying and Land Economy, Kuala Lumpur.

20. Sulaiman, M. S. (1983). The need for technical assistance in surveying and mapping. *Proceedings of Conference of Commonwealth Surveyors*, Cambridge, paper 13.

21. Williamson, I. P. *Op. cit.*, p. 28.

22. For a general discussion of the issues, see Blakemore, M. (ed.) (1985). *Proceedings of Auto Carto London*, Vol. 1, pp. 282–401. Auto Carto London Ltd, London.

23. Williamson, I. P. *Op. cit.*
24. Hawkey, W. (1986). A new department of survey and land information for New Zealand. *Commonwealth Surveying and Land Economy*, No. 23, p. 6.

11. Management issues

In this chapter we examine, from a management perspective, some of the resources and constraints that affect the operation of a land information system.

11.1 The management framework

Management is the art and science of making decisions in support of certain perceived objectives. Like politics, it is the art of achieving the possible. It must achieve the implementation of policy decisions and the accomplishment of objectives in an optimum fashion, as perfect solutions never arise. Management entails extrapolating trends from a limited range of facts. Sufficient information is never available for decisions to be made with certain outcome (see Table 11.1).

Better knowledge and information tend to bring about a better understanding of a system and hence create the possibility for better management. Within many cadastral organizations, for example, the availability of management statistics on productivity and the true cost of the service are severely limited. Productivity is often low, and the total time and cost spent on individual cadastral surveys from initial request to final acceptance is high. On occasions, the real cost of producing a paper description of a land parcel may be higher than the market price of the land itself. There is often

Table 11.1 Three categories of managerial activity

1. **Strategic planning**—process of deciding on organization objectives, on changes to these objectives, on the resources employed to achieve them, and on the policies that are to govern the acquisition, use, and disposition of these resources
2. **Management control**—process by which managers assure that resources are obtained and used effectively in accomplishing the organization's objectives
3. **Operational control**—process of assuring that specific tasks are carried out effectively and efficiently

little analysis of who uses land information and the form in which it is required. This lack of understanding has been reflected in the low operating efficiency of land information systems. Significant cost savings may, however, be possible with improved management and administration. A first step on the road to improvement is to acquire better management information.

System deficiencies

Many cadastral systems are conservative by nature. They are victims of their twentieth century history, following procedures and objectives that were laid down for times and conditions that are no longer relevant. Many practitioners are unable or unwilling to implement change for a variety of reasons. For instance, improvements may appear to need changes in the legislation. People also fear that, without the confidence of those people who have been or will appear upon the cadastral registers, their choices of action are severely restricted. Yet much can in practice be done to improve their system, to increase productivity, to reduce costs, and to increase benefits.

Planning improvements

The first stage in planning improvements is to examine more precisely the framework within which the current system operates. The rights and procedures associated with existing land records should be closely documented and the legal, physical, financial, administrative, social, and political influences upon them identified. The initial analysis should concentrate on the legal cadastre, for all other forms of the cadastre tend to have fewer constraints and can operate on the basis of lower technical standards.

Often the most immediate benefits that arise from the creation or improvement of a land information system come from the fiscal cadastre. The best strategy for improving a system may, in the short term, be to concentrate on those areas that generate revenue. In the overall appraisal, however, all types of land record should be examined, including those relating to the utilities and underground services on the one hand, and to land use and land resources on the other. The development of a multipurpose cadastre or a broad-based land information system may not be a matter of immediate concern. It may, however, be a source of additional benefits at limited additional cost.

11.2   Organizational factors

Part of the management process entails dealing with resources; part is concerned with organization. An inevitable concomitant of computerization is the need for reorganization. A classic statement attributed to Petronius may be translated as:

We trained hard, but it seemed that every time we were beginning to form up into teams we would be reorganized. I was to learn later in life that we tend to meet any new situation by reorganizing and a wonderful method it can be for creating the illusion of progress while only producing inefficiency and demoralization.

Though written in AD 66, the statement above could well have been written today. Organizational and management structures need to be documented if the management process is to be properly understood, so that levels of responsibility and the flow of management information and statistics can be refined. A variety of organizational models exist. Some are based on the pyramid with hierarchical levels of responsibility; others have more worker participation. Since the prime responsibility for land information, especially in connection with land titles, will lie with government, some of the organizational arrangements will lie beyond the control of the land information manager. They raise major institutional issues, some of which were touched on in Chapter 10. Some matters of reorganization are, however, very much within the manager's control.

Organizational structures

The conventional organizational structure, for example, is to adopt a functional approach in which separate departments or sections are responsible for each specialist activity. Thus, in a survey organization, one section may be responsible for control surveys, one for topographic detail work, one for cadastral, one for photogrammetric, one for cartographic, and so on. A production manager is then needed to co-ordinate the work. According to Drucker,[1] functional structures have the great advantage of clarity, for everybody can understand his or her specialist task. As a result, the system is highly stable and is well suited for a workload where there are many small projects that must be completed in relatively short periods of time. This is generally so for land information products and services. The alternative approach is to form a special project team to tackle an assignment. This is more appropriate to specialized projects, for example to establish a totally new system or to undertake major reform and restructuring of an existing one.

Management needs to understand the important elements of what is going on if it is to manage effectively. The type and amount of management information available to managers should be identified, especially that relating to the measurement of costs and productivity. In some countries, such as Bahrain, there is a sophisticated computerized management information system available to those running the cadastral programme. Many countries, however, have limited information on record at the level of detail that is necessary to determine how and what needs to be done to improve matters. Many survey departments in Third World countries cannot even gather enough information to publish an annual report. Survey tasks may simply be given a job number with no indication of their magnitude or complexity. They may then be evaluated on the basis of a scale of fees that is wholly unrealistic in comparison with any true measures of time and cost. Senior management needs enough information to determine areas of weakness and to be able to formulate policies; it should not, however, be smothered by a welter of statistics.

11.3   Matters relating to land registration

Management must be concerned with the technical and administrative framework within which a system operates. The day to day concerns of organizing, scheduling and supervising existing tasks combine with an endless string of meetings to prevent many managers from reassessing fundamental objectives and constraints. Some of these constraints stem from the law. All information systems work within a framework of legislation but those which are concerned with land are more tightly constrained than most. Legislation may affect the licensing of surveyors, adjudication, monumentation, the conduct of surveys and the maintenance and dissemination of information in the registers.

Statutory and customary rights

If the information system is to include matters concerning land tenure and land registration, then it will be necessary to establish what rights in land are recognized by statute and what are adopted by custom. Some of the differences between common or customary law and statutory law may be subsumed within a framework of overriding interests. Some rights may be formally recognized, such as easements, leases, and subleases, but others, such as the rights of squatters, may not be subject to general agreement. The possible contents of the 'bundle of rights' that relate to each parcel of land need to be examined to ensure that only those that are necessary and sufficient for the orderly use of the land are included within the registers. In city areas, for example where high-rise development has become common, it may be necessary to introduce strata titles. Rights to space above and below ground level have often been ignored. In certain environments, they are now of critical importance.

Titles

What legally constitutes the root of any title to land should be linked through a chain of titles to the present, unless the state is to impose a new pattern of ownership by decree. Under a normal system of registration, the state guarantees each title to land. In so doing, it may be anxious to avoid taking risks and hence be overcautious. This results in unnecessary delays and expense. Risk taking is a part of effective management. Gambling is, however, another matter; reasonable precautions need to be taken to minimize the effects of carelessness and corruption. But if every aspect of a Certificate of Title and its supporting survey are to be meticulously checked, then the hidden costs may significantly exceed the benefits gained.

Transfer of land rights

The transfer of rights in land is subject to well-established procedures. Some of these procedures are complex and lengthy. Detailed flow charts should be prepared showing the stages through which an application for land transfer must pass (see for example Table 11.2). The duration of each operation should also be noted. In some systems, the formal transfer of property from one owner to another may take minutes, in some it may take days, and in others months. In some countries, where precise cadastral surveys must be carried out and meticulously checked, the delay in completion may be measured in years. The percentage of time that is accounted for by legislative, administrative, and survey operations should be noted. Every minute of delay can cost money because investment and development are held back.

Table 11.2 Typical sequence for dealing with land application

Application for land parcel submitted:

To **Chief Lands Officer** for processing then
  To **Land Board** for approval then
  To **Chief Lands Officer** for initial then

To **Surveyor General** for survey then
  To **cadastral records** for data then
  To **district office** for local action then
  To **field surveyor** for setting out and survey then
  To **district surveyor** for checking then

To **Surveyor General** for checking then
  To **computing/examination section** for checking then
  To **plans section** for plotting then
  To **fees section** for assessing survey costs then

To **Surveyor General** for approval then
  To **Chief Lands Officer** for approval then
  To **Registrar of Titles** for registration then
  To **cadastral records** for final recording then

Notification and fee sent to applicant

Records maintenance

The maintenance of the records is as important as their initial creation. The manner in which land rights are sold, given away or inherited will, in part, determine how easy it is to keep the records up to date. The maintenance of land ownership records depends upon the existence of a Land Registry or appropriate local court registers, together with compulsory notification of changes in land ownership. There may, however, be no legal requirement to register any sale, gift, or other transfer of rights in land, either in whole or in part. In such cases, existing records of ownership may not be a true reflection of the actual situation. This is particularly so where fragmentation results from the system of inheritance. Fragmentation, leading to the multiplicity of parcels or of owners, causes major problems both for the land and for the maintenance of registers. Changes in the system of inheritance may be beneficial to the use of the land but are unlikely to be practicable, for they raise major social issues. There is, however, little point in improving the record-keeping process if the records are not maintained and rapidly become out of date.

Adjudication

A particular aspect of land registration is adjudication—the legal process for determining rights in land. Adjudication may take place from existing records. These may not, however, reflect the situation on the ground. It may be necessary to hold courts and to take evidence on site from occupiers and other interested parties. The existing procedures for the adjudication of title to land should be reviewed and the economic and social advantages of systematic adjudication weighed against the sporadic. Systematic adjudication is possible only if there are powers of compulsion to bring land on to the register. The acceptance of such powers by the public will, in part, depend on what happens to land where the owner cannot be traced. If an absent landowner becomes dispossessed through no fault of his own, there will be hostility to the whole adjudication process.

Boundaries

The procedures for adjudication may include the determination and demarcation of boundaries. The precision with which boundaries must be determined will depend not only upon the legislation, but also upon local customs and the size and type of monumentation that is adopted. In ex-colonial territories it is not uncommon to find that the standards that have become daily cadastral practice are not in fact legally necessary. The most common example is where there is a conflict of evidence between measurements and monuments. The regulations decree that 'pegs are paramount to plans' and that occupation takes precedence over measurements recorded in documents. However, those responsible for implementing such a policy may, in practice, reverse the process. For this reason, the relationship between the '*de jure*' and the '*de facto*' positions of boundaries often needs to be clarified. The methods by which existing land parcels are described and referenced should be examined and the relationship of the legal position as shown in the records contrasted with the actual practice on the ground. This is crucial to an assessment of the standards needed for survey. If the law lays emphasis on monumentation rather than on measurement, as is the case in many jurisdictions, then the justification for high-class surveys cannot be based on cadastral arguments.

The justification for much of cadastral surveying is often based on the premise that it is to prevent boundary disputes. Disputes exist both over the ownership of whole parcels of land and over boundaries. The solution may, however, lie in adjudication and better monumentation rather than more expensive survey. The cause, frequency, and nature of disputes over land need to be analysed and a distinction made between those that genuinely relate to boundaries, those that relate to the ownership and use of some feature near the boundary, those that are essentially a breakdown in neighbourly relationships, and those that concern a substantial area of land as a whole. It may be that procedures are needed to resolve disputes specifically over boundaries on a sporadic basis; it could be, however, that systematic adjudication is needed. The legal uncertainty about ownership may be easy to remedy if the law provides for the prescription of rights in land through the processes of adverse possession or through the workings of a statute of limitations. These may help to resolve disputes over small areas of land, or over boundaries, by permitting occupation to be the primary source of evidence.

Though some countries may have legislation that requires certain categories of land to be fenced for health and safety reasons, such as along railway lines, there has been in general no legislation requiring people to fence the land along their boundaries. A fence is regarded in most legal systems as an item of defence and a guard against intrusion. In areas of 'open-plan' urban design, the erection of fences may be positively discouraged. If any form of monumentation is laid down in law, then the question of who is responsible for the preservation of boundary marks arises. Some jurisdictions lay down penalties to be imposed if such marks are disturbed though more often than not they are rarely used. The percentage of corner pegs that are disturbed or lost should be determined as this may indicate a need to invoke such penalties, particularly where developers have a cavalier attitude to boundary marks when using earth-moving equipment.

As a general statement of principle, the records of land ownership should be complete in terms of both owners and rights, up to date, and accessible to the public. They should also as far as possible be complete in terms of spatial cover. In order to achieve these objectives, the land information manager will need (Table 11.3) to:

(1) establish the exact legal parameters within which the system must work;
(2) clarify legal priorities such as the precedence of the evidence of pegs and monuments as against plans and measurements;
(3) have statistics available on the numbers of transfers and mutations that can be expected in any area and on the number of land and boundary disputes;
(4) determine suitable criteria by which priority areas may be selected;
(5) take risks, remembering the 50–95 rule that often 95 per cent of the benefits can often be achieved at only 50 per cent of the cost of taking greater care.

11.4 Survey procedures

Survey evaluation

Survey procedures account for 30–40 per cent of the cost of a cadastral system and in some cases up to 90 per cent of the time taken in registering a property. A major factor that influences the cost of a survey is the specification to which the surveyors must work. Any reappraisal of a land information system should evaluate whether the present standards of survey are both necessary and sufficient. It should also consider how these standards are monitored, since the checking and cross-checking of work gives rise to much additional cost (see Table 11.2 above). The cost effectiveness of present procedures needs to be assessed. The average overhead costs of cadastral surveys are normally between two and three times their labour costs. They should be compared with the scales of fees that are currently

Table 11.3 Completing the land registers

Ownership records should be:
- Complete
- Up to date
- Accessible

In order to complete the registers, land information managers should:
- Understand the legal constraints
- Clarify legal precedents
- Have statistical evidence available
- Determine priority areas
- Take risks

charged since the basis on which the fees are assessed frequently does not relate to the true costs of each survey. Governments, consciously or otherwise, almost always subsidize cadastral surveying, for example by the failure to charge for governmental work in the detailed checking of surveys. The level of subsidy should at least be known to those responsible for managing the system. Managers should have a clear understanding of how long an average survey takes to carry out and then to get approval from those responsible for checking it.

Capital investment

Increasingly, surveyors are using high technology to help with their work. Evidence from Canada shows the dramatic increase in capital investment by single licensed surveyors; the value of their equipment has risen almost tenfold from $10 000 to $100 000 over the last decade.[2] In addition, there are higher charges for maintenance and insurance. Plans must be made for new levels of capitalization and a faster recovery on the investment. The higher the capital investment, the greater is the risk of financial disaster for any small company or organization that fails to increase its productivity significantly or to find alternative markets for its products. A twofold increase in productivity can be sustained only if either there is an opportunity for twice as much work or else the workforce is halved.

Legal aspects

In all systems, the written record in a surveyor's field book may be taken as evidence by a court and hence field notes should be treated as legal documents. Fortunately for many surveyors, this is rarely done in practice. None the less, the relative responsibilities of the surveyor and the land information manager need to be determined. Many systems guarantee title to land. Few have established the precise limits to those guarantees. When information systems are opened up to more public access, more users will make decisions on the basis of the information provided. The degree to which the user may sue the land information manager for the consequences of decisions arising from erroneous information needs to be established.

Professional bodies

In many countries, private surveyors are licensed to undertake cadastral surveys and must operate within a particular section of the law. Increasingly, the licensed surveyors are becoming organized into a professional body, through the work and influence of organizations such as the Commonwealth Association for Surveying and Land Economy (C A S L E). The powers and, more importantly, the responsibilities of such a body need to be carefully scrutinized, for its co-operation may be critical to the pace and success of change. Dunkerley referred to:[3]

the need for revisions in policies and a more integrated approach to L I S. 'Integrated' is an appropriate word here. More coordination of interested parties is essential for the development of long-term strategies and for shorter term viable programs which identify priority uses and minimum needs in terms of technologies, staffing, training and financing. Given the severe general resource constraints, an iterative approach seems to me inevitable. Incremental costs and benefits for a variety of major uses need to be considered and subsidiary uses identified, together with both the financial and economic returns. A phased or progressive approach also appears imperative so that the results attained in practice and the actual costs can be monitored and programs modified accordingly. I do not minimize the inherent difficulties of introducing major policy changes and coordinating public agency activities. It will not be easy.

Private and public surveying

Strategies for improving a cadastral system will depend in part upon the percentage of cadastral surveys undertaken by government surveyors rather than by the private sector. Although free enterprise can bring down costs through competition, this often does not apply to the cadastre. Governments often prescribe not only the ways in which surveys must be carried out but also the scales of fees that are acceptable. These may not, on their own, provide adequate remuneration and are often used only as a basis for costing work carried out on behalf of government rather than for private clients. The regulations that govern the licensing of surveyors and the conduct of their work need frequent review, particularly at a time of rapid change in technology and techniques. In many countries, cadastral surveys are now based on the national triangulation network. The density of that control is a major determining factor in the time and cost of surveys. This network is established and maintained by the public sector. If the work of the private sector is to be incorporated into the national archive, then the maintenance of standards and questions of cost recovery will need to be agreed.

Overall there will be a need to:

(1) determine more precisely the costs and times taken for each phase of a survey, from setting out through processing to graphic presentation;
(2) analyse the cost effectiveness of incorporating elements that do not appear traditionally in the legal or fiscal cadastre;
(3) examine the advantages or otherwise of using non-governmental surveyors to gather data;
(4) ensure that adequate standards of data exchange between organizations are available and are implemented (Table 11.4);
(5) structure the data so that rapid access to important features is possible;
(6) maintain disaster copies of essential data.

Table 11.4 Exchanging digital map data

Digital data transfer standards:
1. Must be able to handle all types of data
2. Data must be transferable out from and into the data base with the same integrity
3. Must work with all available computer systems
4. Must be cheap to introduce
5. Must be easy to maintain

11.5 Financial matters

The land information manager should be familiar with accounting procedures and should be able to provide financial justifications for all operations within the system he or she controls. Cost considerations arise when:

(1) choosing optimum techniques;
(2) identifying priority areas for extending the system;
(3) estimating the cost effectiveness of subcontracting more work to the private sector;
(4) evaluating strategies for cost recovery through higher fees, sales of information, and taxes;
(5) analysing the cost effectiveness of linking any existing land records with a wider range of land information.

The average value of the land and the rate at which dealings in land take place are factors to be considered when selecting the areas in which to concentrate resources. The manager should know on what basis the value of land is determined, whether the information on which it is based is currently up to date, and what percentage of properties have been assessed or appraised. If the value of the land is calculated on the basis of the produce derived from it, rather than from the market value of the land, then different information may need to be stored within the system. In either case, the information required by the valuer or appraiser will need to be identified, and the form and nature of the relationship between the legal and the fiscal registers reviewed.

Transfer tax

In determining strategies for cost recovery, it will be necessary to know whether there is a tax on the transfer of land (sometimes referred to as stamp duty), and if so on what basis it is assessed. Stamp duty may provide revenue that helps to subsidize the public costs of conveyancing. Land tax revenue should at least cover the costs of the fiscal cadastre, though in some areas of the world this is not always the case. With low land values or low productivity, the tax may be less than the unit cost of survey and record keeping. In some countries the assessed value may be based on false returns by the landowners.

Charges for information

Appropriate scales of fees to charge for the use of the information in a multipurpose cadastre are more difficult to assess. Too high a charge will discourage its use; too low a revenue will discourage government from investing in the system. In Great Britain, government policies in the 1970s forced the price of the Ordnance Survey large-scale maps up so that, although the sales declined, the revenue from sales still increased. If the value of a map lies in what is saved through its use rather than in the price for which it can be sold, then the greater the use, the greater is the value. The policies adopted for pricing land information systems products will pay a key role in the success or otherwise of their development.

11.6 Co-ordination

Planning regulations

The land information manager will need to be conversant with matters relating to planning and development. Planning laws constrain what can be done with land and hence what information needs to be known about it. In many countries, the law lays down controls over land use and the manner in which these controls are to be enforced. Regulations may, for example, govern the maximum and minimum sizes of land parcels and the width of road reserves and plot frontages. The policing of these will depend on co-operation between the land surveyors who work in the field, those who administer land surveying, and those concerned with town planning development control. At a simple level, it is helpful if town planning boundaries coincide with land parcel boundaries. This has not necessarily happened in the past because plans showing property boundaries have not been readily available.

Assessment of information needs

Frequently the information requirements of planners are unknown outside their own ranks. The surveying and mapping community, for example, provides base maps but has often been unconcerned with the less physical aspects of the environment which are of concern to the land use planner. If the land information system is to serve the needs of a wider community, then the manager must know what land-related information that community uses or would find useful. It may be that sampling techniques will provide an adequate level of information more quickly, more cheaply and more contemporaneously than full-scale surveys. The compilation of comprehensive records of soils, geology, land use, and land potential may be an ideal that is not economically viable at present. An incomplete picture, based on random or systematic sampling, may be both necessary and sufficient for all practical purposes.

Public utility mapping

In similar vein, the land information manager needs to understand the nature and extent of mapping of all public utility services, especially that relating to items buried underground. Although such mapping is generally regarded as desirable, it may be unattainable for both technical and economic reasons. Buried features may be undetectable or locatable at an unacceptable cost. Occasionally, pipelines are recorded as easements in the legal registers. In most countries, the records of underground features are non-existent or very unreliable. Many cities need to renew their underground sewers and stormwater drains, but have no adequate records of where they are. A land information system has a major role to play in support of such refurbishment, provided that the data are structured in a readily accessible form. The public utility companies are a major driving force behind the development of land information systems, with organizations such as AM/FM (Automated Mapping and Facilities Management) spearheading the way.

Data exchange

If there is to be a free exchange of information between users of a land information system then standards must exist for the exchange of digital map and land-related data. The data affected may include basic topographic mapping, local land charges such as for work carried out by a local authority, planning restrictions imposed under town and country planning regulations, compulsory purchase orders, and orders designating specific types of land use. All these items of information are needed every time there is a dealing in a parcel. They should therefore be linked to the proprietary registers with an appropriate unique parcel identifier. It is probable that, in due course, such information will be obtainable from remotely situated terminals in such places as banks, lawyers' offices, or mortgage company offices—much as airline ticket counters now have display screens showing flight reservations. The land information manager needs to anticipate such a development so that the necessary procedures are established to facilitate such data exchange.

Overall, the manager needs to be able to distinguish between:

(1)   what needs to be recorded; and
(2)   what it would be nice to have recorded.

11.7   Human factors in computerization

Management is also about people. Opportunities need to exist for staff development in order to identify those staff who have management potential, but also to provide motivation and encouragement for those who may never make it to the top. In particular, resources need to be allocated to the training and motivation of middle managers; they often hold the key to the implementation of reforms. Senior management inevitably becomes involved in politics and policy formation. It is the responsibility of the middle manager to ensure that the jobs get done.

Much has been written elsewhere about the management of human resources.[4] Governments have their own policies with regard to manpower employment and the extent to which systems must be capital rather than labour intensive. Since the future of land information systems will be closely related to high technology, clear strategies for coping with the impact of such developments need to be worked out. Computerization has far-reaching effects upon the structure of and relationships within organizations. Particular attention needs to be paid to health and safety and to staff motivation. Much of what was traditionally a skill, such as manual map production, is becoming fully automated. Part of the process of map making may still require skills, as in manual digitizing; others, such as raster digitizing, require no craft skill at all. All too often the level of job satisfaction is low and the opportunities for the human to make decisions become more rare. Boredom can quickly set in and with it comes the making of mistakes.

Staff categories

Within the day to day operations of a land information system there are a number of specific tasks that are carried out by different categories of staff. These have been analysed by McGrath as:[5]

(1)   *The system manager* whose task is to take the general overview of the system and its environment, identifying and responding to user needs. He or she should be a graduate with an understanding of computer science and surveying or one of the earth sciences. The system manager must be a good administrator and should if possible have a postgraduate qualification in one of the land or geographic information system courses that are now available.[6]
(2)   *The data base manager*, who is responsible for the design and operation of the data bases. He or she should have a higher degree in computer science and for preference should have gained experience in handling spatially related data.

(3) *The systems analyst/designer*, whose tasks include bench-mark testing, supervising installations, problem analysis, and the evaluation and implementation of design proposals. Such staff should at least have a first degree in computer science.

(4) *The programmer*, who will write any necessary software to implement modifications such as new algorithms or interfaces to new extensions of the system.

(5) *The systems engineer* who is the computer scientist or electronics engineer responsible for the operation and maintenance of the system.

(6) *The systems operator*, who should be a graduate or diplomate and is responsible for the daily operation of the system.

(7) *The terminal operator*, who is responsible for the input of data and for carrying out work at a workstation.

Information flow

In analysing the flow of information in a digital mapping project (Fig. 11.1) and the specialist levels of knowledge between a conventional and a digital

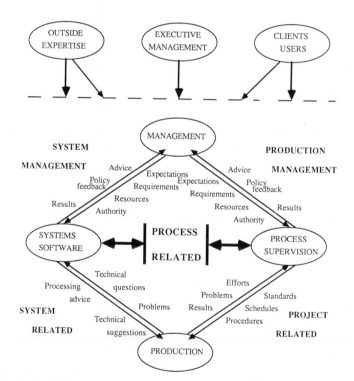

Fig. 11.1   *Information flow: digital mapping project (from Coleman and McLaughlin[7])*

POSITION UNDERSTANDS	Senior Mgt.	Process Super-vision	Technical Expertise	PRODUCTION STAFF Experienced	New
Needs and Demands of Marketplace and Users	● ○	● ○	● ○	○ ▨	▨ ▨
Form of Final Product	● ○	● ▨	● ●	● Hardcopy	○ Digital
Product Strengths and Limitations	● ▨	● ○	● ○	● ▨	○ ▨
Production Tasks	○ ▨	● ●	○ ▨	● ●	○ ●
Data Processing Requirements	○ ▨	○ ○	● ●	▨ ▨	▨ ○
Overall Production Process	● ○	○ ▨	○ ○	○ ▨	▨ ▨

● Yes　　○ Some　　▨ No　　| Manual / Digital |

Fig. 11.2　*Specialized knowledge in mapping operations (from Coleman and McLaughlin[7])*

mapping flowline (Fig. 11.2), Coleman and McLaughlin found that for the latter:[7]

(1) senior management had some appreciation for market demands but rarely understood the processing requirements or production limitations;

(2) technical specialists, if newly hired, understood the hardware and software limitations but rarely had an appreciation of mapping demands;

(3) technical specialists who had been retrained understood the processes but did not fully appreciate the increased management requirements of a major system;

(4) process supervisors, accustomed to labour-intensive operations, were often frustrated by the newly imposed system considerations and the implications of 'black-box' technology on their craft;

(5) production staff viewed both the intermediate processes and the final product in very different ways, according to whether they were veteran conventional mapping technicians or newly trained computer work-station operators.

Medical and psychological effects

The new technology introduces both organizational and physical changes to the way in which staff operate. When using a workstation, or even a word processor, ergonomic considerations must be taken into account. One study has shown that, over a period of time, 69 per cent of operators of workstations had been to see a doctor because they were suffering from back ache, 82 per cent had been for neck ache, and 23 per cent for leg ache. Extensive research has been done into the effects of X-rays on those sitting in front of a visual display unit and who are therefore exposed to unaccustomed levels of radiation. Although there is no confirmed evidence of harm, there has been much anxiety and considerable debate. Many organizations take preventive measures in case of harm to their employees. The manager must recognize such concern and must seek the best working conditions that minimize wasted motion and energy without causing distress to the operator (Fig. 11.3). Psychological factors, including a general awareness of the needs of the individual as a human being in contrast to the needs of the system, are important elements that need to be considered if there is to be any long-term improvement in productivity.[9]

Factors affecting performance

The principle factors that affect mental health and which in consequence affect the performance of an employee (Table 11.5), include:

(1) *Job security.* The threat that machines in particular are about to destroy jobs will tend to give rise to delaying or wrecking tactics.
(2) *Job clarity.* Individuals must know what is expected of them.

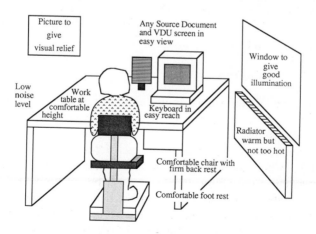

Fig. 11.3 *Working in a comfortable environment*[8]

Table 11.5   Influences on mental health and
performance

- Job security
- Job clarity
- Clear objectives
- Variety
- Use of skills
- Decision making
- Career prospects
- Interpersonal contacts
- Status
- Living standards

(3) *Clearly defined goals.* They must know not only what to do but why
they are doing it.

(4) *Variety.* The continuous repetition of the same task will lead to
boredom, frustration, and the making of mistakes.

(5) *Use of skills.* Craftsmanship still brings its own satisfaction.

(6) *Decision making.* Some part in decision making, even at a humble
level, brings the individual a sense of involvement in the overall
project.

(7) *Career prospects.* Without the chance of career development and the
opportunity for self improvement there will be little long-term commitment to the task.

(8) *Human relationships.* Without at least some interpersonal contact the
human spirit will be demoralized; people need to know that other
people care about them.

(9) *Social status.* Unless society to some extent respects what is being
done then the individual worker cannot be expected to either.

(10) *Standard of living.* At the end of the day if the individual considers
that the standard of living that is attainable from the work is insufficient then he or she will move elsewhere.

Education and training needs

The exploitation of technology is not a matter of replacing humans by
machines, for in so doing there is a danger of computerizing the mistakes of
the past. There is always a danger of treating computers as masters rather
than as servants, most noticeably in the fields of 'turnkey systems' where the
operator must do exactly what the computer package dictates and in the
manner specified. Computers after all are only bits of copper wire, silicon,
and plastic and should be adapted to the tasks. Since the technology of today
is rapidly changing, there is none the less a need for staff to be flexible and
able to cope with such changes. The use of new systems creates a need for
system-dependent and job-specific training. New levels of education and

training and new management skills are needed to exploit modern technology and to maintain the equipment in working order. Many individuals, however, may not have the aptitude for the tasks; others may resent the deskilling that is involved. The use of turnkey systems necessitates a redefinition of educational levels needed to do the job. The need for better educated people becomes less. The higher the education level of the staff, the more they may become frustrated with the bulk of the work. In consequence many decisions will be being taken at a lower education level than previously.

Overall, with the introduction of modern technology, the manager needs to:

(1) identify the human factors involved in the transition;
(2) define new levels of skill and responsibility for each and every task;
(3) consult the staff involved to obtain their confidence and awareness of what is going on;
(4) involve any trade unions who will be affected as their opposition can seriously delay progress;
(5) plan for a more rapid turn around of staff who may not wish to stay in the same job for any length of time;
(6) revise training programmes in the light of changing needs and the consequences of this more rapid turn around of staff;
(7) avoid recruiting staff who are overqualified, for their frustration may rub off on others;
(8) upgrade the education of supervisors who may have management skills but little understanding of modern technology in comparison with younger and more junior staff;
(9) reassess the relationship between what is done in the field and what is done in the office and the linkages between them;
(10) check on ergonomic factors to reconcile efficiency with comfort;
(11) monitor the health and safety of the staff involved.

Of all these elements, the provision of adequate training and the development of motivation in the staff are by far the most important.

References

1. Drucker, P. (1970). *Technology, management and society*, Heinemann, London.
2. *Report of the Task Force on the Surveying and Mapping Industry* (1985). Report prepared for the Department of Regional Industrial Expansion, Ottawa.
3. Dunkerley, H. (1985). Land information systems for developing countries. Paper presented at C A S L E Fifth General Assembly and Symposium, Kuala Lumpur.
4. See, for example, Albers, H. H. (1969). *Principles of management: a modern approach*, 3rd Edition. John Wiley & Sons, New York.

5. McGrath, G. (1986). The challenges to educational establishments: preparing students for a future in LIS/GIS. In Blakemore, M. (ed.) *Proceedings of Auto Carto London*, Volume 2, pp. 296–305.
6. Dale, P. F. (1987). Education and training in land information. *International Journal of Geographical Information Systems*, Vol. 1/1. pp. 89–91.
7. Coleman, D. and McLaughlin, J. D. (1986). Management considerations in the assessment of a digital mapping facility. Resource Information Management Group, Dept. of Surveying Engineering, University of New Brunswick.
8. Health and Safety Executive (1983). *Visual display units*, Her Majesty's Stationery Office, London.
9. Taylor, R. M. (1985). Health and safety factors in relation to the application of the new technology in the mapping industry. Paper B2 in *Surveying and Mapping 85*. Royal Institution of Chartered Surveyors, London.

12. Conclusions and recommendations

In this chapter we emphasize the central issues that have been raised in earlier chapters. We also make recommendations concerning the courses of action that less developed countries might consider taking.

12.1 Land information systems

Land has often been identified as the primary resource from which wealth is derived. Information is also a resource and can be used in the creation of wealth. Increasingly, it is being recognized that the acquisition and effective use of information are fundamental to the survival of any organization, however large or small. The more developed countries of the world are moving into an age of high technology in which information holds the key to their prosperity and development. As Naisbitt has remarked: 'We now mass produce information the way we used to mass produce cars . . . With the coming of the information society, we have for the first time an economy based on a key resource that is not only renewable but self-generating'.[1]

The information society has not, however, reached the poor countries of the world. They are struggling with much more basic technologies and wholly inadequate resources for coping with the social and environmental problems that beset them. According to the *World Bank Development Report* for 1980,[2] 'Nor is there any serious disagreement about who the poor are . . . with the partial exception of Latin America (where about 40% are in the towns) the poor are primarily rural dwellers, overwhelmingly dependent on agriculture—the majority of them landless (or nearly landless) labourers'.

It is therefore not surprising that development projects have traditionally concentrated on the problems of rural communities, helping, for example, in the resettlement of peasant farmers or providing them with some degree of security of tenure.

Recently, however, the problems of the urban communities have become more pressing. A city with a population of 500 000 people and a growth rate of 5 per cent per annum will become a city of 1 million in 15 years, thus doubling the need for land parcels and the infrastructure that supports them. Such a rate of growth comes in part from the increased rate of survival of children up to the age of four years, and in part from the greater age reached by the elderly. The increase in urban population also comes from the

227

migration of those in rural areas who see the higher material standards of living available to their brethren in the towns and cities. In the discussion that follows, it is recognized that the problems of the urban and rural environments differ, the needs and types of information for each environment are not the same, and the type of a land information system that will be most cost effective will be different. The fundamental problems and the methodology for their solution are, however, the same.

Land information is no panacea for the ills of the environment. Naisbitt has warned that 'we are drowning in information but starved for knowledge'.[3] It is all too easy to become confused by superfluous facts. It is, however, arguable that better information increases the chances of making and implementing better decisions. All other things being equal, success in battle goes to the side that has the better intelligence network. This philosophy applies to the management and development of land. Land information systems are the intelligence networks by which land may be successfully administered.

Nevertheless, in almost every society there is a pressing need to:

(1)   acquire, store, and retrieve information about land for the purposes of administration and planning;
(2)   compile some form of cadastral record that is complete, up to date, and reliable;
(3)   display, in graphic form, different combinations of spatial data, especially those relating to topography and to land parcels;
(4)   analyse and process those data to produce meaningful land information.

The development of a land information system is one approach to satisfying these needs. The extent to which they are met, and its manner, will vary among societies depending upon their culture, history, and economic conditions. In some systems, the records may be rudimentary and concerned only with a general level of information. For example, some societies may be unconcerned with the needs or rights of the individual, which may not be formally recognized by the society. Many systems, however, are markedly similar and all are tackling what is fundamentally the same problem.

Much of what has been written in earlier chapters is directed at cadastral systems. Land information systems cover a wide spectrum, of which those related to the cadastre are an especially important subset. It is through the cadastre, in whatever form, that many of the most tangible benefits can arise. The benefits are however difficult to predict in a quantifiable form. The present age is one in which to measure is to know; in the minds of many economists and administrators, that which cannot be measured is deemed to be of no value. The justification for investment in spatial data management systems has yet to be firmly established. The initial costs are high and the benefits are not immediate. A prediction that is 90 per cent accurate after one year is 81 per cent accurate after two years, 73 per cent after three, and 35 per cent after ten. Yet, according to the limited evidence available, it takes ten years before the accumulated benefits begin to exceed the accumulated costs; by this time the prediction would already be at least 65 per cent unreliable. With hindsight it will be possible to produce more reliable figures, but that point has not yet been reached. None the less hard-headed business people and administrators are taking the necessary risks. The long-term benefits are seen to be positive.

12.2   Land registration

Within every society there is a need for some form of land registration. New systems must be created or old systems improved. For as Dunkerley has pointed out:[4]

In most developing countries it is difficult, extremely time consuming and financially costly to identify what land is available, its ownership, the rights and effective limitations to its use and its price as compared to roughly similar lots; and then to accomplish a transfer with clear title. Necessary information is lacking or contradictory. The recording systems function poorly at best.

Even in more developed countries there is often much inefficiency and unnecessary wastage in the operation of existing deeds or title registration systems.

One common characteristic of the various land records that are held by most Third World countries is that they are disparate, incomplete, and very much out of date. Their existence is frequently unknown to other government bodies. However, in the particular case of land ownership, the records cannot be ignored. A new topographic map can always be made without reference to existing maps: a new cadastral map cannot. If a new information system is to be built, then its foundations must stand on what has been agreed in the past. This may be achieved through detailed examination of the old records or through the processes of systematic adjudication.

The single most significant source of improvement to existing systems is good management. Present systems are often steeped in tradition, inflexible in operation, oblivious of true costs, and unaware of alternatives. Effective management statistics are either limited or non-existent. Some changes in the law may be necessary in order to bring about radical improvement. Often, however, greater efficiency can come without such drastic action. A detailed assessment of how the existing system works is a prerequisite to planning any modifications and improvements. A list of suggested questions around which such an assessment might be made is given in Appendix A.

One of the more contentious components of land registration is the survey of boundaries. For many record management purposes, a parcel identifier is the only spatial characteristic that is needed. The survey of the boundaries that enclose that parcel can account for 40 per cent of the costs of the registration process. Where the local population dispute boundaries, adjudication followed by good monumentation solves many problems. Evidence, however, suggests that good-quality mapping of boundaries is necessary in the long term. The degree of precision that is needed for such boundary surveys is less clear—the traditional solution is being to work to what the current technology provides rather than what is cost effective. Realistic evaluation is needed of the causes and frequency of land disputes and of alternative means for their avoidance and settlement. Centimetre accuracy of survey is rarely if ever justifiable for cadastral purposes.

A significant element within a cadastral system is the design and assignment of land parcel identifiers and other mechanisms for accessing and linking the data. The choice of an identifier is of particular importance when extending a land registration system into a multipurpose role. It should, for example, be able to link together legal documents, assessment roles, and planning applications. Its design should be based on such considerations as user familiarity, simplicity, flexibility, data storage, and uniqueness.[5]

12.3   Fiscal cadastres

The most immediate benefits from a land information system often arise when it is linked to taxation and revenue recovery. Often the cost of improving land record management can be more than offset by the increased revenue raised as a result of the greater efficiencies. The use of the land records in this way raises political issues that essentially are not the concern of the land information manager. They are, however, often the concern of those who must pay for the improvements that the manager seeks.

The fiscal cadastre is less dependent on property delimitation than that concerned with land ownership and property boundaries. It should, however, be linked to the latter as the name of the property owner is an integral part of the record, as is the parcel identifier. The levels of information that should be held within the fiscal cadastre need not be sophisticated. The records should, however, be complete in terms of spatial cover.

The data that are held may be of particular value and significance to property agents who are concerned with the buying and selling of land. As such there can be additional benefit if the information stored within the cadastre can be made publicly available for a fee. A land agent advertising a property would then have access to details such as the number of floor levels, square metres of floor space, and rateable value readily to hand.

12.4   Multipurpose cadastres

The terms 'multipurpose cadastre' and 'land information system' are often used synonymously. This is incorrect but understandable. A multipurpose cadastre is a comprehensive set of land records, based upon the land parcel. It is the latter characteristic that distinguishes it from land information systems in general. The compilation and continued maintenance of a set of cadastral overlays are central to the concept of the multipurpose cadastre. The initial compilation of such a cadastre is often as an extension to, or combination of, the proprietory and the fiscal registers. The advantage of using the latter is that the records should cover a whole country.

A great variety of data can be incorporated within the system. Criteria will need to be established to determine what is worth including and what should be omitted. Since many of the data incorporated in the multipurpose cadastre are derived from secondary sources, there is a need to assess the quality and compatibility of these sources. Procedures are needed to ensure the integrity of the system and that the information displayed on the overlays is as reliable as possible. Procedures are also required for refining the overlays over time and for keeping them updated.

A modern parcel-based system will take several, if not many, years to develop. It is therefore susceptible to institutional changes and new user demands. In addition to accommodating such contingencies, it should be able to take advantage of new technologies and system concepts as they become available. For this reason, the conceptual and detailed designs of the system should permit flexibility. Phased or incremental implementation can yield short-term benefits and allow time for the promoters of the system to gain support for further development. Such an approach also allows for reassessment and refinement of the conceptual plan in the light of experience and changing circumstances.

In the incremental approach, priorities will need to be established for choosing which topics and which areas should be tackled first. Since the upfront costs will inevitably be high, those areas that provide the quickest return on the investment will tend to be the most attractive. The temptation to deal only with such areas and to avoid those where the benefits accrue only in the longer term should be resisted.

12.5 Spatial frameworks

Within every country, there needs to be geodetic network able to support basic mapping and to serve as a framework for referencing spatial data. Further densification may be required at the local level to provide coordinate references for parcel information. A geodetic framework is expensive to establish and all such frameworks have been refined and up-graded over time. With current developments in high technology, especially with regard to satellite surveying, further refinements can be expected. Provision needs to be made to handle changes in all coordinate-based files in a land information system, especially where coordinates are used for parcel referencing or for the description of property boundaries. A readjustment of the spatial framework should not interfere with property rights.

Local frameworks serve an immediate purpose. If the local system is subsequently joined to the national, then the network can be readjusted. Subject to the above statement, the new values can then be brought into the system. If the data are already held in computer-compatible form, then the transformation can be an automatic process.

The traditional techniques of triangulation, trilateration, and traversing are being replaced by electronic position fixing. The predictions are that the Global Positioning System will make a major impact on the manner and extent to which control survey networks are densified and on the costs involved. By the end of 1987, the network of satellites was not complete. The extent to which data on their operation will be readily available has not yet been determined. For the present, conventional techniques for densifying networks of control, including those using photogrammetric methods, remain valid. The accuracy they can provide is adequate for almost all land information purposes.

The aerial photograph is a historical document and should be treated as such. The data extracted from it relate to the instant at which the photograph was taken. The framework of ground points, which represent a spatial network, are dynamic and change over time. Some points move, some get lost, and in some areas, the records which relate to them can rapidly become out of date. Maintenance of the framework and the records relating to it are of particular importance if the high investment in the network is not to be wasted. There is safety in numbers so that, with a dense network, the absence of a few points may not be significant. None the less, in many countries, much time is wasted in cadastral surveying, searching for control stations that had disappeared long ago.

12.6   Detail surveying and mapping

Base maps are required both as a reference for cadastral information and for efficiently integrating environmental and other information. The base maps must be at scales large enough to display property information, mapping at 1:1000 or 1:2000 often being the most suitable where parcel sizes are small and the level of detail is great. The type of mapping will depend, amongst other things, on user requirements, cost, and timing. Orthophoto or rectified photo mapping is suitable for some purposes, though conventional line-drawn maps may be preferable where there is to be map maintenance and update.

Data may be acquired through field survey, photogrammetrically, or through the use of remote sensing. The classification of features poses different problems from the measurement of location. The measurement of position is normally more precise when using field survey methods, though aerial survey methods may be better where mass production is required, for instance in the initial compilation of land title records. Remote sensing tends to suffer from overproduction of data and is more suited either to very specific problems, such as in the location of possible mineral sites, or to those areas where a generalized picture is required.

The records within a land information system must be kept up to date. Certain types of data, such as those relating to land ownership, must be updated instantaneously whenever there is a change. For others there is less urgency. On the other hand, procrastination can soon lead to a permanent distortion of the land records, which in turn will lead to great expense in trying to bring them back up to date. Cutbacks in maintenance costs are always an easy source of short-term savings when the money supply is restricted. But it is a certain recipe for higher long-term costs and reduced benefits.

12.7 Digital mapping

One justification for digital mapping is that it makes updating procedures potentially more cost effective. The major objection is the high cost in time and expense of data capture. Digitizing and editing a map sheet may take as long and cost as much as the original conventional compilation. The capital costs of both hardware and software are falling and the technology is becoming more reliable. The volume of data that must be converted to computer compatible form is a deterrent to investment. It is, however, a 'one-off' exercise, provided that maintenance procedures are followed. The process should generate employment over the next decade rather than destroy it.

As a set of techniques for producing conventional maps, the benefits of the digital approach are yet to be proved. In many cases, the overall costs are greater than those that arise in traditional manual methods. The benefits of digital mapping lie in the increased opportunities that are created for data manipulation, analysis, exchange, and display. If these benefits are to be fully realized, then the data that are acquired must be readily available to all potential users. A multipurpose system requires standards and procedures for the systematic collection of information from a number of sources and mechanisms for the exchange of information among data bases. In a digital environment, any incompatibility of data structure or computer configuration can become a major obstacle in developing and expanding the system, particularly when major investments have been made in existing systems.

Standards are required for the definition of features that should be included within the system and how they should be classified; for the accuracy of data collection; for the procedures and responsibilities for quality control, data entry, and manipulation; and for the formats in which the data should be transferred. Provision must also be made to ensure the compatibility of data from different sources within the system, such as between data held in vector and in raster form.

12.8   Data management

Standards are also required for the non-spatial attributes of the data, including those elements that are linked to the digital map only through the land parcel identifier. Standards must encompass both technical arrangements concerning the organization of the information and its flow, and the administrative arrangements for system design, implementation, and development. Considerations include the referencing of the data, mechanisms for efficient and flexible data storage and retrieval, and control over access to the data. Flexibility must be built into the system to accommodate unforeseen applications and inquiries, which inevitably arise as the system expands to meet user demands.

An official policy for land information management can provide the foundation for meeting many of these requirements. Policy will not in itself enforce co-ordination or co-operation. However, it gives a framework within which various groups and agencies can identify priorities and develop co-ordinated programmes and plans. An officially recognized policy will help administrators to obtain the continued institutional support. This is essential when implementation spans years or decades and is subject to changes in government and fluctuating economic climates.

12.9   Economic matters

The most important element in justifying the high up-front costs in developing a land information system is the recognition that information is a basic resource. Information has properties that distinguish it from other resources and make the measurement of benefits derived from it difficult if not impossible. Once information has become available, one can only surmise what would have happened without it. In attempting to quantify both the costs and the benefits that are derived from it, a number of contentious assumptions must be made. Those who have attempted such quantifications have argued in the majority of cases, that the benefits well exceed the costs. Where hindsight has been applied, this has tended to be the case. There are, none the less, levels of investment for which the return will be long drawn out. Even the cost of running many present systems would be wholly unjustified if it were submitted to the same type of critical economic analysis. On the other hand, to abandon rather than reform them would be even more expensive. Much land development would come to a halt, with far-reaching economic and social consequences.

The root of the problem stems from the inability to measure certain benefits. The market-place is not necessarily the right forum in which to attempt to do so. There are some functions that are clearly a responsibility of government and do not respond to present-day econometric analysis. Having said this, there are some components of a land information system that do respond to such treatment. Some types of information are marketable, such as maps, aerial photographs and control survey data. Government may use much of the information for its own purposes, and can also sell it, subject to data protection standards and any Acts governing the freedom of information and the confidentiality of data. People making inquiries from its data base can be charged for the information provided. Any member of the public who goes to a government office and makes an inquiry that does not relate to information that is about him or her personally can be charged; any person or organization such as a bank or mortgage company using a computer network to gain access to the database can be billed automatically. In Sweden, for example, significant revenue is obtained from charges made in this way. It is a question of national policy as to whether such an approach is adopted.

12.10 Institutional matters

Although the evolution of a land information system may be guided by, or respond to, pressure from the private sector, much of the initiative for its development and much of its financing will need to come from government. For, as John Stuart Mill wrote in 1848:[6]

There is a multitude of cases in which governments, with general approbation, assume powers and execute functions for which no reason can be assigned except the simple one, that they conduce to general convenience. We may take as an example, the function (which is a monopoly too) of coining money. This is assumed for no more recondite purposes than that of saving to individuals the trouble, delay and expense of weighing and assaying. No one, however, even of those most jealous of state interference, has objected to this as an improper exercise of the powers of government. Prescribing a set of standard weights and measures is another instance. Paving, lighting, and cleansing the streets and thoroughfares, is another; whether done by the general government, or as is more usual, and generally more advisable, by municipal authority. Making or improving harbours, building lighthouses, making surveys in order to have accurate maps and charts, raising dykes to keep the sea out, and embankments to keep rivers in, are cases in point.

Today one might add to the list the creation of land information systems and the prescribing of national standards for data exchange.

The technical operations of a land information system are becoming largely routine. Given the money and the time, almost anything is possible. The major constraining factor is the institutional environment. Institutional issues, more than any others, determine the effectiveness and pace of development. They directly affect the design and implementation of any system and are themselves affected by its development.

Since a land information system should serve a wide variety of users, both in government and in the private sector, it is essential to understand their requirements. It is also necessary to appreciate the technical, administrative, and institutional constraints under which the system will operate in order to ensure users' support. This assessment should be made not only at the outset of system development, but also throughout its implementation in order to monitor changing requirements. It may be necessary to provide continuing justification for the system; to reassess the level, scope, timing, and source of financial support; and to monitor the direct economic benefits derived from the system (such as the revenue received from fees or the extent of use by government departments and organizations).

Legislative reform is often required before a modern land-parcel based information system can be effectively implemented. Reforms can include provisions for converting customary land tenure into statutory tenure, the registration of documents and plans, and changes in the status of evidence produced by electronic media. Since legal reforms often take several years to accomplish, the system should, if at all possible, be designed to be independent of legislative changes and large-scale administrative reforms.

Many professions and associations will be directly involved in the collection of information for use in a land information system. Amongst the most prominent will be lawyers, land surveyors, planners, assessors, valuers, and land administrators. As reforms in the land information arrangements may require changes in the standards and procedures of these groups, their active support should be obtained. Parcel-based systems, for example, can entail extensive changes in land tenure, conveyancing, and land registration. It is therefore essential that the legal profession, in particular, understands the benefits that the system can offer and supports the initiatives. The support of politicians will also be needed, both at the management and ultimately at the cabinet level, for without it a multipurpose system has little chance of success. Both initial and ongoing political support is needed for the administrative reorganization, legal reforms, financing, and enforcement of other policies affecting the development of a land information system. Also long-term co-operation and communication with political organizations needs to be developed for logistical reasons and to serve the broader areas of education, research, and public relations.[7]

12.11 Management issues

Institutional problems derive from the external relations between a land information system and its environment. The internal problems are the concern of management. The single most effective way to improve the quality of existing systems is, in almost every case, to improve the quality of its management. Management is both a science and an art that is concerned with technology, the people who use it, and the organizational and administrative structures that support them. Senior managers are often preoccupied with matters of a political nature, defending the interests of their organizations from the attacks of their financial masters and, in government, from the ravages of the treasury. They have neither the time nor the skills to get down to the level at which day to day operations take place. Most junior staff are capable of being trained in new techniques but their level of productivity is frequently low, partly through a lack of motivation. Motivation comes from the rewards that are received both financially and in terms of status, and from the concern and leadership that is shown by managers. Good middle management is essential if many systems are to become more cost-effective. Better management skills, better management education, and better management information are essential components of any strategy for progress.

Management must acquire and use appropriate technology. Various strategies are possible, as outlined in Table 12.1. Systems can be developed in house, bought off the shelf, or run on contract by others. Each approach has its own advantages and drawbacks. The technology should be able to handle present system requirements, be sufficiently flexible to meet anticipated future needs, and permit system growth and change. When acquiring new technology, consideration will need to be given to its cost, the technical capabilities of staff, and the availability of space and a temperature- and humidity-controlled environment. The systems chosen will also depend upon the requirements of users, for example their capabilities for manipulating data and their needs for accuracy, precision, and access to the data. In systems that provide legal evidence of land ownership, the reliability of the systems is of particular concern. Large sums of money can be wasted and user confidence in and therefore support for, subsequent system development can be prejudiced, if the wrong technology is acquired or insufficient support is provided during implementation.

Management will invariably need to introduce new personnel arrangements. This may involve hiring new staff for one or more stages of the system development. Current staff will need assistance to obtain the necessary skills and education to work in a new environment. Any systems analysts and computer technicians who may be recruited are unlikely to have sufficient understanding of matters such as land tenure that will be affected by the new system. It is therefore important that existing staff with such knowledge and

Table 12.1   Choosing LIS software and hardware (adapted from Dangermond and Smith[8])

	Create own system	Buy some software	Buy turnkey software system	Buy turnkey software and hardware	Buy LIS services from bureau
Dependence on supplier	Very low	Low	High	Very high	Almost total
Time till operational	Long	Long— Medium	Little	Very little	Immediate
Initial cost	Low	Moderate	Moderate	High	High
Own labour costs	High	Lower	Moderate	Moderate	Very low
Risk	High	Lower	Low	Low	Low
Customized	Total	Total	Moderate	Moderate	Low
Own skill required	Very high	High	Moderate	Moderate	Low
Use of own resources	High	High	Moderate	Low	Very low

experience participate throughout the design and development process. Their co-operation must also be sought in any reorganization that is likely to follow from the implementation of the new system.

12.12   Conclusions

Throughout this report, we have raised a number of issues that must be faced if any country is to expand its land information system. To some extent, the problems facing Third World countries are no different from those faced by everyone else. The difference is in their lack of resources, especially of educated manpower and available capital. Earnings of foreign currency are hard gained and easily squandered. Several things can, however, be done to improve matters.

First there is a need for better education, especially at the management level. Staff need to understand the practicalities as well as the theory of land information management by understanding land, information, and management. The technology must be made to fit into the human, legal, and economic environment and be its servant, not its master. Courses need to be provided to ensure this.

Secondly, those giving help and guidance must become more familiar with the conditions under which the systems they recommend will have to operate. The problems are not simply technical; it is the human dimension that will determine success or failure. Many of the successful systems that are operational today, have behind them one or two individuals whose drive and enthusiasm have carried them through. There is no reason to think that conditions in less developed countries are any different. There must be sensitivity to human aspirations and weaknesses.

Finally, whatever is attempted must be designed as much for the future as for the present. Maintenance is more important than initial system creation; without it, the system will become a historical monument and a folly. The system must be capable of change with growing levels of sophistication of both the hardware and software and the increasing skills of people operating them. If Third World countries are to make a quantum leap forward, if the growth of land information systems is to have the impact on societies that is hoped, if in fact better land information can lead to better decisions about the use of land and resources and better management of that most fundamental resource, then there is a heavy responsibility on those giving aid and assistance to get things right. The affluent can afford the occasional failure. The Third World cannot.

References

1. Naisbitt, J. (1984). *Megatrends.* pp. 16 and 23. Futura, London & Sydney.
2. World Bank (1980). *Development report for 1980*, p. 35. Washington D C.
3. Naisbitt, J. *Op. cit.*, p. 24.
4. Dunkerley, H. (1985). Land information systems for developing countries. Paper presented at CASLE Fifth General Assembly and Symposium, Kuala Lumpur.
5. Moyer, D. D. and Fisher, K. P. (eds) (1973). *Land parcel identifiers for information systems*, American Bar Foundation, Chicago.
6. Mill, J. S. (1848). *Principles of political economy*, Book V, Chapter 1, S2.
7. Ayers, E. H. (1985). Implementation of modern land records systems: politics and institutions. *Wisconsin Land Information Report*, No. 1, University of Wisconsin, Madison, Dec.
8. Dangermond, J. P. and Smith, L. K. (1980). Alternative approaches for applying GIS technology. In *The planning and engineering interface with a modernized land data system.* pp. 97–112. The American Society for Civil Engineers. New York.

Appendix A: Check-list for evaluating a cadastral system

In many cadastral systems, productivity is often low and the total time and cost spent on individual cadastral surveys from initial request to final acceptance is high. Significant improvements are often possible through improved management and administration. Before such improvements can be brought about, the manner in which the present system operates needs to be analysed. The questions listed below are directed at determining the facts upon which such an analysis can be based. They are of course incomplete in that greater attention can always be paid to detail and every environment has its own unique characteristics.

The questions are put forward as a guide so that an existing system can be documented. The aim is, first, to determine the current state of rights and records concerning land parcels and to identify the legal, physical, financial, administrative, social, and political constraints affecting the development of a cadastral system. Subsequently the analysis can be extended to the fiscal cadastre, which has fewer legal constraints and can often operate on the basis of lower technical standards. Finally, any cadastral study should consider those parts of a land information system that integrate a wider range of records, including those relating to the utilities and underground services on the one hand, and to land use and land resources on the other.

Overall any study of existing land information systems should examine:

(1)   institutional matters, by reviewing the procedures whereby land policy is formed and land as a resource is managed, by analysing the relationships and exchange of information between those directly responsible for handling land data, and by assessing present management structures and management information systems within those ministries and departments that deal with land;

(2)   legal matters, by comparing statutary land law with customary tenure and practice, and by examining all legislation affecting the cadastre, including the licensing of surveyors, adjudication, monumentation, the conduct of surveys, and the maintenance and dissemination of information in the registers;

(3)   survey procedures, by documenting resource availability and the technical and environmental constraints on cadastral operations, by determining the cost effectiveness of present procedures, and by assessing the management problems in implementing and monitoring their effects;

241

(4) fiscal matters, by evaluating present policies with regard to land taxation, by examining present methods for land valuation and appraisal and the levels of information that they require, and by determining the updatedness and completeness of cover of existing land tax records;

(5) financial matters, by identifying priority areas for extending the cadastre, by estimating the cost effectiveness of subcontracting more work to the private sector, by evaluating strategies for cost recovery through higher fees, sales of information, and taxes, and by analysing the cost effectiveness of linking the existing cadastral records with a wider range of land information.

Within the cadastral system, four particular areas need close scrutiny:

(1) *Adjudication and the determination of rights in land.* These may take place from existing records, though they may not reflect what is found to be the case on the ground. Alternatively, it may be necessary to hold courts and to take evidence from occupiers and other interested parties on the ground. Clarification of the relationship between the '*de jure*' and the '*de facto*' position will be needed.

(2) *Determination and demarcation of boundaries.* Sources of evidence for the location of boundaries will need to be identified and evaluated. The minimum necessary and sufficient precision with which boundaries must be determined should be established both from custom and procedure and from legislation.

(3) *Conduct of the survey.* The legal, economic, and administrative constraints will need to be examined and an assessment made of the extent to which current techniques conform to these.

(4) *Parcel descriptions and records.* The methods by which existing land parcels are described and referenced will need to be documented and the relationship of the legal position as shown in the records contrasted with that evidenced on the ground. Methods of storage and retrieval of information should also be reviewed.

Finally, before analysing the results of such enquiries it is important to determine what other investigations into land registration and the cadastre have taken place or are currently in progress. Duplication of effort is not uncommon, especially when those subject to scrutiny prefer to hold their own counsel.

Specific factual answers should be sought to the following questions:

On institutional matters

1. Which ministries and departments are responsible for forming and implementing land policies? Which are concerned with land reform?

2. What policies currently exist and are they being implemented? Are urban and rural policies integrated?

3. What mechanisms exist for monitoring the implementation and consequences of land policies?

4. Which government departments handle land-related data? Which are responsible for recording land ownership?

5. What levels of expertise exist within government to formulate and administer such policies?

6. What are the present management structures within relevant ministries and departments? What management information is available to them, especially for the measurement of costs and productivity?

7. What are the present levels and skills of manpower involved in land information systems?

8. What government policies exist with regard to manpower employment and the balance between capital and labour?

9. What opportunities exist for staff development? In particular what resources are allocated to the training and motivation of middle managers?

10. What technical equipment and facilities are available to support education and training in all aspects of land information systems? What computing facilities exist and what national policies relate to their use?

11. Given that the subject of 'land economy' embraces land administration, land management, land development, land valuation, land acquisition, and the implementation of land reforms, what educational and training courses are there dedicated to the subject?

12. What mechanisms exist for the exchange of land-related data between government departments and how do they operate? In particular, what administrative relationships exist between those maintaining land records, such as a register of titles, and those involved in land survey?

13. What access does the public have to government-held land-related data? What protection do they have against the divulgence of personal information?

14. What land data are subject to copyright and what to security restrictions? For example, is aerial photography treated as classified material?

On matters concerning land tenure and land registration

15. What rights in land are recognized by law and by custom? How does common law or customary law relate to statutary in matters affecting land?

16. What overriding interests are recognized, such as easements or the rights of squatters?

17. What constitutes at law the root of any title? Is the chain of title complete?

18. Does the state guarantee title to land?

19. What are the present procedures for the conveyancing of rights in land?

20. How long does it take to transfer a property formally from one owner to another? What percentage of this time is accounted for by legislative, by administrative, and by survey operations?

21. How are land rights transmitted through sale, gift, or through the system of inheritance?

22. Is there a legal requirement to register any sale, gift, or other transfer of rights in land, in whole or in part?

23. Is there a central register or are there local court registers of deeds and other documents that relate to the ownership of rights in land?

24. If such registers exist, what percentage of properties do they cover? What evidence is there that they are up to date?

25. Are leases and subleases recorded and if so how and where? How are easements documented?

26. Are the records of land ownership:
    (a) Complete in terms of spatial cover?
    (b) Complete in terms of owners?
    (c) Complete in terms of rights?
    (d) Up to date?
    (e) Accessible to the public?
    (f) Stored in a form that is physically stable?
    (g) Microfilmed?

27. Are strata titles recognized? What rights exist to space above and below ground level?

28. Does the adverse possession of land lead to the prescription of rights? How does the Statute of Limitations affect land rights?

29. What happens to land where the owner cannot be traced?

30. What procedures exist for the adjudication of title to land? Which specific government department is responsible for the adjudication?

31. If there is adjudication of title, is the approach systematic? What powers of compulsion exist to bring land on to the register?

32. How often do disputes over the ownership of land (as distinct from boundaries) arise?

33. What procedures are adopted to resolve disputes specifically over boundaries? Who resolves the disputes? How often do such boundary disputes arise? Why do such disputes occur?

34. How are boundaries monumented? Is any form of monumentation laid down in law? Are boundaries fully monumented or are some areas 'open plan'?

35. Are boundaries visible from the air?

36. What social attitudes and what elements of the physical environment affect the form of monumentation?

37. Who is responsible for the preservation of boundary marks? What penalties exist if such marks are disturbed? What percentage get disturbed or lost?

38. If there is a conflict of evidence, are 'pegs paramount to plans', that is, does occupation take precedence over measurements recorded in documents?

On matters relating to land survey

39. Is there any legal requirement for land parcels to be surveyed? If so, who issues the instructions to survey?

40. What percentage of cadastral surveys is undertaken by government surveyors?

41. Are private surveyors licensed to undertake cadastral surveys? If so, what laws govern the licensing of surveyors?

42. Are licensed surveyors organized into a professional body? If so, what powers and responsibilities does such a body have?

43. What regulations govern the conduct of cadastral surveys and cadastral surveyors? What provisions do such regulations contain?

44. What methods of survey are currently used to determine the location of boundaries?

45. Would photogrammetric evidence be acceptable in court?

46. What determines whether a survey is to an acceptable standard? What accuracy standards are laid down and how are they monitored?

47. How are survey data stored and retrieved? Are microfilm copies of survey records maintained?

48. What are the average overhead costs of cadastral surveys?

49. What scale of fees is currently charged for cadastral surveys? On what basis are the fees assessed and do they relate to the true overheaded costs of survey?

50. How long does an average survey take: (a) to execute and (b) to get approval from those responsible for checking the survey?

51. What is the current level of national expenditure on surveying and mapping?

52. What are the responsibilities and terms of reference of the national land survey organization? Are separate divisions responsible for cadastre, topographic, and geodetic surveys?

53. If there are separate survey divisions within national mapping, what is the level of co-operation between the cadastral and the other divisions?

54. What technical survey equipment is held by the cadastral survey department? What maintenance facilities are available for the repair of high-technology equipment?

55. What educational and training levels and skills are available and are needed to exploit modern technology?

56. Are surveyors' field books treated as legal documents?

57. What is the availability and quality of the national geodetic control network?

58. Are surveys now based on the national tiangulation network of control? If so, who fixes additional control and to what standards? Who pays for the additional work?

On maps and plans

59. At what scales are cadastral maps and plans produced? Are index plans kept up to date?

60. At what scale are deed plans of land parcels produced? What details do they show?

61. What is the legal status of plans kept within the land registration system? How do they relate to entries on the register?

62. At what scales are topographic maps produced? How complete is the national cover? Are the maps kept up to date?

63. In particular, what co-operation exists between those responsible for cadastral and topographic maps and plans?

64. How are boundaries currently described? Is the method of description governed by regulations?

65. How are land parcels numbered? How are subdivisions numbered?

66. When the field or photogrammetric elements of a survey are complete, how long does it take and what is the cost of producing the related graphic diagram?

On fiscal matters and land valuation

67. Is there a system of tax based on the value of the land owned or on its produce?

68. Is there a tax on the transfer of land?

69. On what basis is the value of land assessed? Is it based on up to date information? What percentage of properties have been assessed?

70. What, area by area, is the average value of land?

71. What is the rate at which dealings in land take place?

72. What percentage of properties are subject to mortgage? If there is no system of guaranteed title, how are these mortgages protected?

73. What is the relationship between the so-called juridical and the fiscal registers?

On matters relating to planning and development

74. What regulations govern the maximum and minimum sizes of land parcels, and details such as road reserve widths and plot frontages?

75. What controls exist over land use? How are they enforced?

76. What is the relationship between the town planning development control regulations and land ownership? Do town planning boundaries coincide with estate boundaries?

77. Is there a system of local land charges covering such matters as:
    (a) charges for work carried out by a local authority;
    (b) planning restrictions imposed under town and country planning regulations;

    (c) compulsory purchase orders;

    (d) orders designating specific types of land use?

78. Have the information requirements of planners and land managers been assessed? If so, what land-related information do they use?

79. What is the present state of land use mapping? What is the level of its completeness and updatedness?

80. What records exist of soils, geology, and land potential?

81. What is the state of utility mapping, service by service? Is it up to date and is it accurate?

82. Are pipelines recorded as easements in any legal registers?

83. What standards exist for the exchange of data including those that are alphanumeric, graphic, and digital? Is there any mechanism to enforce such standards?

Appendix B: Requirements for implementing the multipurpose cadastre

In order to implement a modern parcel-based land information system, there are a series of technical, organizational, and institutional requirements that need to be considered. The following list of requirements has been prepared for North American jurisdictions;[1] it is believed that many, albeit not all, will be relevant elsewhere.

Technical requirements

At the technical level, some of the requirements include:

(1) *Development of data standards.* These standards include: definition of the information content of the system and specific products (e.g., map or CRT screen report); the accuracy for data collection and display, scale, and resolution; and procedures and responsibilities for quality control, data entry, and manipulation. Provisions must also be made for ensuring the compatibility of data from different sources within the system.

(2) *Spatial reference framework.* The geodetic network must be able to support base-mapping programmes and to serve as framework for referencing spatial data. Further densification may be required at the local level for integrated surveys to improve and provide coordinate references for parcel information. The application of new technologies, such as GPS, must be assessed. Provisions must also be made to handle changes efficiently (e.g., network adjustments and refinements) in all coordinate based files in the system, including parcel references where coordinates are used.

(3) *Base mapping.* A standard set of base maps for the jurisdiction is required both as reference for cadastral information and for efficiently integrating environmental and other information. The base maps must be at scales large enough to depict property information, displays at 1:1000 or 1:2000 often being required where parcel size is smaller and detail is greater. The type of mapping (e.g., orthophoto, rectified photo, or planimetric map) will depend on user requirements, cost,

249

and timing, among other factors. For modern LIS, the need for providing base map data and/or cadastral overlay data in digital format must also be assessed.

(4) *Standards for the compilation and continued maintenance of the cadastral overlay.* Owing to cost and time delays in performing systematic field inventories of land tenure, cadastral overlays are generally compiled during initial system development from information already available (e.g., assessment data and maps, survey plans.) There is a need to evaluate the quality and compatibility of these sources and to provide procedures for ensuring that the information displayed on the overlay is as reliable as possible on the first pass to maintain the integrity of the system. Procedures are also required for refining the overlay over time (e.g., intergrated land surveys and registration of plans) and for keeping the overlay updated. Parcel identifiers should be clearly depicted on the maps.

(5) *Design and assignment of parcel identifiers and other access and linkage mechanisms.* PIDs must be assigned to each parcel and should be referenced in as many other records as possible (e.g., legal documents, assessment rolls) to facilitate data input and exchange. The PID design should be based on such considerations as user familiarity, simplicity, flexibility, data storage, and uniqueness. In addition, procedures must be in place to withdraw or assign PIDs when changes in parcel structure occur.

(6) *Acquiring and using appropriate technology.* Not only should technology be chosen to handle present system requirements adequately in a multiuser environment, but it should also be sufficiently flexible to meet anticipated future needs and permit system growth and change. Considerations in acquiring technology include, for example: cost, the technical capabilities of staff, the need for new space and controlled environments, and user requirements such as accuracy, resolution, access, and data manipulation capabilities. The need for reliability in systems that provide legal evidence of land ownership is of particular concern. Acquiring inappropriate technology or not providing sufficient support during implementation can endanger user confidence, and therefore support, for subsequent system development.

Organizational requirements

These requirements encompass both the organization of the information and its flow and the administrative arrangements for system design and development.

(1) *Development of standards for data organization.* These considerations include the referencing and accessing standards for data within the

system, mechanisms for providing efficient and flexible data storage and retrieval, parcel definition, and topology for digital data. There is also a need to incorporate flexibility for unforeseen applications and inquiries to meet expanding multiuser demands.[2]

(2) *Development of standards and procedures for data flow.* A multipurpose system requires standards and procedures for the systematic collection of information from a number of sources and mechanisms for the exchange of information among data bases. In a digital environment, any incompatibility of data structure or computer configuration can become a major obstacle to developing and expanding the system, particularly when significant investment have been made in existing systems.

(3) *Incremental or phased design and development concepts.* A modern parcel-based system will take several if not many years to develop and is therefore susceptible to institutional changes and new user demands. In addition to accommodating these contingencies, the system should be capable of taking advantage of new technologies and system concepts as they become available. For this reason, the conceptual and detailed designs of the system should permit flexibility. Phased or incremental implementation can yield short-term system benefits in order to gain support for further development, and allow for reassessment and refinement of the conceptual plan.

(4) *Appropriate personnel arrangements.* This may involve hiring new personnel for one or more stages of system development. It also entails assisting current staff to obtain the necessary skills and education to work in a new environment. Since many systems analysts and computer technicians do not have an in-depth understanding of the land tenure institutions that will be affected by a modern cadastre, it is important that land officers participate throughout the design and development process.

(5) *Administrative organization and reorganization.* System implementation may require internal reorganization within specific departments or units. They may also require an organizational structure to co-ordinate user input, technology acquisition, development of common standards and procedures, and other system-related decision making.

(6) *Development of communication, co-operation, and support.* The degree to which ideas, requirements, and problems are communicated both vertically (to higher management and political levels and to staff) and horizontally (to other departments, organizations, and users) from the initial stages of system development will help to determine the success of the system. Only through communication will voluntary co-operation be achieved, although co-operation may be enforced to a limited extent through legilsation or policy. Continued system support

is dependent on maintaining a communication network among user communities, administration, and institutions.[3]

Institutional requirements

The institutional environment of the system directly affects design and development, and in turn will probably be affected by the reforms in information arrangements. Perhaps more than other requirements, particular institutional issues will vary from jurisdiction to jurisdiction and with the specific system design. Many organizational requirements have an institutional dimension, but institutional requirements also entail:

(1) *Assessment of user requirements and system constraints.* Since a modern system should serve a wide variety of user communities, an understanding of their requirements and the technical, administrative, and institutional constraints under which the system will operate is essential to developing an appropriate design and receiving user support. This assessment should not only be made at the outset of system development (perhaps in conjunction with economic feasibility studies), but also at some stage after system implementation to monitor changing requirements created by the system or other factors.

(2) *Developing financial arrangements.* These include such considerations as: initial and continuing justification for the system; the level, scope, timing, and source of financial support; and the apportionment of direct economic benefits derived from system implementation (e.g., user fees). System justification generally depends on some form of cost–benefit analysis, which can sometimes be more speculative than scientific in the field of land information management owing to difficulties in measuring intangible and/or multiagency benefits and costs. Although studies in other jurisdictions provide guidelines, the costs and benefits vary with institutional and administrative arrangements and with system design.

(3) *Legal reforms.* To implement a modern parcel-based LIS, legislation is often required. Reforms can include provisions for the conversion of customary land tenure, the registration of documents and plans, and the status of evidence produced by electronic media. Since legal reforms often take years to accomplish, the system should be designed to be independent of legislative changes (or large-scale administrative reforms), particularly in its initial phases.[4]

(4) *Professional support.* Many professionals and associations will be directly involved in the collection and use of information in parcel-based LIS, including lawyers, land surveyors, planners, and appraisers. As reforms in the land information arrangements will possibly require changes in the standards and procedures of these groups, their

active support should be obtained to ensure that related activities are co-ordinated with system development. Since parcel-based systems can entail extensive changes in land tenure, conveyancing, and land registration, it is essential that the legal profession, in particular, understands the benefits the system can offer and supports the initiatives. The different perspectives that each group has towards land information and their role in an integrated system must be taken into consideration in communication of the system concept and in soliciting support.[5]

(5) *Political support.* Without on-going political support—at the senior management and/or cabinet level—a multipurpose system has little chance for success. Administrative reorganization, legal reforms, financing, and the enforcement of other policies affecting the LIS depend on this support. In logistical concerns and in the broader areas of education, research, and public relations, LIS administrators need to develop long-term co-operation and communication with political organizations.[6]

(6) *Land information policy.* An official policy for land information management can provide the foundation for meeting many of the requirements that have been identified to this point. Policy will not in itself enforce co-ordination or co-operation, but it gives a framework within which various groups and agencies can identify priorities and develop co-ordinated programmes and plans. An officially recognized policy will also assist system administrators in obtaining the continued institutional support required when implementation spans years or decades, changes in government, and fluctuating economic climates.

References

1. McLaughlin, J. and Nichols, S. (1987). Parcel-based land information systems. *Surveying and Mapping*, March, pp. 11–29.
2. See for example, Frank, A. U. (1984). Computer assisted cartography—are we treating graphics or geometry? In *Proceedings of the Annual Meeting of the Canadian Institute of Surveying*. Quebec City, P.Q., May, pp. 159–68.
3. See, for example, Hodgkinson, R. (1984). An LIS calls for some hard nosed decision making in individual subsystems. In Hamilton, A. and McLaughlin, J. (eds) *The Decision Maker and Land Information Systems*. Papers and Proceedings from the FIG International Symposium, Edmonton, October, pp. 81–7.
4. Chatterton, W. A. (1984). Legal issues in the development of land information systems. *Wisconsin Land Information Report* No. 1, University of Wisconsin, Dec., pp. 203–9.
5. Portner, J. and Neimann, B. Jr (1984). An overview of the social aspects of land records modernization. *Wisconsin Land Information Report*. No. 1, University of Wisconsin, Dec., pp. 94–108.

6. Ayer, E. H. (1985). Implementation of modern land records systems: politics and institutions. *Wisconsin Land Information Report*. No. 1, University of Wisconsin, Dec., pp. 289–299.

Glossary

Adjudication, the determination of rights in land.

Aerotriangulation, a process for extending horizontal and vertical control from measurements of points on overlapping stereo-photographs.

Appraisal, estimating the market value of property.

ASCII, an acronym for American Standard Code for Information Interchange. It is an international standard that defines how letters and other characters are represented in a computer's storage.

Assessment, determining the tax level for a property based upon its relative value.

Attribute, a characteristic of an object that may be used in its classification.

Backup copy, a duplicate that is made in case original data or software become destroyed.

Batch processing, a procedure whereby the computer collects tasks and then processes the data at one time rather than as each task arises.

Boundary, either the physical objects marking the limits of a property or an imaginary line or surface marking the division between two legal estates.

Cadastre, *Juridical,* a register of ownership of parcels of land; *fiscal,* a register of properties recording their value; *multi-purpose,* a register of attributes of parcels of land.

CAD/CAM, computer-aided design and computer-aided manufacture, namely using the computer to help design and produce a product.

Chain survey, a simple method of survey relying solely on measures of distance.

Clipping, a graphic process of cutting lines and symbols off at the edge of a display area.

Comparator, a device for taking precise measurements of the position of points of single (mono-) or overlapping (stereo-) photographs.

Configuration, the way that a computer and its peripherals are linked together as one system.

Data, a raw collection of facts.

Data base, an organized, integrated collection of data.

Data base management system (DBMS), a set of programs for managing a data base.

Density, the storage capacity of magnetic media such as floppy disks.

Digital elevation model (DEM), a numerical model of the height of points on the earth's surface.

Digital mapping, the processes of acquisition (capture), transformation, and presentation of spatial data held in digital form.

Digital terrain model (DTM), a numerical model of the earth's surface in which the third dimension may be some quantity other than height (for instance, gravity or land value).

Digitizing, the process of converting graphic maps into digital form.

Direct access storage device, a device such as magnetic disk, that allows data to be accessed directly, unlike sequential access where all data must be scanned until the item sought is found.

Doppler Transit Satellite System, a system for fixing position on the earth's surface from measurements to satellites.

Earth anchor, a device that may be driven into the ground to form a firm mark or monument.

Edge matching, the process of ensuring that detail along the edge of two adjacent map sheets matches correctly.

Electronic distance measurement (EDM), the determination of distance from precise measurements of intervals of time taken by an electromagnetic wave to pass between two points.

Entity, an object about which information is stored in a data base.

Feature, another word for an entity (*q.v.*).

File, an organized collection of related records.

Geodesy, the scientific study of the size and shape of the earth and determination of positions upon it.

Geodetic framework/network, a spatial framework of points whose position has been precisely determined on the surface of the earth.

Geographic Information System (GIS), a system of capturing, storing, checking, integrating, analysing and displaying data about the Earth that is spatially referenced. It is normally taken to include a spatially referenced data base and appropriate applications software.

Global Positioning System (GPS), a system for fixing positions on the surface of the earth by measuring the ranges to a special set of satellites orbiting the earth.

Graphic Kernal System (GKS), a system for allowing graphics software to be used on a range of different devices.

Graphics terminal, a device with a cathode ray tube for displaying digital spatial data.

Image analysis, the processing and interpretation of graphic images held in digital form.

Inertial surveying, the determination of position through the use of gyroscopes and measurements of acceleration.

Information, data transformed into a form suitable for the user.

Interface, the connection between two devices that handle data in different ways.

Land, the surface of the earth, the materials beneath, the air above and all things fixed to the soil.

Land administration, the functions involved in implementing land management policies.

Land information management, the managing of information about land.

Land information system (LIS), a system for acquiring, processing, storing and distributing information about land.

Land management, the management of all aspects of land including the formation of land policies.

Land parcel, a tract of land, being all or part of a legal estate.

Land registration, the recording of rights in land through deeds or as title.

Landsat, a series of earth resource scanning satellites.

Land tenure, the mode of holding rights in land.

Land title, the evidence of a person's rights to land.

Land transfer, the transfer of rights in land.

Land use, the manner in which land is used, including the nature of the vegetation upon its surface.

Land value, the worth of a property, determined in a variety of ways that give rise to different estimates of value.

Layer, a sub-set of spatial data, selected on a non-spatial basis, such as all objects in the same category.

Link, a series of consecutive non-intersecting line segments.

LINZ, Land Information New Zealand.

Local area network (LAN), a communication system that allows several processing devices that are nearby to be linked together.

Lot, a land parcel (*q.v.*).

LRIS, Land Registration and Information Service.

Metes and bounds, a property description by reference to the bearings and lengths of the boundaries and the name of adjoining properties.

Microfiche, microfilm, microform, storage media based on photographic processes.

Modem, a 'modulator-demodulator' device that allows data to be converted into a form whereby they can be transmitted as a set of pulses down a cable and then reassembled at the other end.

Network (computer), a system consisting of a computer and its connected terminals and devices. The term is also used to describe two or more interconnected computer systems.

Network (survey), a series of connected survey points that provide a spatial framework for an area.

Node, the start or end of a link.

Optical disc, a computer storage device that uses laser technology to store and read data from disks coated in light sensitive material.

Orthophotograph, a composite aerial photograph from which height and tilt displacements have been removed.

Orthophotomap, a photomap (*q.v.*) made from orthophotographs.

Photogrammetry, the science and art of taking accurate measurements from photographs.

Photomap, a map made by printing photographs rather than using abstract conventional signs and symbols.

Pixel, one of a regular array of cells (picture elements) on a grid, within which data are stored.

Plane tabling, a simple method for plotting survey in the field.

Plot, a land parcel (*q.v.*).

Plotter, any device for drawing maps and figures.

Premarking, the marking of points on the ground prior to the taking of aerial photographs so that the points can be certain of identity.

Presignalization, premarking (*q.v.*).

Private conveyancing, the transfer of rights in land without any public record of the transfer.

Quad tree, an organization of raster data that minimizes data storage.

Raster, a regular grid of cells covering an area, usually recorded by automatic scanning.

Refresh tube, a cathode ray tube in which the image is continuously being redrawn.

Registration of Deeds, a system whereby a register of documents is maintained relating to the transfer of rights in land.

Registration of Title, a system whereby a register of ownership of land is maintained based upon the parcel rather than the owner or the deeds of transfer.

Remote sensing, the technique of determining data about the environment from its spectral image as seen from a distance.

Rental value, the value of a property in terms of the rent that may be derived from it.

Rubber sheeting, the transformation of spatial data to stretch or compress them to fit with other data.

Run length encoding, a method for storing raster data in a data base.

Spatial referencing, the association of an entity with its absolute or relative location.

SPOT, a series of high resolution earth resource satellites.

Stamp duty, a levy charged on the transfer of property.

Storage tube, a cathode ray tube that stores graphic data on the screen without having to continuously redraw it.

Strata title, title to land that is not necessarily divided horizontally, such as in high rise buildings or for mining rights.

String, 2D and **3D,** a set of line elements such as X, Y coordinate pairs, that go to make up a continuous whole.

Thiessen polygon, a polygon around a sampling point that has the property that all points within it are nearer to that point than to any other sampling point.

Title to land, see land title (*q.v.*).

Topography, the physical features of the earth's surface.

Topology, the study of properties of a geometric figure that are not dependent upon absolute position, such as connectivity.

Traversing, a land survey technique of measuring successive angles and distances to establish new positions.

Triangulation, a land survey technique of determining position by measurement of the angles in a series of triangles.

Trilateration, a land survey technique of determining position by measurement of distances only.

Valuation, the determination of the value of property.

Vector, a quantity having both magnitude and direction that in a spatial data base is usually stored as a pair of coordinates.

Visual display unit (V D U), a computer terminal with a cathode ray tube used for displaying data.

Windowing, selecting by area a section of a spatial data base. Also the facility in some systems to display several functions together on one screen.

Workstation, a graphic screen, keyboard and (in digital mapping) digitizing tablet all on one desk and linked together with a computer.

Zooming, proportionally enlarging or reducing an area of a map displayed on a screen.

Author index

261

Subject index